THE FACTORY ACT OF 1833

Eight Pamphlets

1833-1834

Arno Press

A New York Times Company/New York 1972

Reprint Edition 1972 by Arno Press Inc.

Reprinted from copies in the Kress Library
Graduate School of Business Administration,
Harvard University

BRITISH LABOUR STRUGGLES: CONTEMPORARY PAMPHLETS 1727-1850
ISBN for complete set: 0-405-04410-0

See last pages for complete listing.

Manufactured in the United States of America

Library of Congress Cataloging in Publication Data
Main entry under title:

The Factory act of 1833.

    (British labour struggles:
contemporary pamphlets 1727-1850)
    CONTENTS: The factory system defended, by
V. Royle [first published 1833].--Remarks on the
propriety and necessity of making the factory bill of
more general application [first published 1833].--
Letter to the Right Hon. Lord Ashley, by K. Finlay
[first published 1833]. [etc.]
    1. Factory laws and legislation--Great Britain--
Addresses, essays, lectures. I. Series.
LAW   343'.42'07   72-2525
ISBN 0-405-04418-6

Contents

the Ten hour factory bill, assembled at the Yew Tree inn, Birstall, October 28th, 1833. [Bradford, Atkinson, printer, 1833]

Fitton, W.

National regeneration. 1. Letter from Mr. Fitton to Mr. Fielden. 2. Letter from Mr. Fielden to Mr. Fitton. 3. Letter from Mr. Holt to Mr. Fielden. Which letters contain a development of all the principles and all the views connected with this important contemplated change in the manufacturing affairs of the country. London [Printed by W. Cobbett] 1834.

THE

FACTORY SYSTEM

DEFENDED,

IN REPLY TO SOME PARTS

OF

THE SPEECH OF G. CONDY, ESQ.,

BARRISTER-AT-LAW,

AT A PUBLIC MEETING HELD IN MANCHESTER,

On the 14*th of February,* 1833.

"He who goeth about to persuade a multitude that they are not so well governed as they ought to be, shall never want attentive and favourable hearers, because they know the manifold defects whereunto every kind of regiment is subject; but the secret lets and difficulties which, in public proceedings, are innumerable and inevitable, they have not ordinarily the judgement to consider."—HOOKER.

MANCHESTER:

PRINTED BY T. SOWLER, COURIER AND HERALD OFFICE.

1833.

THE

FACTORY SYSTEM DEFENDED,

&c.

" On Thursday last (Feb. 14, 1833,) a public meeting of the electors of the Borough of Manchester was held in the Exchange Dining-room, for the purpose of discussing the propriety of petitioning the legislature to pass Mr. Sadler's *ten hours'* factory time bill, or some other measure equally efficient. The chairman (the boroughreeve,) opened the business. Mr. Condy rose amidst loud cheers, and, after making a speech, moved the first resolution. Mr. Condy, at great length, attacked the factory system and its advocates, combining argument, illustration, and sarcasm with the happiest effect."—*Manchester and Salford Advertiser, of Feb.* 16, 1833.

AT the meeting above mentioned, speeches were made by many of the advocates of Mr. Sadler's measure, to shew the necessity, the urgent necessity, for legislative interference on behalf, as they have it, of suffering humanity—meaning on behalf of all those now employed in cotton and other mills. The speakers distinguished themselves as such speakers generally do, as men who " ordinarily have not the judgment to perceive or to consider that in public proceedings the secret lets and difficulties are innumerable." The abuse sent forth by ignorant and by illiterate men we know is not deserving of much attention, particularly when it is thrown against any particular class in society, or against any particular system ; but we find among these abusive speech-makers an educated man, a barrister of long standing and celebrity, leading on the host, and armed, by what may seem to some men, to be learning and law, and it is to a speech delivered by the learned gentleman, as an advocate for Sadler's bill, that we have to apply our observations.

It is with the greatest reluctance that we undertake the task, for the odds are fearfully against us. We have to contend against a scholar, supported as he is by a numerous class of men, whose minds, to say the least of them, seem to us, similar to the mind of Peter the Hermit, who had such a command over himself, that whatever he wished he believed, and whatever he believed he saw in dreams and revelations, and had sighs, and tears, and ejaculations always in store. Mr. Condy seems to us to have *indulged* in all the prejudices of the party who have instructed him, or have requested his powerful aid ; HE seems to us not to have made himself acquainted with the truth of the case, and therefore it is that we reply to him, and lest the authority of the speaker should be attended to rather than the evidence of facts.

We perceive the danger we run in contending against a distinguished lawyer, *grown grey* in the practice of our courts, a veteran in literary controversy ; a man of learning, and law, and philosophy ; but if we mistake not, with no weapon but truth and reason, aided by experience, and extensive opportunities of observing the wants and necessities of the operatives generally in the neighbourhood of Manchester, we shall be able to hit this second atlas of knowledge right in the forehead; that is, we believe we shall be able to shew that the ground on which he builds the superstructure of his speech is unsound, and utterly unfit even for the foundation of a speech, to say nothing about its being fit to build a law upon. We shall shew that what he states for facts are not facts, and that the law which he is so anxious to obtain would not be a law to improve the condition of those for whose benefit it is intended; in short, that it would be a law of cruelty and injustice, and fitted only to cover the land with poverty and wretchedness. We know that there is not, and there cannot be, a more exalted charity than that which presents a shield against the rapacity of tyrants and oppressors; but we deny that factory owners are either tyrants or oppressors; we contend that the man of property, the capitalist, who devotes all his time, who applies all his energies to increase his wealth, by building mills and factories, and so employing the poor, is the greatest benefactor the poor man can have. One shilling earned by a man's own hand, is worth a pound given to him by the hand of charity, we had almost said mistaken charity.

But to proceed with our work. It will not be denied that the law which Mr. Condy advocates is one of such a character as to demand the most serious attention. And in debating upon what should be contained in a law which will, in a tremendous degree, affect the daily bread of hundreds of thousands of our fellow-creatures, and the value of all the cotton and woollen, and silk and flax mills of the kingdom—a law involving, as the intended law will involve, the very deepest principles of political philosophy, we naturally and reasonably expected that a man of Mr. Condy's learning would have told us something about law, liberty, property, freedom of the subject; we expected he would have begun at the beginning, and told us something about the links by which society is bound together. We expected that he would have told us something about the laws of parent and child, master and servant, instead of explaining to us what they of the law understand by reasonable and unreasonable service. Instead of referring us for further information upon these subjects (all bearing upon the factory time bill) to the works of those who have written in the ablest manner upon the reasonableness and necessity of laws, such as Fortesque, Bacon, Hale, Holt, or Blackstone, we are referred to the ribaldry of Jonathan Swift, the poetry of the king-killing and wife-divorcing Milton, and the supposed wrttings of the drunken and unhappy Porson. Instead of giving us a clear and philosophical exposition of the present condition of the workers in factories and their employers, and then proposing a plan by which that condition can be ameliorated, or by which the load of life can be lightened, (to use a figurative expression,) he dips his pen in sulphur, and says "the factory system is not a whit better than settled legalized infanticide." "The sword has been turned from our enemies and plunged into the bowels of suffering infancy." "Before, you sacrificed men: we now give you children." "Our sympathies are to be extended to the housebreaker, and still not one pang to be deducted from the sufferings of the poor factory children of Lancashire and Yorkshire." He says, "the burden of the poor laws is increased by the factory system;" and that "there is less humanity now in the nineteenth century of Christianity than in the reign of Titus." And then the learned gentleman tells us he has read Adam Smith's book, and considered himself once an adept in political economy; and at last winds up all by declaring that Sadler's ten hours' bill, or some such bill, has become necessary, and will cure all or most of the evils and ills he has so forcibly described. We know not, neither do we care, what the learned gentleman thinks of all this; but we say, and we are sorry to say it, that by condescending to use such unmeaning rant and rubbish, he has bedaubed himself desperately with the mud and slime of field preaching.

We really cannot help thinking that the learned gentleman has, upon this occasion, fallen into the ways of the sophists of old, without intending to do so. We are told that they (the sophists) in their speculative inquiries after truth, made their wisdom (from whence they took their name) to consist in bringing truth to the side of their reasoning; not their reasoning to the side of truth. Hence it became the glory of their profession to demonstrate for or against any opinion indifferently; and they were never better pleased than when that proposition (let it be what it would) was prescribed to them for their subject, which their auditors had a mind should be truth. Hooker said, and said truly, "that he that goeth about to persuade a multitude that they are not so well governed as they ought to be, shall never want attentive and favourable hearers, because they know the manifold defects whereunto every kind of regiment is subject; but the secret lets and difficulties which, in public proceedings, are innumerable and inevitable, they have not ordinarily the judgement to consider."

We fear that the learned barrister has not yet gone the whole round of human learning; let us hope he will read Hooker again, and by harder study, and an increased humility of mind, he may be moderated, and in the next oration which he makes for the good of us, the mob, he will be so kind as to shew what they of the law mean by perfect obligation, and all they can do by law, and what divines mean by imperfect obligation. He may also explain why societies of holy men have been, and are still employed to enforce this latter, viz., imperfect obligation. It would be kind also to convince us that Euhemerus was an imposter, and that there never were men so selfish as to observe one rule or doctrine, and to believe another rule or doctrine for their less instructed fellow-mortals: in short, he might as well shew us at once that Daniel O'Connell and Michael Thomas Sadler never heard a word in all their days about doctrine essoteric and doctrine exoteric: we hope the learned gentleman will understand us.

It is painful for us to remind our learned friend, for we too are as desirous as he is to ameliorate the condition of our fellow-creatures, "that the opinions of him will be disregarded who is proved to be ignorant of the circumstances about which he is speaking."

But to proceed—First, as to the ground upon which Mr. Condy asks for the ten hours' bill with all its penal enactments—without wasting any time in this matter, we mean the evidence taken before Sadler's Committee. Now this evidence, (so says my Lord Morpeth) is merely the case for the plaintiff: so then it comes to this—that the learned Mr. Condy, who is for the plaintiff, states his case, examines his witnesses, and then insists that he shall have a verdict for his client. If such a course is to prevail, then the sooner we come back to the law of nature the better. But we tell him, that the evidence upon which he builds all his argument is, in the fullest meaning of the words, *ex parte*, not upon oath; and what is more,

B

that it was taken with closed doors. We know this of our own knowledge. We were indeed admitted; but not until after half an hour's stormy debate in the committee, as to whether we should be admitted or not. We had heard from a member of the committee, that a witness, whose examination was going on, had charged us with the usual quantity of tyranny, cruelty, and what not; and we very naturally went down to the House of Commons, at the next meeting of the committee, to hear what might be said, having a sort of instinctive desire to proceed upon the old plan of accuser and accused being face to face; no allusion, however, was made to the previous examination: but we heard evidence respecting the Sunday Schools of Manchester, which was utterly untrue, and which we will use, when the proper time arrives, to illustrate the value, the morality, the learning, the philosophy of our would-be statesmen. We repeat, then, the evidence was *ex parte*, and taken with closed doors. And although we were an exception, our admission, at last, we understand, was by special favour; and that the objection to our admission was not because we had no interest in the question, not because we had been vilified and vituperated, but because we were known to have written something of and concerning the venerable and enlightened Mr. Sadler, the chairman of his party. We maintain, therefore, that the evidence is totally unworthy of credit, as yet, at all events; and, consequently, it is unfit to construct a law upon.

The learned gentleman says, that the factory system destroys human life. We say it does no such thing; for that, by a paper in our possession, the population of the Hundred of Salford was, in 1801, 281,413, and in 1831, 612,414. Finlayson and Milne say, in their evidence before a committee of the House of Commons, that the Northampton and Carlisle tables are wrong, and they make no reservation for the manufacturing districts. Mr. Condy says, that the factory system depraves the species. We say, that there are not a greater number of committals to the prison for the Hundred of Salford, than to the prison of any Hundred he can name, number for number in each Hundred; and we tell him, that the men and women in the Hundred of Salford are as hale, and as good looking, and live as long as the men and women of any part of England. We tell him, and we have authority for it, that the battalions of warriors raised in Lancashire, we mean the factory part of Lancashire, hold as well together under fire as any men upon the face of the earth.

We understand Mr. Condy to say, that the people employed in cotton factories are subject to scrofulous diseases, and that those diseases are altogether the consequences of being so employed. Of course it is not expected that we should, of our own knowledge, be able to answer this accusation; we, therefore, put the question, a few days ago, to one of our ablest physicians, who has been nearly twenty years, and now is, one of the Medical Board of our Royal Infirmary. He says, "If the medical witnesses had proper judgment, they would know, by *theory*, that the cotton factories *must* be a *cure* for scrofula; but if they had examined the factories, as the medical witnesses in 1818 did, they would know *practically*, that the factories *are* a cure. The cause of this is, the dryness, the warmth, and the comparative good living which their superior wages enable them to obtain. The scrofulous limbs which are amputated at the Royal Infirmary in this town, are in no instances from cotton factories, but belong to weavers, fustian cutters, calico printers, dyers, hatters," &c.

Mr. Condy says that the factory system has not only a tendency, but does actually increase the poor's rate in the manufacturing districts. We tell him that the facts are all the other way. The poor's rate for the township of Manchester on an average of six years, ending Easter 1832, was 3s. 6d. in the pound,* in which is included county

* RATE OF	DATE.	£.	S.	D.
5s.	Poor's Rates collected from 25th March, 1826, to 25th March, 1827	59216	16	8
5s.	Ditto from 25th March, 1827, to 25th March, 1828	70159	0	5¾
4s.	Ditto from 25th March, 1828, to 25th March, 1829	55704	6	6
4s.	Ditto from 25th March, 1829, to 25th March, 1830....................	52247	16	4½
—	Arrears of 1829-30, collected in 1830-31 ..	9760	15	4½
3s.	Ditto from 25th March, 1831, to 1st March, 1832	44080	0	4

Population of the Township of Manchester 142,026
Ditto of the Parish of Manchester.................... 270,963
Ditto of the Hundred of Salford 612,414
Ditto of the County of Lancaster 1,335,600

Manchester, Town Office,
March 10th, 1832.   GEO. LINGS, *Comptroller.*

rate, constables' accounts, and other charges.—
Looking at the taxes upon all the necessaries of
life, the taxes upon bricks, timber, and glass, we
contend that a 3s. 6d. rate when fairly considered,
is not more than a 1s. rate would have been when
the national debt was one to two or three hundred
millions :*—it should be so, or else all our mills,
machinery, canals, roads, and docks are to no
purpose—all our contrivances by which food,
clothes, and fuel are produced at a less and less
cost of human labour, are also to no purpose; it
must be so, or else all our exertions to support
sunday schools and national schools—all our exertions to give the poor some degree of sound learning, are also to no purpose. We say that the
poor's rate in the manufacturing districts is not
heavier than in other districts; and if it is heavy,
the factory system is the only system by which
you can lighten it, keeping faith with the national
creditor.

Mr. Condy says that the overseers of the poor
will not give relief if the children of the claimant
are not sent into factories. The overseer must in
all his doings keep close to the law. The public
ought to be in no worse situation than the father of

* Lands are better tilled ; the quality of agricultural produce is improved ;
exports are increased ; a larger revenue is collected ; the price of all our
produce is improved ; the intercourse with England is enlarged ; absentees
are increased in numbers ; and wealth, rents, and tithes have advanced from
one hundred to five hundred per cent. on those paid at the commencement
of the French revolution.

DOYLE'S LETTER to Mr. T. S. RICE.—*Ridgway,* 1831.

a family. It may seem absurd for a layman and a worker in a factory to read law to Mr. Condy. However, absurd as it is, we must do it. Blackstone says, book I. chap. 16,—" No person is bound to provide a maintenance for his issue unless where the children are impotent and unable to work either through infancy, disease, or accident: and then only is obliged to find them necessaries." And then the Judge goes on to shew the reasonableness, or spirit of the law, (as Montesquieu has it,) and says that " the policy of our laws, which were ever watchful to promote industry, did not mean to compel a father to maintain his idle and lazy children in ease and indolence, but thought it unjust to oblige the parent to provide them with superfluities."

But with respect to the state of the poor in days of old, let us beg of him to look over again his copy of Latimer's Sermons, Harrison's Description of England, Dalton's Justice, and his copy of Eden. In his Harleian Miscellany, he will find a curious pamphlet entitled " Greevous Grones of the Poor." Davison and Bichero too, he should read : lastly, the evidence lately given before a Committee of the House of Commons by those able men, the Catholic Bishop Doyle and Dr. Chalmers. Harrison wrote in 1577, and says, " there is no commonwealth, *at this day*, in Europe wherein there is not great store of poor people, and those necessarily to be relieved by the wealthier sort, which otherwise would starve and come to utter confusion :" and he says, too, "that at that time there were three or four hundred rogues hanged every year." All these authorities are agreed, that the people are poor because they have nothing to do, because they have no trade, no tools, nor can capitalists be found to lend them any ; all we contend for is, that there is less suffering among the poor, at the present time, in the manufacturing districts, than there was in those districts before manufactories were established in them. Mr. Condy seems to be of a different opinion. We are aware of the argument of Malthus, and (if we understand it correctly) it comes to this, that the English poor laws give a security for food and clothing to all, which is neither just nor reasonable : we agree with him ; he is no doubt right in the abstract, and so say Mr. Davison and Dr. Chalmers, and, in some degree, Bishop Coplestone. By the law of nature, it is not denied that the ownership is accorded to him who with his own bow kills the deer ; who with his own hand digs the well in a piece of ground which others had abandoned. But what says expediency : *expediency*, where all our arguments about perfect rights and perfect wrongs terminate ? Expediency says, that as the law will not punish a man who steals a loaf to save his life, you people of property had better settle the matter among yourselves, you had better all subscribe a fund, to which all who are suffering under disease, or are in distress, or in want, shall flee, and shall be relieved; and so save your persons from violence or death, and your property from spoliation or destruction. Hence come poor laws*. We are the more particular in this matter, because it does seem more than strange to us to be told, that when a man goes into a parish and finds the inhabitants have only spades and pick-axes, ploughs and harrows, and cart gear, by which they live, and when he has built a mill of the value of ten, or twenty, or sixty thousand pounds, and is then to be told that by so doing he has not only

* We are aware of the argument of Bishop Doyle, which is set forth in his letter to Mr. Spring Rice ; and it is excessively curious to perceive the ingenuity and the concealment with which the bishop approaches the defences of his adversaries. The concealed argument is this, that when man abandons the rights, or supposed rights, which he had under the law of nature, and surrenders himself into the compact of society, from that moment he has not only *a right* to the full protection of the laws of that society, but he has *a right*, being in distress, to a participation in the food and the clothes which the society may have accumulated. The bishop seems to us, in proving his proposition, to have, from the very first, thrown overboard the learning of the man, and the sagacity of the statesman ; and uses just such metaphors and matter as are used by our sectarian ministers, when they are holding forth at a missionary club, or such as our Cantwells use when they are making a preachment about factory children. He, like them, takes authority for truth, and not truth for authority. To our great mortification, the bishop all at once stops short, as if his head was giddy, and says he dares trust himself no further, (knowing very well how far he was safe,) and then goes on to prove his case by turning to the scriptures of our Church, and to the scriptures and traditions of his own; and this latter, viz., tradition, as did the sanctuaries of old belonging to his Church, covers a multitude of sins. The bishop disdains to accept, as we have done, a refuge in expediency. The whole letter, however, is full of information, and will repay the reader well for the perusal. The bishop asks for a poor law for Ireland; but he " seeks only to provide bread to the orphan, shelter to the aged, and food to the weak and decrepid," who have no friend to support them. He says not a word for the able-bodied poor ; nor will he suffer, in his system of poor laws, an appeal to the magistrates. In England we abound with uneducated magistrates, whose chief work seems to be to order money to be given to the able-bodied poor. Often, very often, have we heard a sage upon the bench put these questions to the lusty claimant.

17

not added a single tool to the chest, but has absolutely taken out of it the rule and the square, seems to us a monstrous absurdity. We are disposed to say with the writer of old, not only that the heart of man is desperately wicked, but the head of man is desperately ignorant; eyes has he, but sees not; ears has he, but hears not; understanding has he, but it is clouded by ignorance and prejudices of thick darkness.

Our readers (if we shall have any) will perceive why we have said so much about the poor and the poor laws; for, if we have demonstrated that the factory system does not destroy life, if we have demonstrated that the factory system does not increase the poor's rate, and we humbly think that we have so demonstrated, certainly we may say, that we have answered the most fastidious objector, although that objector should be an able and accomplished scholar like Mr Condy.

We have mentioned the name of Bishop Doyle;

How many children do you say you have? What do you all earn? Well, then, what is it you want? How much can you do with? and after a little huckstering a bargain is struck, the pauper receiving town's money, and the magistrate receiving—the sacred spirit of independence and the feeling of personal responsibility. The whole man is changed; the cries of his helpless children no longer rouse him to exertion; to provide for the sorrows of his wife no longer calls all his energies into action. No, no, why should they? Alas! they are all transferred to the justice—to the magistrate. The only joy the lusty pauper feels, is when he looks at the frugal and thriving farmer; the active and industrious factory owners exerting themselves: the one to obtain a better crop, the other to obtain a larger mill; for without toil or care, he knows he shall partake with them to the extent of his wants. Mr. Condy might, in candour, have told us something about this part of our law, for he must have seen much of it, and of its effects.

C

we shall hear what he says about the poor of Ireland; but the answer we are about to give applies to the poor of all countries. The bishop is asked, (see parliamentary paper, June 3rd, 1830, question 4447,) "Do you consider that any *alteration of law* could be made that would have a *tendency* to lessen or to terminate the distress among the poor in Ireland?" He answers the question by saying, "I believe *no legal enactment* could terminate the distress among the poor, for *the providence of God is* that there will be *always poor in the land;* but, I think, legal enactments might diminish, very much, the stock of misery which now exists, and provide, in *a reasonable manner,* for the wants of the destitute *who may be* hereafter."

Mr. Condy says the law interferes in regard to minors in the wealthy classes. And here again we have the odious task of reading more law. Blackstone, book 1, chap. 16, "A father has no other power over his son's estate, than as his trustee or guardian; for though he may receive the profits during the child's minority, yet he must account for them when he comes of age. He may, indeed, have the benefit of his children's labour while they live with him and are maintained by him; but this is no more than he is entitled to from his apprentices and servants."

Factory time bill makers should look carefully to this part of the law; for it seems to us, that if a child can maintain itself by the labour of its hands, conducting itself with propriety and according to law, it may leave the roof of its parents; and there is no law by which it can be compelled to return.

So much, then, for the ground upon which Mr. Condy raises his arguments, and so much for such of *his facts*, as seem to us of importance; and we cannot help saying here, that when we look at the way in which the contemplated law will work; when we look at the alarming consequences which will flow from it, should it become law; when we look at the way in which it is advocated; when we see men, who should know better, ready to discuss without accurate information, and when the daily bread of millions of our fellow creatures is at stake; when we see men ready to decide without reflection; we are humbled and mortified beyond what we can express. We always be-- lieved that educated men, at all events, considered, that "to examine we should be serious," and "to judge we should be attentive to the argument:" it seems we were wrong in this respect: we are, how- ever, taught a lesson of humiliation, and a lesson to lower the pride of all those who were wont to "exult in the progress and advancement of human reason."

Before we proceed to the most difficult part of our task, namely, to shew that a ten hours' bill would impoverish, and be a law of cruelty and injustice to, those for whose benefit it would seem to be in- tended, we must be permitted to notice several of the quotations which the learned gentleman made use of in the course of his speech; one, at least, seems somewhat to our purpose, and if we can strengthen our case by an argument from the other side ; if we can shew that learned men do not always deliver the whole text and nothing but the text ; if we can do this, we will challenge the thanks of the learned gentleman himself. We begin with what is said about a paper of Dean Swift's :—the Dean proposed to have children made fat and sold, but our learned friend is reported to have said or suggested, that the same mode might now be adopted with the useless parents of the factory children. The Dean's paper is entitled " a modest proposal," and may be found in the seventh volume of Scott's edition of the Dean's works. Now the Dean was continually complaining that the poor of Ireland had little or no employment ; and he says in the paper alluded to, " These mothers instead of being able to work for their honest livelihood, are forced to employ all their time in strolling to beg sustenance for their hopeless infants, who as they grow up, either turn thieves *for want of work*, or leave their dear native land to fight for the Pretender in Spain." The Dean had a mortal hate of thieves and soldiers, and he said, that rather than children should be brought up in idleness, and so become thieves or soldiers, he would have them made fat at about a year old and sold for food.

We venerate the memory of Dean Swift, passing strange as the expression may appear in the eyes and ears of the learned : we venerate his memory for his patriotism, for we will consider him

an Irishman ; we venerate his memory for the
many rules he has left us, by which we may easily
detect a knave under the garb of religion. He
mourned over the miseries of his country, arising
from the want of employment and consequent poverty. He lamented that capitalists, to use a
modern term, could not be induced to live there :
the want of such men the Dean saw and felt most
severely. The Dean was not a sickly sentimentalist ;
he saw human nature as it was, and still is, and
ever will be, darkly as he described it. The Dean
did not, like our humanity-moved men, believe
what he wished, and what he believed, see in dreams
and revelations. The Dean, like a true friend to
the poor, did all he could to find them employment, he knew that life, without honest and independent means of supporting it, was utterly worthless, and therefore at last, as it were in an agony
of feeling, he says, rather than children should be
brought up in idleness, he would " that they
should be made fat and sold for food."

Thus then we have the testimony of Dean
Swift, that children should be employed, and not
left to become thieves for the want of work.

The learned gentleman quotes some poetry
about a pig swimming across a river, which he has
fetched out of the Devil's Walk, a beastly piece of
ribaldry which is attributed to Porson, and which,
possibly, the Professor may have parted with when
he was spouting drunk in the cyder cellar. If we
could demean ourselves so as to aspire to a place

among the Cantwells, the Dogberrys, the Duber-
leys, the Sea Coles of our mighty city, we might
be tempted, particularly if we were holding forth
against factory time bill makers, to say, that such
or such a one reminds us forcibly of the following
lines of Porson.

> " A gentle pig, this same, a pig of parts,
> " And learned as F. R. S. or graduate in arts,
> " His ancestors, 'tis true, could only squeak,
> " But this has been at school, and in a month will speak."
>
> *Kidd's Collection of Porson's Tracts and Criticisms.*

The learned gentleman goes on and calls in the
aid of Milton; and then to express his hatred of
factory masters and factory systems, repeats the
lines—

> " —————— Immediately a place," &c.

Now the learned gentleman will not be offended
if we quote some lines of an abler poet than
Milton; not to shew our hatred of factory time
bill makers, but to remind them that in days of
old there was a certain play written which was
called "The Clouds," and in it there is a description of a noisy set of bipeds, who, notwithstanding all that was said and written for their learning,
would everlastingly take authority for truth and
not truth for authority, and thereupon the great
master satirist of antiquity, when speaking of the
numerous family of whom the clouds were the
nursing mothers, says that they were

> " Famous sophists, fortunetellers,
> " Quacks, med'cine mongers, bards bombastical,
> " Chorus projectors, and star interpreters,
> " And wonder-making cheats.

The learned gentleman will easily perceive a sort of family likeness. He will see here the faces of many of his speech-making coadjutors in the factory time bill making line.

But to return to our subject. It is asserted that the factory system, under its present regulations, impoverishes and demoralizes all those who derive their bread from being employed in our factories; that they are *compelled,* by the factory owners, to labour more hours than they ought to labour: in short, it is asserted that the factory system is a system of blood and slaughter;—and that a ten hours' bill, or, in other words, a bill to limit the hours of labour to ten hours per day, will be a full and efficient remedy; and the legislature are asked by the commercial philosophers of Manchester, with the boroughreeve at their head, and others, to pass such a bill. It is said, indeed, that the bill shall take under its protection only such as are under twenty-one years of age: but from the arrangement in all mills, by which persons under twenty-one years are furnished with employment adapted to their age, their experience, or their strength, comes, what we call a full and effectual division of labour. The younger prepare certain parts of the work, and the older, or more experienced, complete it; each becoming by practice more expert and more accurate. The old and the young are essentially necessary to each other, and form a whole, and make a full and beneficial division of labour: to say, therefore, to the young, you shall

work ten hours a day, and to the old, or all above
eighteen or twenty-one years of age, you may work
as many hours as you please, would be just the same
as if you said to a bricklayer, you, Mr. Bricklayer,
may work as many hours as you please, but your
labourer shall give over work at four o'clock in the
afternoon. Now, in considering this question, it
appears to us necessary to begin at the beginning,
and ask, have the legislature power to pass such a
bill? for even the power of legislators is limited.
In this matter the authorities from Aristotle down
to Locke are all agreed; and Locke says, "Their
power, (the law-makers) in the utmost bounds of
it, is limited to the public good of the society. It
is a power that hath no other end but preservation;
and, therefore, can never have a right to destroy,
enslave, or designedly to impoverish the subject."

Next we have to shew what law is, and here too
we believe there is not, nor has there been much
difference of opinion since the days of Demosthenes.
"The design and object of laws," says Demosthenes,
" is to ascertain what is just, honourable, and expedient, and when that is discovered, it is proclaimed
as a general ordinance, *equal and impartial to all.*
This is the origin of law, which for various reasons
all are under an obligation to obey; but especially,
because all law is the nomination and gift of heaven;
the sentiment of wise men; the correction of every
offence; and the general compact of the state; to
live in conformity with which, is the duty of every
individual in society." We see then, that law-

that the ear of the magistrate is deaf to any case of cruelty committed in a cotton mill; that cotton spinners have no notion of justice; that the rule of doing as one would be done to is unknown to them. We tell the objectors to the factory system, who call upon us to believe all this, that the cotton spinners know their interest as well as other men, and none but a fool is incapable of perceiving that "honesty is the best policy;" and we believe there are not more foolish cotton spinners than foolish linen drapers.

If need be, instead of addressing our remarks to, or intending our remarks to be read by legislators chiefly, we will address ourselves to the workmen particularly, and shew them how they stand with regard to their masters; why it is that they often see bread rise, whilst no advance takes place in their wages; why bread is sometimes dear after a good harvest, and comparatively cheap after a scanty one; we will tell them why trade is good now, and why it was bad in the autumn of 1831, or at any other time. We should be ashamed to do this upon this occasion: as we said before, our remarks are meant for men who know the first principles of political philosophy, but seem to be mistaken as to the right application of them.

"The care of the poor," as Paley says, "ought to be the care of all laws, for this plain reason, that the rich are able to take care of themselves." But in

makers ought not, at all events, to make a law which shall designedly impoverish—or shall be unjust, or inexpedient. Yet we find that the legislature is required to make a law which shall say: all you who derive your daily bread by working in cotton, and woollen, and silk, and flax mills, and who have no other means on earth of providing for the day which is passing over you, save the labour of your hands, you shall employ the labour of those hands but ten hours out of the four and twenty, be your wants, be your necessities, what they may.

We have no occasion to write a history of trade, a history of a bale of cotton, or of a pound of gold; we have but little occasion to shew that it pleases God, for the wisest purposes, to give us bad seasons and scanty crops; for it is evident that trade is the very creature of the seasons, and a good demand or no demand depends upon the earth yielding or not yielding her increase. Therefore, to say to the workers in cotton, and woollen, and silk, and flax—you shall hold on, in a constant unvarying rate of work, is to say, you shall endure all the privations and hardships arising from a want of demand for your labour; and you shall not improve your condition or be enriched when your labour is in demand. The people of other nations, your competitors, your neighbours, employed in other trades, may adapt their exertions to the times and seasons; but you shall have no such advantage.

We say, therefore, that the ten hours' bill is

partial and unjust, and calculated to impoverish the subject. We will next inquire if a ten hours' bill will be expedient; that is, fit, proper, or suited to the occasion. It is said that a law has become necessary to protect the young people employed in cotton and other mills against the tyranny, the cruelty, and the unreasonable exactions of their masters; that the hours of labour are too many; that the mills are dirty, ill ventilated, and destructive of health, and so forth. It has been shewn by several cotton spinners, who have written books upon the subject, that the operatives in their own mills, or in mills generally, are not ill-treated in any respect. One of these gentlemen tells us how much his operatives earn a-week; and then says, that if there are any evils to be complained of they may be cured by a steam engine restriction act. Another tells us, "that his operatives, and the operatives in other mills, are as well off, and much better, than the workers in metal at Birmingham, or the pitcher makers of Burslem." Another *of these learned men* tells us, among other things, how many tons, hundred weights, quarters, pounds, and ounces of cotton his mill spins up in a year, and the proportion that that lot bears to the whole lot. However these books may have satisfied and pleased the writers of them, they seem to have satisfied no one else, as they certainly ought to have done. Perhaps it will be no answer to say that the cotton and other spinners have their full share of under-

standing, and that they know it to be ag interest to be tyrants, to be cruel and un exacting, to have their mills dirty and ill and therefore it follows, that but few, v any such abuses exist. At all events, it much to say that a man knows his own proportion to the quantity of learning information he may possess; and it see that master cotton spinners, and silk spi wool spinners are as well informed as iro master farmers, master potters, or mast and do therefore conduct their trades wi abuse of any authority they may have.

To believe all, or any part, of what is suffered in cotton or other mills, requi believe that the people, or operatives, in the fullest meaning of the word—that th are in a sort of combination, and that t together and consider how they can op grind down the workman; and that but combination and unjust conduct of the m should never hear of *long hours* (to us venient term) and low wages; that but (the masters) wages would be good, and t in continual prosperity; *just as if the inc decrease in the value of money had to do with trade,* and as if it never the master at all; as if the storm which the cottage of the workman, flew over the of the master. We are required also t

the terrible mania of act of parliament making, which this country labours under, we seem to forget that the foundation of all moral feeling, and moral conduct, is in a man's personal responsibility for the consequences of his own conduct. A sense and perception of this responsibility is the spring of the practical principles of virtue. It enters into our highest duties. We forget that "the efficacy of human laws," to use the words of Mr. Davison, "may be cast, perhaps, nearly in the following scale: their direct power to inspire men with the love of probity, diligence, sobriety, and contentment, by positive commands, is small; their power to restrain the opposite vices is greater; their power to discourage, or hinder, good habits of character, by mistaken institutions, is greatest of all." Now every thing is to be done by Act of Parliament. Bishop Fleetwood tells us in his Chronicon Preciosum, and Lord Liverpool, in his book on the coins, says the same thing, that laws and proclamations were made to keep up the value of clipt and debased coin—Laws have been made to prevent the coin of the realm being exported, let the foreign exchanges be ever so unfavourable— Laws have been made to fix the price of bread— Laws have been made to set a rate upon victuals in a time of famine—Laws have been made to regulate the working of cotton mills; but then, as Locke says, "these were laws to hedge in the cuckoo, and to no purpose."

But to return to the proper consideration as to the fitness or expediency of Sadler's ten hours' bill: let us admit only for the sake of argument, that the operatives in these districts are enduring an intolerable load of life, and then let us inquire if a ten hours' bill will lighten that load. If the operatives work many hours, and are ill paid, it must be in consequence of the supply of labour in the market being greater than the demand,—in other words, there are too many labourers, and too few masters who want labourers; and hereby hangs "all the law and the prophets." There is a want of employment; "and the labourers," as Adam Smith says, "bid one against another in order to get it, which lowers both the real and the money price of labour." The fact that the supply of labour in the market is greater than the demand, need not be insisted upon; for even at this time, February, 1833, when the circulation of the Bank of England is at the very highest point, and higher than can be maintained steadily many weeks or months, the overseers are paying a considerable sum, weekly, to poor who cannot find employment. In this state of things it is proposed to reduce the working days of the week from six to five, by a ten hours' bill, which, to us, appears an absurdity. A ten hours' bill seems to us to be likely to cover the land with poverty and wretchedness. One can hardly believe that men can be found so visionary as to believe that an Act of Parliament can regulate the hours of labour, can create food and a demand for labour. "The belly has no ears," says the old adage; nor has necessity any law.*

The contracts between master and servant, in the manufacturing districts, are made for one week, which, in our view, is a matter to be remembered. "Service," says Paley, "in this country is as it ought to be, voluntary and by contracts; and the master's authority extends no further than the terms or *equitable* construction of the contract will justify." Again, we will suppose that the ten hours' bill has become law, then either the present rate of wages must be raised one-sixth or one-fifth part, or they must not; if they are raised, it can only be by a demand for our merchandize at a corresponding advance. In our competition with foreigners, does any one believe that we can obtain a higher price than they obtain, because of some act of our

* In 1822, when the farmers were in great distress, they petitioned the legislature for relief, when Lord Liverpool, whose greatest failing was not a want of compassion, or of a desire to do good, said in a memorable speech, " Ask the farmer in his sober reason, when he is divested of the delusions instilled into him by the sophistry practised at public meetings, what it is that he really wants, and he will tell you, a market. But," continued his lordship, " it is not in the power of parliament to give the farmer a market adequate to his wants." Here then we have the cultivators of the soil appealing to the legislature in a most earnest manner. The farmers appeal to land owners, who not only knew, but *felt* the sufferings they were enduring; and are told by one of the most benevolent of men—the minister of the day—that although they only ask for a market, it is not in the power of parliament to give a market. But parliament are asked to make five days a-week serve all the purposes of six: they, in short, are asked to find a market for all productions of labour, at an advanced price, and they will, to a moral certainty, give the same answer,—that it is not in the power of parliament to give, to find, or to create a market.

parliament? When the foreign exchanges are against us, when, consequently, the circulation of the Bank of England is reduced from twenty or twenty-two millions to sixteen and a half millions, as it was in January, 1832, does any one expect that a ten hours' bill will secure constant employment at good wages?—will a ten hours' bill ever enter into the consideration of either master or man for one moment? But, if we had no Bank of England, the same effects would be felt; because whenever we import more merchandise from foreign countries than we export,—in other words, when our imports exceed our exports,— away will go our metal money to pay the difference, and whilst the settlement is going on, (and the whole of 1831 was a settling year,) low wages, "long hours," and more work are the inevitable consequences. But all this is burning candles by day, and proving not only what no one denies, but what every 'prentice boy knows to be true. If there are abuses under the factory system, (and we doubt whether there are any except such as are inseparable from all systems and inherent in our nature,) we can see no remedy for them by a ten hours' bill; and we believe, therefore, that such a bill is neither fit nor expedient.

Do the promoters of the ten hours' bill think that by acts of pains and penalties against the capitalists and master manufacturers, they can increase the means by which the poor are employed—that by acts of pains and penalties against mill owners,

they can induce them to enlarge what mills they
have, or build new ones—that by acts of pains
and penalties against mill owners they can induce
our youngest and most enterprising capitalists to
remain in England rather than go into Switzerland,
as some have done? Seeing that the population
of the Hundred of Salford has increased in thirty
years, from 287,413 to 612,414, will they, by acts
of pains and penalties insure an increased means of
employment; in other words. can they, by acts of
pains and penalties, provide a corresponding increase of mills and works for the increasing population? It seems to us certain that the population
will go on increasing for many years to come, but
it is by no means seems so certain that there will be
a corresponding increase of mills, machinery, and
means of employment.*

* " They would fix a limit to the working of the steam engines and water
wheels employed in all the cotton, woollen, silk, and flax mills in the kingdom ; they would have one of the king's men to watch the mill owners by
day and by night, and with the king's lock, the king's key, and the king's
seal, open and lock up our furnace doors by act of parliament. Can they
not see that thousands upon thousands of industrious and well-disposed
work-people are daily and hourly pressing upon the mill owners for employment and for bread, and yet do they propose to restrict the moving powers
of our mills ? Can they not perceive the imminent danger of not keeping
the mighty masses of population which are crowded together in the manufacturing districts in employment, and in tolerable comfort even ! Can they
not perceive, that if these masses before mentioned are meddled with rudely,
if they are interfered with in their pursuits, and hindered by unjust and
unreasonable enactments—such as Mr. Sadler's or other factory time bills—
that they will, like the whirlwind, in an instant lay temples, and palaces,
and laws, and order, prostrate ! Will they say that the steam engine has
not become essential to the very existence of millions of their fellow-
creatures, and it may be said, to the peace, to the order, to the government,

E

The factory time bill makers tell us, that their work is a work of benevolence, of kindness; they would have us believe that they are creatures of pure reason and enlightened beneficence, that theirs is an exalted charity: but we tell them that there is poison, deadly poison, in the alms of their mistaken charity. If they would really improve our condition, let them lower the price of our food, or increase the demand for the productions of our hands, and fewer hours of labour will be the consequence:—it is an over load, an unnatural load of taxation which cuts us to the heart. Our bread is taxed, our beer is taxed, our tea is taxed, our sugar is taxed, our building materials are cruelly taxed,

and to whatever makes life desirable in this country? And yet, to use their own words, they would place "restrictions upon the moving power" of our mills.

"Again; according to the wisdom of these men, we have been mistaken all these years in speaking of the philosophic Dr. Black with the purest veneration, and the sincerest affection and gratitude; we have been wrong in our estimate of the services of the ingenious and able Watt. These philosophers left us the steam engine nearly forty years ago, as it is unaltered at this moment: but it would seem they did too much for their fellow men. Will they say, that in cultivating the arts of peace, we are multiplying by means of the steam engine the necessaries, the comforts, and the elegancies of life, at too low a cost of human labour, and that we have arrived at a point from which we are to retrograde, to turn back, for that onward there is nothing but "rocks and brawling waves, and mists and fogs, and murky darkness." It was a holy Christian Bishop in his blind zeal who destroyed the valuable library at Alexandria (called the new library). Christian Baptist saints have lately preached one of our oldest colonies into rebellion; and in England, in the nineteenth century, Christian *philosophers* and *saints* would lay their rude hands upon our proudest triumph of philosophy (the steam engine,) and place a limit to its usefulness."

From a Pamphlet, published by Ridgway, entitled "Mr. Sadler, his Factory Time Bill, and his Party.—1832.

the very light of heaven, which the God of the universe allows to fall upon us fréely, is taxed ; but the most cruel tax of all is the tax upon raw cotton. But for these taxes, with all our roads and canals, and steam engines, and mills, and machinery of every kind, does any man think that children of nine years old would be set to work ten, or eleven, or twelve hours a-day? But it will be as well to inquire more particularly into this matter, viz., the employment of children in our factories under ten years of age.

Burke says, " It is one of the finest problems in legislation what the state ought to take upon itself to direct by the public wisdom, and what it ought to leave, with as little interference as possible, to individual discretion." It is in vain to refer factory time bill makers to this valuable specimen of the master mind of Burke. Parental affection, perhaps, the noblest gift of heaven, is to be regulated, and its place usurped, by act of parliament. One would have thought, from what Blackstone says as to the law of parent and child, enough had been done ; but it is not so,—a father is not to be the judge as to the time when his child shall be set to work, or how it shall work. No, no ; this must all be done by act of parliament.

Now we shall endeavour to shew how the ten hours' bill will act with respect to children under ten years of age, who are to become the objects of its protection in an especial manner, and who are now employed in our factories. If we take twenty,

or any given number, of children under ten or
eleven years of age, and inquire carefully into their
circumstances, and the circumstances of their parents, we shall find that by far the greater number
are either orphans, without father or without
mother, or that they are the oldest of numerous
families, young as they are; or that they are children of the poorest of the community. Many of
their parents, from age, sickness, or incapacity to
provide for their children, have assistance from the
poor's rate. Others of these parents are exerting
themselves to the utmost of their power, to rear
their children without parish pay, and many of
these are widows, who have a laudable pride by
which they will endure any hardship, face any
danger, submit to hunger and privation in silence,
rather than apply for parish relief: we know many
of this class who would submit to the last extre-
mity of distress, rather than it should be said after
their deaths, and thrown in their children's teeth,
that they had been reared in the poor house, that
they had been fed by parish pay.

Now let us suppose the ten hours' bill has
become law, and that all the children under ten
years of age are deprived of their employment.
Does any man suppose that they will be sent to
school? Will overseers pay school-wage? The
national schools cannot contain a fiftieth part of
them, but if they could, how are they to be fed?
We have seen that they are now, many of them,
assisted by the parish, or striving hard and enduring

privations, laudably to do without such assistance.
Well, they are driven from their employment
into the poor house, or to prowl and beg in our
streets, where they learn to pick and steal. Thus,
then, the ten hours' bill says to all children under
ten years of age—orphans, without father or without mother, but mostly without father, or the
children of the poorest of the community—you
shall be driven from your employment into the
poor house, or into the streets, to beg and learn to
pick and steal: and this is precisely what the ten
hours' bill will do. We say again, and the observation cannot be repeated too often, that there is
poison, deadly poison in the alms of the ten hours'
factory time bill makers. Humanity, indeed!—
The ten hours' bill or any bill of the kind, will be
a bill to impoverish the poor and cover the land
with wretchedness. Factory time bill makers are
mockers of the poor and the needy, there is poison
in the alms of their charity.

The magistrates of Kent and Sussex would interfere between the farmers and their servants;
they would regulate wages; they fixed a rate, and
what was the consequence? why, night-fires, bur-
glaries, and rebellion, and then special commissions,
transportations, and deaths by the hands of the
public executioner.

By regulating, as it is called, the hours of labour
in these districts, would they expose us to night
fires ? Would they have master manufacturers

murdered in broad day light, as Mr. Houstun was ? Do they wish to renew the days of the Special Commissions ? Some dozen or more mills or factories might be burnt in a night for several weeks together, and each mill of the intrinsic value of fifty thousand pounds; but to rebuild and refit them is quite another affair.

Professor Senior says, " the principal means by which the food for the maintenance of labourers can be increased, is by increasing the productiveness of their labour; by allowing every man to exert himself in the way which, from experience, he finds most beneficial; by freeing industry (not by making fetters in the shape of ten hours' bills) from the mass of restrictions, prohibitions, and protecting duties, with which the legislature, sometimes in well-meaning ignorance, sometimes in pity, and sometimes in selfish jealousy, has laboured to crush or misdirect her efforts."

M. Garnier said long ago, " let government no longer attempt to impede the efforts of industry by regulations, or to accelerate her progress by rewards; let it leave, in the most perfect freedom, the exertions of labour and employment of capital; let its protecting influence extend only to the removal of such obstacles as avarice or ignorance have raised up to the unlimited liberty of industry and commerce; then capitalists will naturally develope themselves by their own movements in those directions which are at once most agreeable to the profit of the capitalists, and most favourable to the increase of national wealth."

It would be a waste of time to go further to shew that the capitalists and their work-people should be let alone. The one supplies himself with the best servant he can find,—the other supplies himself with the best place he can find, and the contract, as we have shewn, lasting but for a week, or at most a fortnight, if any difference arises, it is settled either by arbitration or by the magistrates, who, both paid and unpaid, always lend a willing ear to every complaint of oppression or unfairness.*

We shall proceed to shew, in as few words as possible, what the factory system has done for this country; and we shall point out the names of the benevolent men to whom gratitude is due; but to describe, in adequate terms, what these men have done for this country in particular, and for all civilized men, is a task fit only for a much abler hand.

---

* The public are probably not generally aware that the author of the last factory time bill was Worsley, of Stockport,—a person well known to the factory owners in this part of the kingdom. He was assisted by Mr. Joseph Brotherton, at present the member for Salford. When the bill was before the committee of the House of Commons, a gentleman appealed to the chairman respecting the wording of the clause that fixes the time after which an information should not be laid, when Mr. Hobhouse, turning to Worsley, said, " Mr. Worsley, will that do? Mr. Worsley, do you think it should be as Mr. —— has put it?" Worsley replied, "All the other statutes allow a longer time between the committing of the offence, and receiving the information;" and then he muttered something to his co-adjutor Brotherton, who went up to the chairman, and with an expression of countenance peculiarly his own, said, " Well Mester Ob—bouse, ween agreed toot, and I agree toot.'

It may be said, that the factory system began
at the period when Mr. Watt effected his great
improvements in the steam engine. As soon as
that great work was accomplished, an efficient
moving power, easily repaired, was to be had at a
moderate expence, and could be set up in or near
any of the towns and villages upon the great coal
fields of the kingdom. Power was taken to the
people; and after these moving powers were so
placed, their numbers increased with astounding rapidity. We see next a rapid increase of
population wherever these moving powers are
placed. The " busy hum" of man is heard on every
side. The population of the Hundred of Salford,
we have seen, in thirty years is increased from
281,413 to 612,414. Land becomes better cultivated, and bears an increased value. Mines of
coal, iron, lead, and copper are opened, and
become beneficial. Next we have improved
roads ; rivers are made navigable ; canals are
formed, and made also navigable ; increased
accommodations are required, and made in many
of our sea ports. The port of Liverpool attests
the stupendous increase of ships and commerce;
her magnificent docks, and the last triumph of
philosophy—the railway, which bears her name—
all, all are derived from the factory system.

Our schools, our ancient halls, our colleges, are
found scarcely equal to the accommodation of
those who seek to be instructed in those venerable
institutions—those purest foundations of sound

learning and philosophy: they are crowded with the sons of our merchants and manufacturers.

England, by her factory system, was able to carry on a war unequalled for duration and waste of human life; in spite of a monetary system—the most vicious and the most wicked—the standard of value being then, as now, entrusted to a club of dealers and chapmen, who use it for their own profit, and for no other consideration. Scraps of paper were current coin—daring, and mad, and rash speculation prevailed in all its frightful mien. The wealthy merchant of to-day was the next day an inmate of a mad house or a poor house. Fortune and misfortune went hand in hand; "the rich, under this vicious monetary system," says the able Bishop Coplestone, " have been made poor; the creditor has been paid off with less than he lent; the hapless annuitant has sunk amidst the general rise;—and he who sold his land for what was deemed an equivalent, has lived to see the price dwindled to less than half its value." Under all this load of dishonesty and misgovernment we see the commercial navy of Great Britain visiting the remotest corners of the earth, laden with the produce of our factories, and carrying in her train mutual good-will, civilization and peace; teaching men to regard each other as brethren and children of one parent; teaching men that in order to possess the greatest possible quantity of this world's good, they have but to beat their spears and swords

F

into plough shares and pruning hooks, and to culti-vate the arts of peace.

Great Britain owes her eminence in arts and in arms, and her proud rank among the nations of the earth, to her factory system : by it she has become a land mark of liberty ; and, as a tower of strength, she maintains her rights as a nation, and the rights of all civilized men.

We may now inquire which of her sons have contributed in the greatest degree to raise their country to this distinguished rank. Who are the benevolent men who have invented the machinery by which all this astounding progress has been made ? who are they by whose master minds such mighty advancement has been made ? by whose inventions are the wants, the comforts, the ele-gancies of life supplied at a less and less cost of human labour ? who are they by whose inventions commerce is promoted, and learning and civiliza-tion is extended ? who are the benevolent men who, by their inventions, lead and induce men to cultivate the arts of peace ? We instantly recog-nise the names of Black, Watt, Heys, Hargreaves, Horrocks of Preston, Crompton, Adam Murray of Ancoats, John Kennedy of Ardwick, George Sidebottom of Mottram, and Thomas Ashton of Hyde, and to these must be added the names of Brindly, Murdock, the Rev. Mr. Lee, and the Rev. Mr. Cartwright; and whenever the educated man, the man of letters, or the historian who in-

quires into the causes to which Great Britan owes
her eminence in arts, and we may add in arms, the
names of the distinguished men we have just written will stand forward not only as benefactors to
this their native land, but as benefactors to the
whole family of man, and the expression of gratitude of intelligent men in all time to come, will
be made to the God of the universe, for having,
by these his servants, so clearly maintained his
power and his goodness.

Such is the factory system, and such are the
men to whose master minds we owe it. To mark
its progress with accuracy, to develope its power as
a means, or an instrument of civilization, is a task
to which we intend to devote the leisure hours of
the few remaining years which may be left to
us ; for the present we shall close our remarks with
the words of Bacon, for whose comprehensive
mind nothing seemed too vast, for whose sagacity
nothing was too minute or intricate, and who says,
when speaking of inventions—

" First, then, the introduction of great inventions
appears one of the most distinguished of human
actions, and the ancients so considered it. For
they assigned divine honours to the authors of
inventions, but only heroic honors to those who
displayed civil merit, such as the founders of cities
and empires, legislators, the deliverers of their
country from lasting misfortune, the quellers of
tyrants and the like. And *if any will rightly com*

pare them, he will find the judgment of antiquity
to be correct. For *the benefit* derived from inventions may extend to mankind in general, but civil
benefits to particular spots alone; the latter moreover last but for a time, *the former for ever.* Civil
reformation seldom is carried on without violence
and confusion, whilst inventions are *a blessing* and
a benefit without injuring or affecting any. Inventions are also, as it were, new creations and imitations of divine works."

VERNON ROYLE.

Manchester, Feb. 1833.

T. BOWLER, PRINTER, COURIER AND HERALD OFFICE, MANCHESTER.

REMARKS

ON THE

PROPRIETY AND NECESSITY

OF MAKING

THE FACTORY BILL

OF MORE

GENERAL APPLICATION.

LONDON:

LONGMAN, REES, ORME, BROWN, GREEN, AND LONGMAN;
T. SOWLER, MANCHESTER; AND ROBINSON, LEEDS.

1833.

REMARKS, &c.

It is now upwards of thirty years since the first legislation on Cotton Mills, when Sir R. Peel, in 1802, obtained an act of parliament for the protection of parish apprentices employed in them.

In the year 1819 the first act was passed restraining the *hours of labour* and *ages* of ALL children working in Cotton Mills; since when, and up to the year 1831, four other Acts have followed, with further restrictions on *both*.

In the last and present years Bills have been brought into the House of Commons for extending the principle to a few other trades, besides the cotton; pushing the limitations to the ages of children and their hours of labour a great deal further than before, and with a ruinous increase of severity in the penal enactments.

It is manifest to the most common observer, that the whole manufacturing system of the Empire has, of late years, been undergoing a regular and radical change, by the concentration of numbers of persons, of all ages, in establishments or Factories; instead of being carried on, as formerly, in detached portions—partly in buildings provided by the employers, and partly by the work-people at their own homes, spread over the whole face of the country. And however deeply such a change, which has altered the domestic state of a great part of the manufacturing community, is to be regretted, it has become unavoidable from the force of circumstances. Whether our principal manufactures are carried on by the aid of machinery, or by mere manual labour, this principle of concentration is alike common to all.

So great a deviation from the old system attracted public attention in the year 1815, when a Bill was brought into the House of Commons to regulate the hours of labour in ALL mills, manufactories, or buildings in which TWENTY or more persons should be employed under the age of eighteen years. This Bill was entertained by the House for the greater part of the session, was referred to a Committee, but did not pass into a law *.

In the years 1818 and 1819, when evidence on Cotton Factory labour was taken in both Houses of Parliament, it was proved upon oath before the House of Lords, by a list given in of thirty or forty other trades, that the ages of children, and the duration of their labour, differed but little from those in the Cotton Trade, or from each other. The particulars of this evidence are given in an appendix. As these facts cannot, or ought not to be unknown to those philanthropists who have so frequently brought this subject

* This Bill, as amended in the Committee (13th June, 1815), enacts, that " this Act shall extend and be construed to extend to all Cotton, " Woollen, Flax, and other Mills, Manufactories, or Buildings, in which " twenty or more persons shall be employed under the age of eighteen " years."

5

before Parliament, it seems no less extraordinary than unaccountable, *why*, for a period of sixteen years (viz. from 1815 to 1831) their attention should have been confined to Cotton Factories alone; and *why*, when in the year 1832 they thought fit to bring an extension of the principle before Parliament, they selected some other trades, as the woollen, linen, and silk, to be also regulated by law, while they left all others (and even a principal branch of the cotton trade, calico printing, namely) untouched and unnoticed; though notoriously performed under similar circumstances as to the congregation of numbers, hours of work, and ages of the children employed in them.

It has been observed by the Editor of a leading London evening journal, "That it is doubtless very difficult, how-" ever desirable, to protect children from oppression, and " from labour beyond their years, under all circumstances; " but the COMMON-SENSE-PRINCIPLE appears to be, that " the legislature should interfere whenever persons of ten-" der years are brought together for purposes of labour in " such numbers in single establishments, that interference " in their behalf becomes matter of public concern, and " may be enforced without danger and injustice by reason " of the notoriety of the condition of numerous bodies of " such persons. This was the principle of the Bill brought " in in 1815, which dropped; and on this principle the " legislation for the protection of infant work-people should " be founded. To proceed on this principle is due, not " only to the helpless beings whom we wish to protect, but " to the employers, also, against whom we intend to pro-" tect them. Any regulations really unwise and oppressive " to employers will be less likely to be carried through " Parliament when it affects ALL branches of labour, than

" if we singled out for the ostentation of cheap philanthropy
" some one branch of manufacture, while we left scores of
" others untouched."

Partial legislation is as invidious as it is unjust. " It
" should be the object," the same writer goes on to say,
" of those persons, who desire the interference of Parlia-
" ment, to make the protection against destructive toil as
" general as the evil. It is difficult to conjecture on any
" principles of legislation, *why* limitations in particular
" branches should be introduced—*why* the fibrous, metallic,
" or other nature of a material, should determine the hours
" a child ought to work upon it; or *why* the power which
" moves, the machine should make him more or less an
" object of pity and protection. We have no desire to
" exclude from our minds the difficulties and even danger
" of rash legislation on this subject to our manufactures,
" and even the manufacturing population themselves; nor
" are we sure that Parliament has all the information before
" it, necessary for safe legislation."*

Such *excessive* restrictions as are now sought to be
enforced by law, might be less injurious were the subject a
mere home question. The first effect felt in the half dozen
manufactures proposed to be limited, would be a general
derangement and disproportion of parts. Some dependent
portions deprived of employment from a want of materials
until new establishments could be raised to supply the
deficiencies. The earnings of all the poor work people,
adults as well as children, necessarily lessened in proportion
to the shortened time of their labour, and the cost of pro-

* See *Globe* Newspapers of 10th, 11th, and 18th January last.

duction to the manufacturer as necessarily increased. From
the great competition of foreign nations in the chief
branches of our leading manufactures, the question assumes
a different character, as the major part of them are exported.
We have not only to contend against cheaper labour arising
from cheaper food, but against untaxed materials and protecting duties also. Further, we have to contend against
similar machinery and concentration of labour as our own,
with unrestrained time of work.

The measures proposed by our own restrictionists,
" would " (as stated in the Resolutions of Manufacturers
at Leeds, in 1832,) " produce effects precisely similar to
" those which would follow the annihilation of a large
" portion of national capital, or from any sudden retro-
" gression in manufacturing skill." Further competition
with foreign nations would be a hopeless task, as in the
present existing state of things profits are not only greatly
reduced, but many of our manufactures do not yield a
remunerating price. The whole of our manufactures for
export must, in a very few years, fall into their hands.
Indeed, no surer mode of their transference from ourselves
to our foreign rivals could possibly be devised. When too
late, we may wish to retrace our steps ; but when once lost,
there is no recovery.

" The warmest philanthropists, while indulging their
" feelings of gratuitous humanity, by pushing restrictions
" to so great an extent, would shudder at the adoption of
" their own measures, if they could perceive all their con-
" sequences."*

* " Exposition of the Factory Question," published at Manchester, 1832.

Let the principle of the Bill of 1815, as to generalization, be adopted. If the number of *twenty* young persons be considered too small, at the present day, to *constitute* a *Factory*, let a greater be taken as the criterion. Let there be some limitation of time, but not such as is now sought for; and let there be moderate penal enactments. Thus, instead of harassing the legislature and individuals year after year, as has been the case for the last fifteen or twenty years, about particular manufactures, let one general law embrace all which come under the definition; and thus let this long agitated question be set finally at rest.

March, 1833.

APPENDIX.

Hours of Labour of Other Trades than Cotton Spinning, in which Children are employed in conjunction with Adults, (delivered in and proved on Oath, in the House of Lords in 1818 and 1819, and inserted in Appendix to Evidence, No. 34.)

Earthenware and Porcelain......	Staffordshire and Derby........	....	12 to 15 hours daily
File Cutters ..	Warrington...		72 hours weekly
Nail Makers ..	Birmingham	Children begin at 9 years old	12 hours daily
Iron Works, Forges, and Mills	Warwickshire and Staffordshire ..	Boys employed at 8 years of age	12 hours daily, and in alternate weeks 12 hours nightly
Iron Founders..	Ditto	ditto.. Ditto	ditto.... 12 hours daily
Collieries	Ditto	ditto.. Boys begin at 8 years old	12 hours daily, under ground
Ditto	Lancashire	Ditto	ditto.... 11 hours daily, under ground, 12 and 13 above ground
Ditto	St. Helen's and Worsley	Girls as well as Boys are employed...........	Ditto ditto
Glass Trade..	Warwickshire and Staffordshire ..	Children employed from 9 to 10 years old......	12 hours daily—12 hours nightly
Wire Card Makers ..	Halifax, &c.	Employ *chiefly* Children..	12 to 13 hours daily
Watch Makers..	Coventry.................................		12 hours daily in winter — 14 in summer
Pin Makers....	Warrington......	Employ younger Children than the Cotton Mills of that place............	14 hours daily
Needle Makers..	Gloucester		13 hours daily
Manufactrs. of Arms ..	Birmingham	Children begin from 7 to 9 years old	13 hours daily
Calico Printing.	Lancash. Cheshire Yorkshire, &c..	Boys employed from 8 years old upwards	12 to 14, 15, and 16 hours daily, sometimes all night
Worsted Mills..	Leeds	....	13 hours daily
Ditto	Halifax		14 to 15 and 16 daily, and sometimes all night
Ditto	Keighly		Some of them all night
Ditto	Exwick		12 hours daily

Worsted Mills..Norwich...........	Girls begin at 10 years old	14 hrs. daily, part of the people all night	
Ditto .... Manchester......................	14 hours daily		
Flax Mills .... Leeds, &c.	13 hours daily		
Ditto .... Halifax	14, 15, and 16 hours daily—several of them all night		
Ditto .... Shrewsbury...............................	71 hours weekly		
Hosiery ......'Leicester.........	Boys, Girls, Women, and Men employed	12 hrs. daily in winter and 13 in summer	
Ditto .... Nottingham	15 hours daily		
Ditto .... Mansfield .....{	Employ a great number of Children	Hours longer than at any Cotton Mill in that neighbour-hood	
Lace Manu-factory....} Ditto	Children employed as soon as they can use the needle	Ditto ditto	
Ditto ....Nottingham ...	Children employed at 7 years old and upwards..	12 hours daily	
Ditto .... Tiverton	14 hours daily		
Silk Mills .... Derby	72 hours weekly		
Ditto .... Macclesfield	76 hours weekly		
Ditto .... Nottingham	Children employed at 8 years old and upwards..	13 hours daily	
Ditto ....Congleton	Employ near 2,000 per-sons, of whom the great-er part are Children from 5 years old up-wards	12 hours daily	
Ditto .... Stockport	Children as in Cotton Factories	Hours as in Cotton Factories	
Power Loom Weaving..} Ditto .... Ditto .... Ditto ditto			
Cotton Wea-vers by hand} Lancashire, York-shire, Chesh. &c.	Children at all ages work the same hours as Adults	14 to 16 hours daily	
Draw Boy Weaving..} Paisley..........	Children from 7 years old upwards extensively employed as Drawers to Weavers....	15 hours daily	
Ditto .... Glasgow	In One Village near 1,000 Children from 8 to 12 years old are employed	Till 11 or 12 at night or even till 1 in the morning	

T. SOWLER, PRINTER, MANCHESTER.

LETTER

TO THE

RIGHT HON. LORD ASHLEY,

ON THE

COTTON FACTORY SYSTEM,

AND

THE TEN HOURS' FACTORY BILL.

" Manufactures dependent on foreign consumption, never can continue to flourish in a country where they are subject to duties, or fettered by restrictions. To be prosperous, they must be free."

By KIRKMAN FINLAY, Esq.

GLASGOW, 1st MARCH, 1833.

" Every person employed in a Weaving or Spinning Factory, is supplied with a powerful assistant—a Water Wheel or Steam Engine—and with tools of the best and fittest description for performing that part of the work in which he is engaged.

" Thus, a capital is furnished, by the owner to the workman, amounting to from L.40 to L.150. For the capital, management, and risk attending this joint partnership, a portion of the value of the work must be paid.

" At present, the prices obtained for Cotton Twist and Power Loom manufactured Cotton Cloth, in most cases, barely pay the interest, in some cases fall below it.

" Whatever lessens the productiveness of the sunk outlay, must therefore necessarily fall as a tax upon the worker, and lessen his wages."

TO THE

RIGHT HON. LORD ASHLEY,

&c., &c., &c.

GLASGOW, 1*st March*, 1833.

MY LORD,

I DO not offer any apology for thus publicly addressing myself to your Lordship. I observe by the votes of the House of Commons, that you have given notice of a motion in relation to a Bill or other proceeding, regarding what is called Mr. Sadler's,* or the Ten Hours' Bill of last session, affecting the workers in Factories.

It is not necessary for me to say, that in approaching this subject, and in attempting to substitute facts and reasoning for the misrepresentations and declamation with which the public press has been filled, and the public mind abused, I am far from regret-

---

* The merit, if merit there be in originating this proposal, does not belong to this Gentleman. It is one of the visionary and impracticable schemes of the philanthrophic enthusiast, Mr. Robert Owen, who proposed and urged it in 1816.

ting that the attention of good men, and of the nation generally, has been attracted to it.

I rejoice that a subject so interesting and important, should engage a large share of public notice, that every inquiry should be made, and exact knowledge should be acquired of all the evil and all the good which belong to the system. The condi-tion of the working classes, the education, comfort, and pros-perity of their children, can never be objects of indifference to me, but when matters of such deep importance are propounded to the Legislature on a subject with which I have some acquaint-ance, I wish to examine whether the measure recommended is likely to attain its purposes, or does not rather contain within itself the seeds of many evils which it is meant to avert.

My connexion, which is of long standing and of some con-siderable extent, is with the Cotton Factories alone, both spin-ning and weaving. Of other Factories for spinning or weav-ing woollen, silk, and linen, I know but little, of their internal regulations absolutely nothing, and therefore, every thing I mean to take the liberty of stating to your Lordship, has refer-ence to Cotton Factories, and to them alone.

It cannot be unknown to your Lordship, but it is not gen-erally known to the public, that these Factories are placed at present in situations very different, in as much as the Cotton Factories are, and have long been, under the regulation of Acts of Parliament, whilst the other Factories are not affected by any Legislative enactment.*

Your Lordship is well aware, that in Cotton Factories, no child can be legally employed, till it has attained the age of nine years, and that no person under eighteen can be suffered to remain in the Factory more than twelve hours in any day, that besides on Saturday, dismissal must take place on the expiration of nine hours.

Your Lordship is, no doubt, perfectly well informed of the laws to which I have alluded, and also of their history; but as

---

* In all, three Acts have been passed, the first relates to apprentices only, the second was passed in 1816, generally called Sir Robert Peel's Act, and the ast brought forward by Sir J. Hobhouse.

the public who form themselves into a body of controlling judges on all such subjects, do not appear to think inquiry at all necessary before sentence; and, as most of them are not instructed in these matters, I think it proper thus to mention them.

I do not question, that your Lordship, before undertaking the duty you have imposed upon yourself, has taken ample pains to acquire correct information respecting the existing laws, and how far these have been obeyed, also as to the practice in well regulated Factories, and how far the whole system works to the advantage of the children and others employed in these establishments. I doubt not you have likewise maturely considered every circumstance by which your proposed measure may probably affect the maintenance of the Cotton Trade in this country, to its present extent.*

I concede at once to the supporters of the Ten Hours' Bill, if it can be shown that the employment of persons in Cotton Factories, in the manner and for the time fixed by the present laws, is incompatible with health and proper instruction, some further interference may be necessary, but when I can point out as it would be easy to do, many large Factories in England and Scotland, where the whole of the workers, children and adults, enjoy better health, are better educated, have more comforts and better food, are as sober and well conducted as any other class of persons in the same parish, I think I at least show grounds for believing that the present system, where the law is obeyed, does not require farther legislative interference.†

* The Cotton Manufacture employs in Great Britain not only a large population directly, but affords support indirectly, to a vast many more, for there is no trade or occupation that is not assisted by it. Of agriculture it is a main support, and it contributes more largely than any other employment to the payment of the public creditors.

† It is generally supposed that the poverty of parents is the cause of children being put into Factories at too early an age ; but in fact it is not so, for it is a common thing for respectable workmen, earning high wages themselves in Cotton Factories, to send their children to work in those Factories as soon as they arrive at nine years of age, and become legally admissible, which

It has been admitted by owners of Factories in Lancashire, that the laws are not enforced, that various plans have been successfully adopted for their evasion, and that both with respect to the ages of children employed, and the hours of working, little attention is paid at some Factories to the legal enactments.

But does the fact, that it is found impossible to enforce the present law, invite any one to proceed to enact a new law farther restricting the hours of labour.

It is admitted on all hands that the law at present only requires that owners of Factories should do what most of them did before any Act was passed. It enjoined every one to act in the same manner, and to work the same hours as was the practice at the best conducted Factories previously to the passing of any law. It was therefore, if universally observed, not contrary to the interest of the owners of Cotton Factories, or of the trade in general. Still that law is in some instances evaded. But were a law to be passed, such as is now proposed, what additional inducements would be held out for evasion ! *

The Cotton Manufacture of this country, yields the most

---

they never would do if the employment was hurtful; especially as a child of that age cannot earn above two shillings or eighteenpence a-week. In many cases, parents have their children working along with themselves, in the Factories, and where a man has several children, there is nothing to prevent him from having them, under the present law working by turns six hours each per day ; but such a thing is never thought of, because twelve hours is not found to be oppressive. A child may be taught to read and write before it is nine years of age ; at some Factories, no child is employed, unless previously instructed in reading; besides, after it has been sent to a Factory, there is nothing to prevent the parents taking it out of that employment for a few months and sending it to school. There are instances in Scotland of clergymen and medical men who were once Factory children, and commenced their education at the Factory school.

* The wish to have the hours of labour reduced, would not prevail generally among the workers themselves, if they were not persuaded by demagogues or ignorant persons, that they would receive the *same amount of wages working ten hours, that they receive now working twelve hours.*

profitable, and with the exception of agriculture, perhaps the most extensive employment for the labouring classes that exists in any country in the world. It employs, in many counties in Great Britain more than one-half of the population; and by its means, either directly or indirectly, a vast portion of the whole people is maintained. Take any large part of it from us, or adopt any measure which will materially affect its wages, and the condition of the working classes must become truly wretched.*

It is known to every person conversant with the history of the rise and present state of this manufacture—which has grown to its incredible height and importance within the last fifty years—that we possess no particular advantages for carrying it on with success, but such as depend on our skill, industry, and capital, that other nations may even surpass us, and that some of them whom we formerly supplied, do now not only supplant us in their own markets, but are making inroads upon our sales in other quarters.†

The Americans, in the cheapness of cotton wool, possess a very great advantage over us,‡ especially in the manufacture of

---

* The wages paid to Factory workers have always been, and are now good and regular, much beyond what weavers can earn, working much longer hours in their own damp shops. It is a great matter for a poor family to have some of their number employed in a Factory, for their earnings materially assist the pittance otherwise obtained.

† In any country, in the infant state of manufacture, and indeed up to that period in its progress when the supply does not exceed the demand but is just equal to it, it may be true that the Home market is the best; but so soon as that stage is attained, when the supply is greater than the demand, it is manifest that the Foreign market becomes the most important, and, indeed, the only quarter to be looked to, as capable of absorbing the surplus supplies. The Home market, then, stands in the same relation to the Foreign market as a limited, and always fully supplied market, to what under a free commercial system, may be regarded as an unlimited and never glutted market.

‡ A heavy duty on the importation of Foreign cotton wool is imposed in this country, amounting to 12 per cent. on its cost in America; this, added to the freight and charges, loads the manufacture of coarse cotton goods with a very heavy disadvantage in Foreign markets.

8

low qualities of cloth, and, being both active and ingenious, have incredibly succeeded in not merely making machinery for themselves, but in contriving new inventions which have proved greatly beneficial to the manufacture generally.

It is true that their manufacture is confined to the coarse and more common kinds of cotton cloth.* But of this description, the great bulk of the consumption consists, a large part of the employment of the workers depends, not on the fine, but on the common fabrics. Besides, wherever the first inroad is successfully made, wherever the ordinary kinds of cotton cloth are produced to the most advantage, the manufacture of the finer will gradually follow, and the transfer of a large part of the employment of the people of this country, will become inevitable.

It is always to be recollected, that not only do we depend on Foreign nations for the supply of the raw material, but that we also depend on them for the consumption of nearly three-fourth parts of all the cotton wool spun in this country, and sold as twist or goods.†

It is not asserted that three-fourths in value of Cotton Twist and goods are exported, but that nearly three pounds in every four of weight are exported, and a judgment may be formed, when, in addition to this the extent of our export of printed cottons is considered, of the importance of the foreign trade to the cotton manufacture. Were the foreign demand to fall off materially, the effect on the wages of Factory workers must be in proportion severely felt.

This most impolitic duty, contrary to all sound principles of taxation, bears with particular severity on the poor: it is the cause of reducing the wages of the worker lower than if no duty were payable,—and its being recently and absurdly altered, from an *ad valorem* to a rated duty, makes it to be highly oppressive on that very description of cloth which the poor chiefly consume.

* The Americans first manufactured a kind of stout cloth, known by the name of domestics, now in general use in this country, on the Continent, and in Spanish America.

† The *real* value of Twist and Cotton manufactures exported in 1832, exceeded twelve millions.

I think it must be obvious to the most superficial observer, that were the cotton trade of this country to suffer any serious diminution, the labouring classes, and all other persons connected with it, would be injuriously affected, the national resources proportionally impaired, and consequences follow, which it is not possible to contemplate without serious apprehension.

The question is not whether Factory children are as well off in all respects as the children of parents who are themselves living comfortably, but whether they are made better or worse by their Factory employment? Compare them with the children of the poor at other employments, or those who can find none. Do not attempt to compare them with those from whom their situation is wholly different, and ever must be different.

The proper way to attain this information in an authentic and complete manner, is by means of one or more commissions. Gentlemen of perfect impartiality and knowledge may be appointed to visit the Factory Establishments in all parts of the country, compare the condition of the young so employed, with the state of those who have other occupations or none, and on their report some judgment may be formed of what it may be wise to propose, and practicable to carry into execution.

What I now say, is for the purpose of entreating that portion of the public who think themselves advancing the interests of persons employed in Factories, by advocating a Ten Hours' labour measure, calmly to reflect on every step they take, to examine the subject well before they proceed to act, and to satisfy their own minds after patient investigation—for the subject deserves it—whether by the proposed interference with Cotton Factories, they can really promote the purposes contemplated, without endangering the comfortable maintenance of a vast part of our industrious population, and hazarding their steady and regular employment.*

---

* This measure, to give it a true name, should be entitled, " A Bill to Transfer the Cotton Manufacture of Great Britain and Ireland to Foreign Countries."

It is not a subject upon which an experiment can be tried, and abandoned should it not succeed. If a strong hold of the cotton manufacture be once obtained by other countries, it will be found impossible to wrest it from them; *once* removed, the progress is certain; it is what cannot stand still; once before us, they will keep the lead, and deprive us by degrees of a great part of our present advantages.*

The owners of Cotton Factories may be divided into two classes. The first, those who adhere exactly to the provisions of the Act of Parliament, as they relate to the hours of working; and as far as possible to the ages of the children, and other enactments. The second consists of those who evade, as far as they can, the existing law, and work as long as their people will agree to remain at their labour.

It must be evident that the first class of persons are exposed to two species of competition in the market; the one from foreign manufacturers, whose produce now meets theirs for sale in every market in the world,† and the other from that body of Spinners and Power Loom manufacturers who work beyond the legal hours.

---

* The present comparative extent of the Cotton Manufacture in Great Britain, France, and America, can best be known by reference to the published accounts of the consumption of cotton wool in each, and which stand thus :—

> In 1832, Great Britain, 865,000 packages.
> „　　France,........ 272,463　　„
> „　　America,...... 173,800　　„

It is however to be recollected, that in America the Cotton Manufacture has grown up since 1813, and that it was then very small in France.

The importation of Cotton into other parts of the Continent, independent of France, was, in 1832, 200,000 packages.

† By statements lately received from the United States, of most respectable authority, I find that wages paid there to workers in Cotton Spinning and Weaving Factories, are rather under what are paid in Glasgow, as will be seen by the annexed Schedule, whilst from the duty on cotton in this

If a Spinner or Power Loom manufacturer, working with
machinery, which requires little or no bodily labour to assist

---

country, and the difference in charges of laying it down at their Works, they
have the raw material at 15 to 20 per cent. lower than we have it.   The
value of cotton manufactures exported from the United States in 1831,
amounted to 1,126,313 dollars, and these manufactures have not only been
meeting ours with a powerful competition in all the South American markets, but even in our own colonies; considerable imports of them having
lately made their appearance in Calcutta, where they have been sold, notwithstanding the additional duty they have to pay, at prices which would
not remunerate the British manufacturer.   I have not yet any return of
their exports for last year, but from the rapid increase that was making in
their machinery, there can be little doubt that it will be considerably greater
than in 1831.   In 1831, the machine makers had orders for more machinery
than they could turn out for 12 months; and in the small town of Patterson
alone, between the months of July and November, no less than five new
Factories were begun to be erected.

Their machinery is of the best description, and it is well known, that the
most important improvements which have lately been made in Cotton
Spinning Machinery, are of American invention, for which patents have been
obtained in this country.   No better proof of their excellence need be
given, than that some of our principal manufacturers here have been putting
out large quantities of very valuable machinery, which had been only in operation for a very few years, and replacing them with these American machines.

With regard to the competition of the manufacturers on the Continent, it
is well known that in Germany, the Cotton Spinning trade was making very
considerable progress until 1831, when the low price of yarns from this
country, compelled many of the Spinners on the Rhine, to stop their works;
from this we may judge, that Spinning in Germany can only be kept in
check by our being enabled to supply the market upon the lowest terms.

In Switzerland, the trade has made great progress within the last ten
years, and is still on the increase—the quantity of cotton now consumed
there, is, I believe, fully greater than what is consumed in Scotland.   Ten
years ago, the Swiss imported from this country, all Nos. of yarns from No.
20 to 200, but each year as they have made progress, their imports have
fallen off, beginning at the lowest Nos., say 20—and they have now so
extended and improved their spinning, that they require to import no second
quality below No. 60—they have, in consequence of this progress, within
these few years, begun to supply that part of Germany bordering upon their

its motions,* has it in activity for fourteen hours in the
day, or, as is sometimes the case, during the night, then it is easy
to see that he can greatly undersell the first class of persons,
who work only twelve hours in the day.

I have already said that no owner can legally employ, in a
Cotton Factory, children under nine years of age, nor work
longer than twelve hours in the day, provided he employ persons under eighteen years of age, but if he employs none under
twenty-one years of age, he may work without any sort of
restriction, either in the day or in the night.

It is notorious, and has been publicly avowed by owners

---

own country, with both Mule and Water Twist. These were formerly
drawn entirely from this country.

The Report of a Committee of Congress, states that the twist spun in
America in 1831, was 67,862,000 lbs. ; while we know, from our published
states, that what was produced in Scotland in that year, only amounted to
28,112,000, being about one-third part of what is produced in America.

Since the preceding was written, the following information has been
received :—

It appears from the " *Review of the New York Market*," published on the
5th January, 1833, that the shipments of Domestic Cotton goods to Foreign
Parts, from New York, in the year 1832, exceeded those of any former years
by 2239 packages. The export having been—

In 1828,................1900 packages.
„ 1829,................2804 „
„ 1830,................5306 „
„ 1831,................3030 „
„ 1832,................7545 „

* A great part of the machinery moves by itself, requiring only a
person to mend threads, to stop it if wrong, to set it on, and such other
operations which require merely attention, and moving from one place to
another. Many, when the work goes well, sit down and look at the machine
for some time together;—a machine of this kind does work exactly in proportion to the time it is in active operation, and it follows that a spinner
working in this way, who works longer hours than his neighbours, can
undersell those who confine their time to twelve hours in the day.

of works in some parts of Lancashire and Cheshire, that they
have worked regularly beyond the legal hours, while I cannot
learn that in this part of the country, and my information is
pretty extensive, a suspicion of such conduct attaches to
any person doing business to extent. In small works, evasions
may be practised, but no considerable establishment in this
part of the country infringes, in the smallest degree, the regulations, in respect to hours of working, established by law.

I am free to confess, there is one of the provisions of
the Act of Parliament which it is not in the power of the
owners to say they can comply with, and that relates to
the age of children employed. At every work with which I
am acquainted, care is taken only to employ those who have
attained the legal age; it is, I am confident, not the wish or
interest of owners to have younger children in their works,
but they do not, and cannot, possess the means of *really* knowing, whether every one they employ is truly arrived at the age
prescribed by law or not.*

Another provision of the Act of Parliament, is very generally
neglected in this part of the country. By Section 14 of the
Act first and second, William IV., " It is provided that one
" hour and a half shall on *every* day be allowed for meals."†

Now the dinner hour here is two o'clock, and if a work is to

---

* How is it possible to prove that there is no one under 18 years of age,
or below 21 ? Such enactments show the absurd nature of Legislative interference, for they open a wide door for the evasion of all who choose to disregard them. Many Factories are at work fourteen hours in the day, and all
night; yet surely no practical man believes that they employ only persons
above eighteen or twenty-one years of age. How is it possible to ascertain
such facts with any degree of accuracy, especially when it is the wish and
interest of both parties that they should not be precisely known ?

† The inconvenience thereby created, was probably not foreseen when the
Act was passed, otherwise it would have been provided against; but I
understand the circumstance has prevented informations against more serious
and hurtful transgressions, since those who did not literally comply with the
law, even in this trifle, could not prosecute a more formidable breach of it
in others.

be dismissed on Saturday after nine hours' working, and which is universally the case at every respectable establishment with which I am acquainted, it would be necessary to stop the work at two, and bring the workers back at three, in order to work an hour and a half, so as finally to dismiss them at half-past four o'clock. This would be done at great inconvenience to the workers; and the usual practice is to keep the work going till half-past three, when it closes, and the workers are dismissed.

From what I have myself observed, I can very truly assert that the people employed by the first class of Spinners and Power Loom Manufacturers, who work for twelve hours on five days in the week, and nine hours on Saturday, and no longer, are as steady, healthy, comfortable, and well-behaved workers as are to be found in any part of the Country, in any Manufacture whatever, or employed even in agriculture itself.

Indeed, in many of these establishments, especially in the country, they are perfect examples of what the working classes ought to be; are well instructed, in schools established by the Owners for the purpose, and are regular and exemplary in the discharge of their duties, forming altogether a society of as sober and well-conducted persons as are to be found in any community; living in good houses, some of them their own property, and enjoying comforts to which most other classes of working persons are entirely strangers.*

---

* It would be easy to give certificates of this fact from the clergy and resident magistrates in the neighbourhood of many of these establishments, but the following from the Rev. Dr. Murray, of a large Factory in his Parish, where he has lived for above forty years, is a proof that there is nothing in the hours nor in the employment which ought to be a hinderance to education and to exemplary conduct. Similar evidence can, I believe, be given of a large proportion of the country parts, and what is done at one Station may be done at others; there is at least nothing in the hours of working nor in the nature of the employment to prevent it.

(Minister's Certificate.)

As minister of the parish in which the Deanston Works are situated, I feel myself entitled to state, that the children employed in these works are kindly

I am well convinced that if the present Laws were enforced and effectual means taken, to put a stop to every kind of Factory working above twelve hours in the day, also to abolish night working, under any pretence, no complaint whatever could justly be made of working in Cotton Factories.

But it must be abundantly evident that till some means are found adequate to compel adherence to the present Law, it will be not only idle, but most mischievous to the trade, and ruinous to respectable Factory Owners—who must, and will obey any Law that is made—to enact a new one farther restricting the hours of labour and thereby inviting the regardless portion of the trade to contrive fresh modes for evading and setting it at nought: for, can it for a moment be imagined that persons who now commit a breach of the Law in working fourteen hours in place of twelve, will not continue, by some contrivance, the same hours of working when the reward becomes higher by the first class of Factory Owners being compelled to restrict their hours of working to ten?

It is not the general opinion that *in all cases* it is a matter of great profit to Mill Owners to work more than twelve hours; in some cases where the work is done solely by machinery, it

---

and tenderly treated; that the mode of conducting their education is excellent and that the manager studies how to promote their comfort in all respects. The schools are annually strictly examined by a Committee of the Presbytery of the bounds, and a report, attested by the examinators, sent regularly to the General Assembly of the Church of Scotland. I can also state with great truth, that there is no portion of the inhabitants of this parish, consisting of 3,700 souls and upwards, whose moral conduct and general behaviour, is more correct than that of those employed at the Deanston Works. Further, having been forty years minister of this parish, and well acquainted with the habits of all my people, I hesitate not to say, that whatever changes may be thought necessary as to other works of a similar kind, in my humble opinion, the system of management in the Deanston Works, might be with safety adopted as a model for ensuring the health, promoting the virtuous and religious education of the young, and improving the conduct of all connected with such establishments.—Given at the Manse of Kilmadock by me,

PATRICK MURRAY, D.D.,

Minister of that parish, this 13th day of June, 1832.

undoubtedly is so ; but then, *in every case*, it must be profitable to work twelve or thirteen hours in place of ten, and he who works the longer time will be able effectually to ruin and supplant a rival who only works ten hours.

If such a Law as that for restricting labour to ten hours were established, not only would the first class of Manufacturers and Spinners be exposed to the competition of their rivals in Europe and America,* where labour is unrestricted, but also to the equally ruinous competition of those at home, whom no laws can restrain.†

It is very easy for benevolent and well-meaning persons to talk at Public Meetings of what can be done by legal enactments,

---

* On the Continent the hours of labour in Factories are always above twelve, frequently as much as fourteen. In America generally thirteen.

If a law were passed restricting the labour in Factories in this country to ten, while Foreign Factories continued to work as they now do, it would be quite impossible for our Factory Owners to stand up in the competition— the struggle might for some little time be continued but it would be in vain. The throstle spinner whose produce depends solely on the hours of active work, and where there is no labour, would sink if compelled to work only ten, while others worked twelve, thirteen or fourteen hours.

† By a calculation which has been carefully made, it appears that a Manufacturer, whose machinery is only permitted to be in operation ten hours per day, must, in order to enable him to produce his goods at the same cost as a Manufacturer whose machinery is in operation for twelve hours, reduce the wages of his workers, at least 25 per cent. An amount which would reduce the great body of workers employed in our Factories, from a state of comfort to one of great privation; and although the artificial and temporary scarcity of goods which would be occasioned by a measure like the one proposed, might so raise prices as not to operate to this extent on wages *immediately*, yet since whatever enhancement may take place on our cost of production, cannot fail to act as a bounty in favour of the foreign manufacturer, and give a stimulus to the increase of machinery in other countries, it must be evident, that as soon as the deficiency occasioned by the reduced productiveness of our machines, is filled up by the erection of new machinery, a re-action must take place; and when this emergency arrives, the loss must inevitably fall upon the workers, as in the present state of profits in the Cotton Trade, there is no fund except wages, out of which the unnaturally enhanced cost of production could be compensated.

but every one knows that the power of Parliament can never compel large bodies of men to forego great advantages, and that in a short time after passing such a Law as is now contemplated, both masters and workers would combine, to set it at defiance, as is already the case with regard to the existing Laws in some parts of Lancashire and Cheshire.*

Indeed, so very little were the Laws on this subject ever regarded in these districts, that I assert, without fear of contradiction, the provisions of the Acts of Sir Robert Peel and Sir John Hobhouse were till lately unknown to many and disregarded by a great proportion of the Spinners and Manufacturers in them.

If your Lordship can succeed in obtaining an Act which shall compel all owners of Factories to obey the present Law in regard to the hours of working, and to alter the clause regarding the Saturday's working, so as to make it really capable of execution here with conveniency to parties, you would con-

---

* It has been thought that the Factory owners in many parts of England have been waiting without resistance the passing of this law, either in expectation that its impractical character would lead to its early repeal, or in the intention of evading its enactments. No doubt their conduct appears to lend colour to the latter suspicion. For on no other ground than this, is it possible to believe that they would calmly, patiently, and without resistance, contemplate a measure which they must be convinced would lead by no indirect road to the ruin of the business in which they are engaged, and the ultimate abandonment of many manufacturing establishments on which millions have been expended.

No man acquainted with the subject can believe it possible that a work to spin and manufacture the coarse and ordinary wear of the country, of which three-fourths of the manufacture consists, could support the competition of the European and American Continents, should this proposal be enacted into a Law. The thing is impossible.—In Flanders there is much wealth, and a population more dense and better adapted for manufactures than in any part of Europe, with the exception only of Great Britain. They also possess an inexhaustible supply of excellent coal.

Throstle spinning, and Power Loom Factories established there, and working, for fourteen hours a-day, or longer, as with two sets of hands might be easily done, would utterly destroy any Factory owner in this country, confined to work only ten hours in the day.

fer a benefit on the first class of Spinners and Manufacturers who are now oppressed by the illegal proceedings of others ; but if an attempt be made farther to restrict the hours of labour, it will not only fail, but it will prove destructive to the interests of those who have obeyed, and will continue to obey the enactments of the Legislature.*

---

* It has been proposed to allow Factories to work as long as they please, provided no person, under a certain age be employed more than six, eight, or ten hours in the day. But, besides all the objections which apply, as already stated to age, and not merely the difficulty, but the impossibility of ascertaining it, it is very clear, that such an enactment would afford, in great towns, the easiest means of evasion, and that children would be allowed to attend more than their present hours, although in different Factories.

Besides, in many places, especially in the country, where the workers are, in all respects, better cared for, and more comfortable than in towns, two sets of hands could not be procured, and thus an advantage and encouragement would be given to town Factories, over the better establishments in the country.

In many cases, the Manufacturer who employs Power Loom workers carries on his business unconnected with any Spinning Factory. He purchases the Twist from spinners. In this way, a much smaller capital is requisite for getting into the trade, and many individuals who had not sufficient funds to embrace both branches, have been induced to embark small capitals in the weaving department. Farther facilities have also been given to these parties, by capitalists building Factories with steam engines, and great Gearing, and letting them on leases for terms of years to the Manufacturer, who puts in the small Gearing, Looms, and other necessary machinery, the landlord supplying the power requisite for driving, and the tenant paying a fixed rent, which may average from L.3 10s. to L.4 per loom per annum.

These contracts have all been entered into on calculations made from the existing state of the trade ; the landlord receiving a fair remuneration for outlaid capital, and the tenant reckoning on a certain known produce from his looms. It is quite evident to any one acquainted with machinery, that the tenant cannot, without inevitable ruin, fulfil his part of the contract by paying the same rent for a loom, which will only turn off 5 pieces per week, as for one which (as at present) turns off 6 pieces per week. How are these existing contracts to be adjusted ?

I am aware that there are demagogues travelling every part of the country to excite the feelings of the whole nation on this subject. These men have found it for their interest to live upon the earnings of their more laborious brethren; they persuade them that something will be done to give them *more wages and less work.* These very individuals have been busy for years in the same cause; they have found it a most profitable employment, much more to their taste than any work of spinning or weaving, and they will not willingly or readily abandon it.

There is another very different set of gentlemen, Mr. Sadler, Mr. Oastler and others, whose benevolent feelings have been excited, and who in their amiable eagerness to suppress what they are persuaded is wrong, would adopt ruinous and impracticable measures to the manifest danger of the comfortable existence of those young persons they mean to protect and assist.

It was wisely said by the French minister a few days since, in his address to the Agriculturists, Merchants and Manufacturers of France, "that no great change is ever beneficially made, that is hastily made"—I implore you, therefore, my Lord, not rashly to proceed in this business—to let ample inquiry precede any measure you may think it your duty to propose to Parliament, and not to fetter a trade which is, next to agriculture itself, the main pillar of the national resources, with such restrictions as must soon paralyze, and ultimately strangle its beneficial existence.

I have the honour to be,

With sentiments of the highest respect,

My Lord,

Your Lordship's

Most Obdt. humble Servant,

KIRKMAN FINLAY.

APPENDIX.

In regard to health, and to labour, the employment of Factory workers on Power Looms is greatly preferable to that of persons employed on Hand Looms. The latter work in damp shops, where labour is not only severe, but must be continued at present for sixteen hours in the day, to enable them, at similar work, to earn even one-half of what a boy or girl of 16 or 18 will gain at the Factory, where there is nothing approaching to labour, where the room is comfortable with good stone or brick flooring, where there must be no heat beyond 45° if possible, and where it is always warmer than the outer air in winter, and cooler in summer.

In respect to education, I am informed that many families are indebted to their Factory children for the means of affording it : one child working in a Factory enables a widowed mother, or poor parent, to send other children to school, and this, I am assured, is known to be done to a great extent.

The cases of cruelty, of which the details were so eloquently given, are only fresh proofs of the barbarous dispositions in some savage natures ; of these there are abundant instances to be found, I fear, in all occupations. The thong and the strap are instruments of which I never heard till I saw them mentioned in the report of Mr. Sadler's eloquent speech in the House of Commons ; but their use is not necessarily the consequence of any fixed hours of labour. The savages by whom they are employed, may use them during six or seven hours' working, as well as more.

But least of all, is such, or indeed any punishment, required in Cotton Factories, for the heaviest affliction that can befall the young workers is dismissal ; and when that is the sure follower of negligence, no other punishment is called for.

The employment in Cotton Factories well managed, and spinning ordinary Nos. of yarn, is perfectly healthy, as shown by the testimony of medical men who have been for years regular attendants on the inmates of such establishments. The theoretical opinions of medical men, however eminent, are entitled to all the weight, and no more, which my Lord Eldon said they merited in the Case of the Berkley Peerage.

In the great proportion of spinning it is only necessary that the air should be dry, not that the rooms should be more than comfortable, or the thermometer above 65°

One of the most difficult parts of factory-spinning management is to get the people to allow the rooms to be kept sufficiently cool. The workmen are themselves great foes to the admission of fresh air, and this observation applies to all who are engaged in indoor occupation—tailors, &c.

SCHEDULE,

Showing the PRICES paid in Weaving and Spinning Factories in the United States, with the comparative Prices paid for same work in Glasgow.

The general price paid on Mules of 300 Spys. each for Power Loom shuttle cops, is 10 cents per 100 skeins, Nos. 10 to 20, being equal to 4s. sterling, per 1000 hanks. } Paid in Glasgow for 1000 hks. No. 16. 4s. 11d.

Wages of Girls in carding-rooms run from 75 cents to two dollars ; average about 1 dollar, 65 cents, or equal to 6s. 7¼d. per week. } Paid in Glasgow,...7s. 1¼d. per week.

Wages of Girls and Children at Throstle Spinning, 6 cents per 100 skeins, No. 30, equal to 2s. 6d. per 1000 hanks. } Paid in Glasgow,...2s. 3d. per 1000 hanks.

Wages of weaving an 800 reed, with 11 or 12 shots, yarn No. 16, 22 cents for 31 yards, equal to 1s. 7¾d. for 58 yards. } Paid in Glasgow,...1s. 7½d. pps. of 58 yards.

Wages of weaving a 1000 reed, with 16 shots,25 cents, for 28½ yds., yarn No. 30, being equal to 2s. pp. of 57 yards. } Paid in Glasgow, for 57 yards, 1s. 11¼d.

Dressing the above, when done by men, 7 cents pp. ; but this work is generally done by girls, at 3½ cents.
at 7 cents, equal to 6¾d. pp. of 57 yards, at 3½d,.........3⅜d. } In Glasgow, all done by men, price 6d. pps.

N. B.—The above are the prices paying in the United States in 1832.

SCHEDULE

Showing the Ages of Workers and Average Wages, being from Returns made by twenty-nine Spinning Mills in Glasgow and Neighbourhood.

AGE. Nine to ten.				AGE. Eleven to twelve.				AGE. Twelve to fourteen.				AGE. Fourteen to sixteen.				AGE. Sixteen to eighteen.				AGE. Eighteen to twenty-one.				AGE. Twenty-one upwards.			
Males.	Weekly Wages.	Females.	Wages.	Males.	Wages.	Females.	Wages.	Males.	Wages.	Females.	Wages.	Males.	Wages.	Females.	Wages.	Males.	Wages.	Females.	Wages.	Males.	Wages.	Females.	Wages.	Males.	Wages.	Females.	Wages.
	s. d.		*s. d.*		*s. d.*		*s. d.*		*s. d.*		*s. d.*		*s. d.*		*s. d.*		*s. d.*		*s. d.*		*s. d.*		*s. d.*		*s. d.*		*s. d.*
122	2 0	107	2 1	331	2 8¾	447	2 10¼	408	3 9	460	3 8	268	5 4	402	5 2	212	7 0	503	6 2½	139	11 8	563	7 2¼	924	21 11	387	7 11¾

GLASGOW :
EDWARD KHULL, PRINTER TO THE UNIVERSITY.

LETTER

TO THE

RIGHT HON. LORD ASHLEY,

ON THE

Cotton Factory Question,

AND THE

TEN HOURS' FACTORY BILL;

WITH

AN APPENDIX,

CONTAINING

AN ABSTRACT OF THE BILL.

———

BY A LANCASHIRE COTTON SPINNER.

———

Manchester, 30th March, 1833.

━━━━━

Manchester:
PRINTED BY HENRY SMITH, ST. ANN'S SQUARE.
1833

RIGHT HON. LORD ASHLEY,

&c. &c. &c.

—————————

Manchester, March 30th, 1833.

My Lord,

      A Bill has been recently brought into the House of Commons, by your Lordship, to regulate the labour of children and young persons in the Mills and Factories of the United Kingdom.

      I should have presumed, my Lord, that you would have hesitated to bring before the House of Commons, a Bill of any description, before you had sufficiently inquired into its necessity, and have become fully convinced of its judicious application; more especially one which involves in its operation, the immensely extended field of manufacturing industry, engaged in the Cotton, Woollen, Worsted, Hemp, Flax, Tow, and Silk Mills of the United Kingdom; one branch alone, that of the Cotton Manufacture, employing a Capital of fifteen Millions sterling, and one hundred and fifty thousands of workpeople.

      Previous to bringing in a bill containing such singular provisions and highly penal enactments, a proper feeling should have induced your Lordship to have ascertained, whether the evidence adduced before Mr. Sadler's Committee, was a faithful account of the condition of the *whole* Trade, or whether it applied only to a very limited portion of it, and whether that defective portion, if any, was faithfully described.*

---

* *Eighty-nine Witnesses were examined on the subject of Mr. Sadler's Factories' Bill.*

	Witnesses.	woollen and worsted	Flax.	Cotton.	Silk.	other persons.
Witnesses from Yorkshire..............	52	28	12	4	1	7
— — — Scotland	9		6	2		1
— — — Wales	1	1				
— — — Watford, Hertfordshire..	1				1	
— — — Lancashire & Cheshire...	11			8	1	2
Medical Men *resident* in *London*	15					15
Total....	89	29	18	14	3	25

This evidence may be applied as follows :—

29 of them were connected with the Woollen and Worsted Trade.
18———— were on the subject of Flax Mills in Yorkshire, and the neighbourhood of Aberdeen, in Scotland.
4———— were on the subject of Cotton Mills in Yorkshire,
2———— were on the subject of Cotton Mills in Glasgow.
8———— were on the subject of Cotton Mills in Lancashire and Cheshire.
3———— were upon Silk Mills.
2———— were Overseers of the Poor from Yorkshire.
1———— Minister from Aberdeen,
1———— Clergyman from Yorkshire.—The Rev. G. S. Bull.
1———— Mr. Richard Oastler, from Yorkshire.
3———— Medical Men from Yorkshire.
2———— do. do. do. Lancashire.
15———— do. do. do. London.
—
89...Total.

The following are the Witnesses examined upon the subject of Cotton Factories from Lancashire and Cheshire:—

Joseph Sadler, Dresser, Stockport } Dressing is an occupation not necessarily connected with Cotton Spinning—and is considered a wholesome employment.
James Turner, ditto Manchester }

William Longston, experienced in Spinning, Stockport.

Charles Aberdeen, Card Grinder, Salford, *aged* 53.

David Rowland, Agent to the Bootle Water Works Co., Liverpool, aged 38, stated that he had worked in a Cotton Mill when about six years old, but it appears that his evidence applied to Cotton Mills, probably 25 years ago—when they worked 14 to 16 hours a day.

Thomas Daniel, Cotton Spinner, Manchester.

George Downes, Ashton-under-Lyne, } Cripples.
Isaac Openshaw, Halliwell, }

Thomas Young, M.D., Bolton.

John Malyn, Surgeon, Manchester.

I am not prepared to deny, that so far as relates to the evasion of the present Law, abuses do exist in Cotton Mills, but however fully the state of Woollen, Worsted, Flax, and Silk Mills, may have been shown, it must be allowed that the evidence produced, relating to the state of Cotton Mills, has been extremely limited and insufficient.

I will endeavour to show you, my Lord, that the leading objects and provisions of your Bill, are immensely perilous to the welfare of the parties they are intended to serve; that they are uncalled for, and much too severe as a remedy for any abuses alleged to exist in the Cotton Manufacture; and I assure your Lordship, that the master manufacturers of this country, as a body, are totally undeserving of the gross imputations upon their humanity, which your Bill is made to insinuate. I am sorry to remark, that a degree of injudicious and unkind feeling is discoverable throughout the provisions of your Bill, which in my opinion, ill accords with the spirit of a wise and benevolent legislation;—a striking instance of which occurs in the unheard of permission given to informers, of selecting any magistrate within twelve miles distance, for the hearing of their complaints.

Your Bill uncandidly infers the existence of an habitual disregard of the sabbath, by providing against the performance of Mill Labour on Sundays;—already known to be unlawful. Such a practice is very uncommon, if not totally unknown in this Country; and the assumption of the existence of such an offence, is a gratuitous and unmerited insinuation, altogether unworthy of a legislator.

Your Lordship is aware that 69 hours weekly, or 11½ hours per day, for 6 days' labour, are now allowed to Cotton Mills; and you propose to limit them to 58 weekly, or little more than 9½ per day, and to include in the operation of your Bill, all other descriptions of Mills, which have not hitherto been restricted. Do you think, my Lord, that the working man will thank you for limiting his labour to an average of little more than 9½ hours in a day, whatever may be his wishes or necessities?

You make owners of Mills liable to severe penalties for the untimely working of a Steam-Engine or a Water-Wheel, unless such Mill owner is able to prove that at the time stated, he was NOT GUILTY of having any child or young person in his Mill, engaged in any manufacture ; and you require the Mill owner to enter in a book, every day, the hours of starting and stopping his Steam-Engine or Water-Wheel; and compel him, under heavy penalties, to hand this registry of his guilt to the clerk of the peace, within four days of stated periods, four times every year :—and your Lordship's Bill also provides the Mill owners with the form of a declaration, which they are to fill up and deposit four times a year, with the clerk of the peace, stating that they have not employed any child or young person, against the provisions of your Bill. This declaration being signed by the Mill owner, is to have the force and validity of an oath ; and that it may agree with the other imputations of your Bill, you do not forget to put the Mill owners in mind of the punishment awarded for perjury. This, my Lord, is a novelty in British Legislation—to compel a man to provide a registry of his own offences, upon which to procure convictions against himself contrary to every principle of British Law ; and we question the right of parliament to enact such a regulation; and, I ask, are we, as Englishmen, bound to obey it ?

By the provisions of your Lordship's Bill, you appear conscious, that accidents may happen in Factory employment, as in all other trades and occupations of life; and your Lordship knows, that the Common Law as regards responsibility of masters, is extremely severe.—It is therefore a gratuitous injury to single out the masters of Factories alone, and to make them the objects of a Special Law, and of severer penalties.

Your Lordship, amongst other things, appears to think that the architectural construction of Mills should be determined by Law; and magistrates are to inflict an annual penal rent upon every Mill (if any Mill owner shall dare to offend by building) containing a room less than ten feet high.—Where does your Lordship find a precedent for such a Law ?

Is your Lordship fully satisfied as to the character of your advisers ? Are you fully aware of the extent of the Fines imposed by this Bill, and of the livelihood provided for a numerous race of common informers, by the threatened penalties ? For I assure your Lordship, that no Mill owner can work a single day free from inevitable liability ; and may, in a single week, incur penalties to the amount of £1,200.* In short, at the proposed rate of only one conviction per day, and the limitation of thirty days for informations, (to say nothing of the 3 months allowed by the time book) the majority of the masters would, within six months of the passing of your Lordship's Bill, become liable to penalties amounting to the confiscation of their whole property, to say nothing of the imprisonment of their persons.

Whatever you may think, my Lord, this Bill of yours is a very serious affair :—it may not be within your Lordship's intention or expectation; but should it ever come into complete operation, this country will become a wreck of ruined manufactories. Where are your Lordship's feelings of humanity and justice, when you empower a Magistrate and an Informer, to punish and degrade

---

* *Penalties for Cases of infraction of Lord Ashley's Bill for regulating the labour of Children and Young Persons, in Mills and Factories.*

Offences by acting contrary to the Provisions of this Bill.	Lowest penalty	Mean penalty	Extreme penalty
Allowing any person under 18 years of age to work more than 10 hours in a day	£. 5	£ 20	£. 60
Not allowing the hours of refreshment	5	20	60
Employing a Child under 9 years of age	5	20	60
Neglecting to inquire into the validity of Certificate	5	20	60
Allowing the Cleaning of Machinery on a Sunday	5	20	60
Obtaining a False Certificate	100	100	100
Not Whitewashing	5	20	60
New-built Mill, having a Room not 10 feet high, an annual penalty to be charged by a Magistrate			
Not having Rules and Regulations hung up in a Mill	5	20	60
Not delivering a Time Book to the Clerk of the Peace	5	20	60
False Entry therein	50	100	100
False Entry therein committed by a Servant	5	20	20
Refusing or neglecting to transmit a Declaration	50	100	100
Accidental death ; if proved Manslaughter, trial at the Assizes			
For not providing a Clock	5	20	60
Accident by Machinery ; pay the sufferer by order of a Magistrate	50	200	200
If the Steam-Engine or Water-Wheel is working at an untimely hour, the Mill owner must prove that he is NOT GUILTY of working any Child or Young Person, or pay a Penalty of	5	20	60
	305	720	1120

A Mill Owner is liable for all Penalties for offences which he may have committed during the 30 previous days ;—also for such Penalties as are obtainable from his own confession in the " Time Book," during the previous three months.—Besides imprisonment for not less than 3 nor more than 12 months.

an honest manufacturer ; to take an industrious and enterprising
British tradesman from his family, his friends, and his lawful
occupation, and to imprison him in the Common Gaol, amongst
thieves and felons ?—to double his legal liability of commitment
for manslaughter, fine him to a ruinous extent, and possibly
transport him to New South Wales, for life ; and subject him to
all this barbarous treatment, for a few inconsiderable offences, or
alleged offences, which as I have before told your Lordship,
may happen in a single week, and which by reason of sickness or
absence, he may be entirely unconscious of having committed ?
Does your Lordship really think you can mend the condition
of the workman by ruining the employer ? Pause my Lord :—
have you forgot the Fable of killing the goose which laid the
golden eggs ?—Did it ever occur to your Lordship, that this Bill
of yours may, by possibility, be made to imprison the *Key of the
Mill*, as well as the *Master ?*—and did you never think of the
probable starvation, that you might bring upon thousands and
possibly millions of industrious unoffending work people, in case
the masters, consulting not less their honor than their safety, refuse to work their Mills under such ruinous and ignominious
restrictions.—My Lord, do not think that this is either an idle
threat, or an improbable event.—It was the impression of many
of the largest and most respectable masters on the first promul-
gation of your Bill; and the policy and necessity of such a measure acquires more weight, the farther it is considered.—But,
supposing that all the manufacturers of the kingdom, included in
your Lordship's Bill, continue in activity, but strictly observing
its provisions for only ten hours per day, is your Lordship aware
of the necessary consequences, which such a limitation of productive industry entails ?—Is it a trifling evil that twenty-four millions of people in this country, and fifty millions of people in other
countries, shall be compelled to pay ten per cent more for their
clothing ?—or if they cannot afford the advance, to be deprived
of a portion of it?—Is it a trifling evil, that one tenth of the
shipping now employed in importing the raw materials, and
exporting the manufactured articles, shall be thrown idle; and
that a diminution of one tenth be caused in the consumption of Coal, Iron, Wood, and the thousand other articles
in use in the manufactories ?—Is it a light evil that one tenth of

the artisans and labourers in all the collateral branches of employment, be thrown out of work altogether, and left to starve, or to seek relief from the parish, or a support in foreign countries, which a mistaken and sickly legislation, denies them in their own?

Your Lordship may perhaps imagine, that I am tiresome and captious in saying so much about this Bill of yours, and of course you wish to know how it happens that I should dislike it, since there is so much petitioning to obtain it.—There are two ways of shewing you this, my Lord; but I will begin with proving that the condition of the work-people engaged in the Cotton Manufacture, under *judicious management*, requires no further legislative interference, than the enforcing of Sir J. C. Hobhouse's Act, —allowing 11½ hours labour per day, for six days in the week; and permit me to assert my belief, that it would be more judicious on your part to admonish the work-people, and desire them to seek employment with humane and provident masters, rather than support so many of those insidious characters, who seek to obtain, through your Lordship, these severe enactments.

To convince you of this, I beg to call your Lordship's attention to the following extract from a publication by Dr. J. P. Kay, of Manchester, "On the Moral and Physical condition of the Working Classes employed in the Cotton Manufacture." It is an account of a Cotton Manufacturing establishment at Hyde, belonging to Mr. Thomas Ashton.—Your Lordship will find it a very good account, and perhaps may imagine it is selected as the best that could be found;—this is not the case;—it is the *only* description of such an establishment that I have ever seen published.

"Twelve Hundred persons are employed in the factories of Mr. Thomas Ashton, of Hyde. This gentleman has erected commodious dwellings for his work-people, with each of which he has connected every convenience that can minister to comfort. He resides in the immediate vicinity, and has frequent opportunities of maintaining a cordial association with his operatives. Their houses are well furnished, clean, and their tenants exhibit every indication of health and happiness. Mr. Ashton has also built a School, where 640 children, chiefly belonging to his establishment, are instructed on Sundays, in reading, writing, arithmetic, &c. A library, connected with this school, is eagerly

B

resorted to, and the people frequently read after the hours of labour have expired.—An infant school is, during the week, attended by 280 children, and in the evenings, others are instructed by masters selected for the purpose. The factories themselves are certainly excellent examples of the cleanliness and order which may be attained, by a systematic and persevering attention to the habits of the artisans. The effects of such enlightened benevolence, may be, to a certain extent, exhibited by statistical statements. The population, before the introduction of machinery, chiefly consisted of colliers, hatters and weavers. Machinery was introduced in 1801, and the following table exhibits its consequences, in the augmentation of the value of property, the diminution of poor rates, and the rapid increase of the amount assessed for the repairs of the highway, during a period in which the population of the township increased from 830 to 7138."

Township of Hyde, in the Parish of Stockport, in the County of Chester.

Year.	*Estimated value of Property assessable to the Poor's Rate.* £	s.	*Sums Assessed for the relief of the Poor.* £	s.	d.	*Sums assessed for repairs of Highways.* £	s.	d.	*Population*	*Remarks.*
1801	693	10	533	12	0	2	11	6	830	Machinery introduced.
2	697	0	394	19	4	51	19	5		
3	697	0	336	8	0	52	3	0¾		
4	697	10	325	10	0	52	5	9¾		
5	724	0	385	17	4	100	6	11½		
6	786	0	339	6	0	110	12	11½		
7	829	0	276	6	8	172	7	9½		
8	898	10	223	1	4	177	6	10		
9	915	0	286	16	8	152	17	9		
1810	935	0	345	10	0	146	18	3½		
1	945	10	417	6	4	199	19	3½	1806	Riots, Machinery broken
2	975	15	471	8	4	168	11	1		in various places.
3	986	0	687	7	8	148	18	11¼		Power Looms introduced
4	997	0	630	6	8	144	18	8¼		
5	1029	15	508	18	0	99	9	3½		
6	1079	5	390	2	0	156	9	5¼		
7	1109	15	502	3	6	150	2	8½		
8	1142	0	421	2	0	171	15	9		
9	1242	0	431	6	0	201	8	7½		
1820	1272	0	355	4	8	229	11	7		
1	1371	15	274	7	0	265	1	1		New County Rate made;
2	1429	5	435	10	6	440	12	0¾	3355	from this time the county
3	1570	0	479	8	0	454	8	8¾		rate, together with the
4	1792	0	348	17	0	506	2	2½		salary of the serving of-
5	1957	0	398	11	0	524	19	3½		ficer averaged £200. per
6	2093	10	438	7	6	573	10	7¾		annum.
7	2354	15	479	6	3	598	10	5		
8	2533	0	502	7	4	732	4	3½		
9	2623	0	790	11	9	681	19	6½		Vestry built this year.
1830	2727	0	549	16	0	578	10	1		
1	2783	0	*834	18	9	359	5	5½	7138	
	Total in 31 years.		13995	13	4	8405	19	7		
	Average ..		451	10	0	271	7	2		

* A considerable balance in the Overseer's Hands.

" This table exhibits a cheering proof of the advantages which may be derived from the commercial system, under judicious management. We feel much confidence in inferring, that where so little pauperism exists, the taint of vice has not deeply infected the population: and concerning their health, we can speak from personal observation. The rate of mortality from statements * with which Mr. Ashton has politely furnished us, appears to be exceedingly low. In thirteen years, during the first six of which, the number of rovers, spinners, piecers, and dressers was one hundred, and during the last seven, above two hundred, only eight deaths occurred, though the same persons were, with rare exceptions, employed during the whole period. Supposing for the sake of convenience, that the deaths were nine; then by ascribing three to the first six years, and six to the last seven, the mortality during the former period was one in 200, and during the latter, one in 233. The number of weavers during the first six years was 200, and during the last seven 400; and in this body of workmen 40 deaths occurred in thirteen years. By ascribing thirteen of these deaths to the first six years, and twenty-seven to the last seven, the mortality during the former period, was one in 92, and during the latter, one in 103."

---

* Minute of deaths amongst Spinners, Piecers, and Dressers, employed at the Works of Mr. Thomas Ashton, in Hyde, from 1819 to 1832, thirteen years, viz.—*Spinners*, Richard Robinson, James Seville, David Cordingly, Eli Taylor. *Piecers*, James Rowbotham, William Green. *Dressers*, John Cocker, Samuel Broadhurst.—There are employed at these Works 61 Rovers and Spinners, 120 Piecers, and 38 Dressers: total 219; among whom there are at this time, 10 Spinners whose ages are respectively from 40 up to 56 years; and among the Dressers there are 12 whose ages are equal to that of the above Spinners. We have no orphans at this place, neither have we any family receiving parochial relief, nor can we recollect the time when there was any such.—The different clubs or sick lists among the Spinners, Dressers, Overlookers, and Mechanics employed here, allow ten or twelve shillings per week to the members during sickness, and from six to eight pounds to a funeral; which applies also to the member's wife, and in some cases, one half or one fourth to the funeral of a child; the greatest amount of contributions to these funds have in no one year exceeded five shillings and sixpence from each member. The weavers (chiefly young women) have also a funeral club, the contributions to which are fourpence per member to each funeral. In the above period of 13 years, there have happened among them only forty funerals. Total number of persons employed, twelve hundred, who maintain about two thousand.

JOSEPH TINKER, *Book-keeper.*

Hyde, March, 1832.

" These facts indicate that the present hours of labour do not injure the health of a population, otherwise favourably situated; but that when evil results ensue, they must chiefly be ascribed to the combination of this, with other causes of moral and physical depression."

" Capitalists, whose establishments are situated in the country, enjoy many opportunities of controlling the habits and ministering to the comforts of those in their employ, which cannot exist in a large manufacturing town. In the former, the land in the vicinity is generally the property of the manufacturer; and upon this he may build commodious houses and surround the operative with all the conveniences and attractions of a home. In the town the land is often in the possession of non-resident proprietors, anxious only to obtain the largest amount of chief rent; it is therefore let in separate lots to avaricious speculators, who (unrestrained by any general enactment or special police regulation) build, without plan, wretched abodes in confused groups, intersected by narrow unpaved or undrained streets and courts. By this disgraceful system, the moral and physical condition of the poor, undergo an inevitable depression.

A list of persons in the employ of Mr. Thomas Ashton, of Hyde, with an account of their respective ages and capabilities as to reading and writing, taken 25th of March, 1833.

Age.	Cannot Read.	Can Read.	Can Read and Write.	Total.	
9	1	12	4	17	
10	2	33	6	41	
11	4	34	14	52	
12	4	34	15	53	
13	4	32	17	53	
14	2	43	30	75	
15	3	21	18	42	
16	3	31	29	63	
17	—	28	29	57	
18	6	31	42	79	
19	3	22	36	61	
20	1	22	33	56	
21 to 30	28	104	180	312	
31 to 40	11	36	72	119	
41 to 50	6	20	29	55	
51 to 60	5	7	16	28	
61 to 70	4	1	6	11	
71 & upwards	—	1	—	1	
	87	512	576	1175	

From this account your Lordship will readily perceive what an extent of prosperity is diffused over a country, by the exertions of such an industrious, enterprising, and wealthy individual, as Mr. Thomas Ashton. He provides the poor work-people in his employ, with comfortable dwellings, *regular* wages, averaging twelve shillings per week to every individual, and the means of education for their offspring; he has found abundance of employment for masons, carpenters, bricklayers, labourers, and other artizans in the building of his mills, cottages, and premises;—he has benefitted the farmer by bringing an extensive market to his homestead, and the landlord, as you will perceive by the immensely increased rental of the township, has not failed to benefit by the advantages arising out of Mr. Ashton's well-directed abilities.

Dr. Kay tells you, that in this establishment there are twelve hundred persons employed. 1 understand they work 69 hours per week, and you will have observed that they never require parochial assistance, but have funds provided amongst themselves for relieving the necessitous.

Calling your Lordship's attention to Dr. Kay's remarks on the healthy appearance of the work-people, and his opinion of the duration of the hours of labour at present allowed, I beg to inquire of your Lordship, in what way you think your bill would increase the prosperity of the Township of Hyde, or improve the condition of the work-people? Surely you will conclude with me, that to degrade and imprison Mr. Thomas Ashton is not the way to do it.

I beg to ask, can your Lordship find me in the county of Dorset, so cheering a picture of prosperity and comfort, or shew me any Agricultural district, where the moral and physical condition of the people, has not retrograded during the same period, *even with the undue protection of the Corn Laws.**

Perhaps your Lordship may inquire, whether there are any more such pictures of prosperity to be found in the manufacturing districts. I say there are, but that many Mill owners feel a delicacy—a reluctance to have the prosperity of their manufacturing establishments, and the condition of their work-people, publicly exhibited; however, as I do not choose to take a liberty

---

* *The following are the average amounts per head of the population, expended on the relief of the Poor, in each of the respective Counties of England, in* 1831. *It will be seen that these sums are much smaller in the Manufacturing and Mining Counties, than in those which are entirely Agricultural Counties. The former are distinguished by an asterisk.*

	s.	*d.*		*s.*	*d.*
Bedford	16	11¾	* Monmouth	5	5
Berks	15	10	Norfolk	15	4¼
Bucks	18	8¾	Northampton	16	9¾
Cambridge	13	8¼	* Northumberland	6	7¾
* Chester	6	2¼	* Nottingham	6	5¼
* Cornwall	6	9	Oxford	17	1½
* Cumberland	5	5¼	Rutland	9	1
* Derby	6	7	* Salop	7	9¾
Devon	9	0	* Somerset	8	8½
Dorset	11	4¾	* Stafford	8	11½
* Durham	6	5¼	Suffolk	18	3¾
Essex	17	2¼	Surrey	10	11
* Gloucester	8	8¼	Sussex	19	4½
Hereford	11	3¼	* Warwick	9	6¾
Hertford	13	1¾	Westmoreland	15	2
Huntingdon	15	2¾	Wilts	16	1¾
Kent	14	5¼	* Worcester	7	10¾
* Lancaster	4	4¾	York, East Riding	9	10
Leicester	11	6	——North do.	8	9¼
Lincoln	10	11½	* ——West do.	5	7½
Middlesex	10	0¼			

with the affairs of other people, I may be allowed to state (though reluctantly) what I should be highly gratified to show your Lordship personally, the condition of the work people employed in the Cotton Manufactory under my own direction.

The concern in which I am interested is situated in the country; and has not long existed as a manufacturing establishment. It furnishes employment for 561 work-people, whose earnings vary from two shillings to two pounds a week, and form an average of 9s. 5d. for each person.

I cannot show with the exactness that Mr. Thomas Ashton does, what effect this manufacturing establishment has yet had, upon the poor's rate; or the rental of land in the neighbourhood: I do know, that the effect has been highly favourable hitherto, and well estimated; and I can say with him, that none of my work-people have any parochial assistance, as they support those who are sick or needy, from a fund that has been established amongst themselves. The farmers, shopkeepers, tailors, shoemakers, &c. of the neighbourhood, have been very much benefitted by the advantages of a greatly increased population; and the masons, carpenters and labourers, have had a very regular source of employment in erecting mills, building cottages for work-people, and other premises; and the poor funds of the township, have received a considerable accession of income, by the rates which are charged upon the mills and premises; and the overseer of the poor, has perceived a diminished expenditure of considerable extent, by reason of the necessitous poor obtaining a regular source of employment for themselves or their children in the mills.

Many poor families have obtained work in the mills, who have previously been accustomed to weaving or to some other ill-paid employment; some had incurred heavy debts with shopkeepers, which they were unable to pay, and most of them were in arrears of rent with their landlords. I rejoice to say, my Lord, that I can shew you many of these families still working at the mills, who can tell you, with an honest countenance, that they have paid off their arrears of rents and accumulations of debts, and are living in comfortable well-furnished dwellings, having regular employment, and who by the skill and ability which they and their children have acquired, are enabled by their joint earnings to obtain more than three pounds a week of wages; I will also gladly shew your Lordship, that these people have not had the education of their children neglected; that out of 561 persons employed, 549 of them have learnt to read, and 253 of them can write also. Of the remaining 12 who cannot read, 9 of them have been recently engaged, mostly from other employments, and the other three persons have worked two or three years at the Mill, but have not resided on the premises.

The neighbourhood, as your Lordship may easily imagine, forms a sort of manufacturing colony; a school-house has been built, and on Sundays, the school is well attended by the children, and well supplied with teachers from amongst the work-people; and on the evenings of that and other days, they provide for themselves a minister of the gospel of their own choosing, to attend and instruct them.

On other days of the week, and in the evenings, the school is well attended as an infant school, and as an evening school; and it is used occasionally as a lecture-room.

I will not unjustly offend my work-people with attempting to make your Lordship believe, that they have been provided with education at my expense; it is no such thing,—they owe it to their own exertions; and I would rather be esteemed even parsimonious, than see them deprived of their independence.

The teacher of the infant school, had a small pecuniary allowance from me for a month or two at the commencement; but this was discontinued as soon as the work-people, who had little prejudices to overcome, saw the advantages of educating their children; and the teacher has since received ample remuneration from them.

The feeling of good order and wholesome discipline, which exists amongst the work-people themselves, may be estimated by their uniform practice of appointing, from amongst their own body, a number of judicious persons, whom they authorise to act as sabbath-wardens or constables, who take charge of the peace of the neighbourhood, and apprehend or admonish any such idlers, as may happen to intrude; and thus they endeavour to enforce the salutary regulations of the sabbath.—Their appointment is not an enforced one on my part, but is based upon their own desire for the dutiful regard of that day.

C

You may next be ready to inquire, my Lord, what degree of general health these people enjoy;—whether they wear the " *haggard looks,*" the " *pallid ghastly cheeks,*" the " *emaciated frames,*" that you have heard so pathetically described. I tell you no :—And you will not find any evidence of the existence of " haggard looks " in any cotton mill, working no more than twelve hours a day, and nine hours on Saturdays; which is the limitation allowed by the act of Sir J. C. Hobhouse.

I speak with candour, when I assert, that the general health of persons working in the mill, will bear comparison with an equal number of unselected persons found in any other occupation, with the exception of those engaged in husbandry labour.

I find my opinion upon this subject fully corroborated by the following extract from the letter of Kirkman Finlay, Esq. to your Lordship, dated 1st March, 1833. p. p. 14, 15.

" From what I have myself observed, I can very truly assert, " that the people employed by the first class of Spinners and " Power-loom Manufacturers, who work for twelve hours on five " days of the week, and nine hours on Saturday, and no longer, " are as steady, healthy, comfortable, and well-behaved workers, " as are to be found in any part of the country, in any manu- " facture whatever, or employed even in agriculture itself."— Again, " I am well convinced that if the present laws were en- " forced, and effectual means taken, to put a stop to every kind " of Factory working above twelve hours in the day, also to " abolish night-working, under any pretence, no complaint what- " ever could justly be made of working Cotton Factories."

And also by the following, " It would be easy to give certi- " ficates of this fact from the Clergy and resident Magistrates in " the neighbourhood of many of these establishments, but the " following from the Rev. Dr. Murray, of a large factory in his " parish, where he has lived for above forty years, is a proof that " there is nothing in the hours nor in the employment, which " ought to be a hindrance to education, and to exemplary con- " duct. Similar evidence can, I believe, be given of a large pro- " portion of the country parts; and what is done at one station " may be done at others ; there is at least nothing in the hours of " working, nor in the nature of the employment, to prevent it."

MINISTER'S CERTIFICATE.

" As minister of the Parish in which the Deanston Works are
" situated, I feel myself entitled to state, that the children em-
" ployed in these works, are kindly and tenderly treated ; that
" the mode of conducting their education is excellent ; and that
" the manager studies how to promote their comfort in all respects.
" The Schools are annually strictly examined by a committee of
" the Presbytery of the bounds, and a report attested by the
" examinators, sent regularly to the general assembly of the
" Church of Scotland. 1 can also state with great truth, that
" there is no portion of the inhabitants of this parish, consisting
" of 3,700 souls and upwards, whose moral conduct and general
" behaviour, is more correct than that of those employed at the
" Deanston Works. Further, having been forty years minister
" of this parish, and well acquainted with the habits of all my
" people, I hesitate not to say, that whatever changes may be
" thought necessary as to other works of a similar kind, in my
" humble opinion, the system of management in the Deanston
" Works, might be with safety adopted as a model for ensuring
" the health, promoting the virtuous and religious education of
" the young, and improving the conduct of all, connected with
" such establishments.

" *Given at the Manse of Kilmadock, by me*
" PATRICK MURRAY, D. D.
" *Minister of that Parish, this* 13*th day of June,* 1832."

You may very properly inquire, my Lord, whether I do not
think that it is hard for children to be called up early in a morning, and walk a long way to the mill, as described in the evidence?
I answer, that I really think it is a hardship.—Such children ought
to go to Infant Schools; and not be allowed to enter mills before
they are eleven or twelve years of age.

You know, my Lord, these children are free agents, or at all
events, their parents are. The mill owner cannot compel them
to work for him ; they, or their parents are at liberty to choose
their own business or master; and if you ask the parent of one
of these children, perhaps a weaver or labourer, or some one engaged in an uncertain employment, what are his reasons for
sending his children to a mill, he will tell you that his own busi-

ness is not worth following; that it makes his family but a scanty subsistence ;—perhaps only 7s. to 10s. a week ; but that his children's wages, added to his own, maintain them pretty comfortably. Again, he will tell you, that by obtaining employment for his children in the mills, whilst they are young, they are learning a business which will enable them hereafter to obtain a regular employment, and twice or thrice the amount of wages that he himself is earning.

You will next very naturally inquire about the old men, who are said to die or become unfit for work when they attain forty years of age, or soon after. I tell you, my Lord, (and I will convince you more of it hereafter) that you will find from the evidence which follows, that there are but few men, in any business, who much exceed the age of forty ; and even these will be found more or less incapacitated. However, I beg to assure you, that as far as regards cotton spinners, a full proportion of old men may be found in some establishments, although there are other mills where but few are employed. As all spinners, whether young or old, are paid the same price per lb. for spinning, the production of an old man is at a greater expense, by reason of the diminished quantity : this, and not ill health, may sometimes occasion his discharge ; but he frequently receives indulgence in this respect, on account of length of servitude, or otherwise.

It may also be added, that old men of every description, adhere to habits contracted in early life ; hence, they are troublesome to manage, and often disagree with the overlookers, who are younger than themselves ; this may sometimes lead to their discharge, but it happens not unfrequently that they become disinclined to work, when the earnings of their families are sufficient to maintain them.

It may also happen that the number of men, of forty years of age, engaged in cotton-mills, appear to be comparatively few, because the trade itself is yet but young. Probably one half of the cotton mills have been erected within the last twenty years.

It is well known amongst the mill-owners and managers, that many parents seek mill employment for *delicate* children, because a warm occupation suits their constitutions, and they find a difficulty in meeting with any other suitable business,

With regard to the alleged extensive mortality of those towns, in which large manufactories are carried on, allow me to assert that the case cannot be otherwise, whatever be the nature of the employment, so long as an immense population are crowded together in unwholesome streets and miserable dwellings.—Hence, the bills of mortality cannot be deemed a proper criterion of the salubrity of manufacturing employments.

In order to disabuse your Lordship of the impression, now unfortunately become so general, and diffused by over zealous and inconsiderate persons, that mill occupations cause a greater mortality than the average of other employments, I have taken the liberty to extract the following accounts (which may probably not have come before your Lordship's notice) of the effects of various trades, upon the health and longevity of persons employed therein; from a publication by Mr. C. T. Thackrah, Surgeon, Leeds, 1831.—It appears to have been the result of an investigation entered into by Mr. Thackrah as a professional study. In curtailing his remarks, I have endeavoured to keep their substance as accurate as possible; and have made no intentional omission which would deprive them of their proper conclusions.

EXTRACT

FROM

Thackrah's remarks on the health and longevity of persons engaged in Trades, Manufactures, &c. in and about Leeds, 1831.

He states that fifty thousand persons spend their lives in the manufactories of Leeds, or in occupations allied to them ; he examines their condition, in comparison with those engaged in agriculture, and shews that the duration of life is considerably less in the West Riding, the manufacturing district, than in other parts of Yorkshire.

He shews by the census of 1821, that the mortality in Leeds, is one in fifty-five ; that of Ripon, one in sixty-seven and a half; and that of Pickering-Lythe, which he considers an entirely natural mortality, is only one in seventy-four.

It may therefore be presumed, that about four hundred and fifty persons die annually in the borough of Leeds, from the injurious effects of manufactures, the crowded state of population, and consequent bad habits of life.

" We need scarcely remark, that the air of a town like Leeds is always in an unnatural state: this state of the atmosphere affects, in a greater or less degree, all the inhabitants; the complexion is pallid and the digestion is disordered and imperfect:— I should think not *ten per cent* of the inhabitants of towns like Leeds enjoy *full health.*"

" The following statements are conceived to approach to the truth. They are drawn up from an examination of the agents believed to be injurious, and from conversations with masters, overlookers, and intelligent workmen. They begin with those operatives who approach nearest to the perfection of the Physical state : they are men of active habits, and whose employments are chiefly in the open air."

" BUTCHERS—take strong exercise, much in the open air, they eat fresh-cooked meat twice a day, look plump and rosy, are not subject to such anxieties as the fluctuations of other Trades produce. They are subject to few ailments, and these the results of plethora. Notwithstanding these favourable circumstances, longevity is not greater in them than in the generality of employments, but perhaps shorter than amongst others who spend as much time in the open air.—Butchers live too highly, not too highly for temporary health, but too highly for long life. It may be assumed, that every man is gifted at birth with a portion of the pabulum of life, which he cannot increase, but which he may prematurely consume by profligate indulgence."

Dr. Murray, of Scarborough, concurs in the statement relative to butchers. " The high living of butchers, assuredly leads to plethora and premature dissolution."—He adds.—"Thus Coal meters, &c. of London, rarely if ever attain the age of 40, though men remarkable for bulk and muscular strength;—they work most laboriously, perspire immensely, and supply such waste by extraordinary and almost incredible potations of porter, which ultimately, without much positive and actual intemperance, bring on irregularities of the digestive system, structural changes, and death."

" CATTLE AND HORSE DEALERS—lead an active life in the open air; would be generally healthy were it not for their habit of drinking."

" LABOURERS IN HUSBANDRY, ROAD MAKERS, &c.— would be healthy were their means of subsistence adequate to their wants.

" BRICK MAKERS — have full muscular exercise in the open air, and illness is not frequent among them; some of them are found of great age."

" CHAISE DRIVERS, COACHMEN, GUARDS, &c. — have plenty of fresh air, but not much exercise, they suffer from irregular living. The whole of this class are short lived, and generally die before they reach the age of fifty. Only three old men of this class could be found in Leeds, and they had the character of great temperance."

" CARPENTERS, WHEELWRIGHTS AND MILLWRIGHTS—appear to receive no injury from their respective employments, they receive high wages; and that class who are temperate are healthy, and sometimes live to sixty years of age; but others suffer from their debauched habits, and are short lived."

" TAILORS—sit all day in a confined atmosphere, with the legs crossed and spine bowed, and therefore cannot have circulation, respiration, or digestion well performed. We see no plump, rosy tailors; none of fine form and strong muscle. The prejudicial influence of their employ, undermines rather than destroys life; of 22 workmen in Leeds, not one had attained the age of 60; two had passed 50; and of the rest, not more than two had passed 40. They suffer very much from intemperate habits."

" MILLINERS, DRESS MAKERS AND STRAW BONNET MAKERS—suffer from being in crowded apartments, working *long hours*, sometimes from 5 or 6 o'clock in a morning till 12 o'clock at night, and some of them from lowness of wages."

SHOE MAKERS—like tailors, suffer from sitting in a very bad posture,—are often unhealthy, and injure themselves by irregularities, drinking, &c."

" CURRIERS—are subjected to a disagreeable smell; but are generally healthy, and many of them live to old age."

" PRINTERS—live in a confined atmosphere; they suffer from effluvia emitted from the types, and a compositor is seldom found above 50 years of age."

" CLOCK-MAKERS—are generally healthy; but WATCH-MA-

KERS have a much worse employ. Sitting with the trunk bent forward, affects the lungs, and injures the eyes. They rarely live to old age."

" SMITHS—have an employment remarkably conducive to muscular power; and for youths of strong constitutions, no labour is better than that of the smith. The exertion is too great for delicate persons.—When smiths are ill, it frequently arises from intemperance.—They do not arrive at great age; only one old smith being found in the town of Leeds."

" COLLIERS—have considerable muscular labour in an unnatural atmosphere, and with an artificial light, are greatly exposed to changes. They have the spine almost always curved, and the legs often bowed ; and they are very liable to accidents.—They do not generally exceed fifty years of age."

" CORN MILLERS—breathing an atmosphere loaded with particles of flour, suffer considerably.—Several who had borne the employ from boyhood to the age of 50 or 60, were by no means robust ; and an aged and healthy miller could not be found."

" MALTSTERS—are exposed to much dust, and suffer from the heat of the kilns.—They are affected with bronchial inflammations, and many become asthmatic for life.—They often leave the employ at an early age."

" COFFEE ROASTERS—are affected by the heat and vapour; and are said to become asthmatic."

" WORKERS IN FLAX.—In the Flax Mills, all the departments with the exception of spinning and reeling produce dust ; but the worst department is certainly the heckling."

" The majority of the operatives in the great Flax Mills, are young women, girls and boys."

" Persons in the dusty departments are generally unhealthy ; they are subject to indigestion, morning vomiting, chronic inflammation of the bronchial membranes, inflammation of the lungs, and pulmonary consumption."

The process of heckling Flax is generally the most injurious to health ; a large proportion of men in this department die young ; very few can bear it for thirty years ; and not one instance could we find of any individual who had been forty years either in this, or in any of the dusty rooms.—We find indeed comparatively few old persons in *any* of the departments of the

Flax Mills. On inquiry at one of the largest establishments in this neighbourhood, we found that of 1079 persons employed, there are only nine who have attained the age of fifty; and besides these only 22, who have reached even forty.—They work twelve hours a day; and in some cases, thirteen hours a day, for six days in the week."

" MASONS—inhale particles of sand and dust, which arise from chipping the stone; they use great muscular exertion, and are exposed to vicissitudes of the weather from exertion in the open air; their face has colour, and the figure is muscular and robust; they suffer from inhaling dust; their habits are dissipated; they are addicted to intemperance, and die generally before they attain the age of forty."

" MINERS—in the North of England, (I am indebted to an intelligent friend for the information) when employed in ore in the Sand Stone, suffer considerably from particles of dust, but not so much when the ore is in limestone; they work only six hours a day; take immoderately of ardent spirits and seldom attain the age of forty:—last year in the village of Arkendale, there were not less than thirty widows under thirty years of age."

" Smelting is considered a most fatal occupation; the appearance of the men is haggard in the extreme."

" GRINDERS OF SHEFFIELD.—Dr. Knight, in the North of England Medical Journal, states, that the fork grinders who use a DRY grindstone, die at the ages of twenty-eight or thirty-two: while the table-knife grinders, who work on wet stones, survive to between forty and fifty."

" THE FILERS—in the Machine Manufactories of Leeds, suffer from inhaling particles of metallic dust, and are almost all unhealthy men and remarkably short lived; only one instance being found of a man's following the employ for twenty years. At two of the principal of these manufactories in Leeds, there are only two filers of the age of forty-eight; and in neither case had they pursued this labour from boyhood.—The work-people employed in this occupation were not considered intemperate, but generally steady."

" PLUMBERS—though sickly in appearance do not generally complain.—It is apparent that the occupation undermines the constitution; as there are but two individuals in the neighbour-

D

hood of Leeds who have pursued this employment, beyond the age of forty."

" PAINTERS—are unhealthy in appearance, and do not generally attain full age."

" WOOL SCOURERS—are in a wet room inhaling steam, and are exposed to currents of cold air; yet they are not sensible of any unusual ill effects."

" DYERS—are exposed to the same agents. As a body they are generally healthy and long lived; individuals may be found who have been dyers forty or fifty years."

" BRUSHERS OF CLOTH BY STEAM—chiefly boys, are immersed all day in dense vapour, and a room of considerable heat; they have a sickly appearance."

" MILLERS OF CLOTH—are exposed to cold and wet; yet they are generally healthy."

" SPINNERS OF WORSTED—inhale fine dust; but this is not in such quantity as to produce a marked effect."

" PAPER MAKERS—work in very wet rooms; the arms and feet are exposed; they are alternately engaged in warm vapour at the vat, perspiring at the press, and at another time at the cold employ of putting up the paper to dry. They are not subject to any serious illness; and individuals have borne the employ to the age of seventy."

" Whether we examine the agency of moisture on men in the open air or those under cover, we find it much less than common opinion would expect."

" COTTON AND SILK SPINNERS—are not numerous in Leeds, for there is but one mill; the rooms are kept in a high temperature, heated by steam. We found the thermometer stand at 70. —The carding-room is dusty, but much less so than similar rooms in the Flax mills.—Adults who have been long in the employ, not unfrequently suffer from affections of the lungs, but they are not subject to urgent diseases.—The young suffer less than the adult. It is stated, that of the 300 individuals in this establishment, not more than ten in a year are incapacitated for work."

" DEALERS AND SHOPKEEPERS—live in a confined atmosphere; they move about, but do not take much exercise; they are engaged till late in an evening, are temperate in their diet, but suffer from want of fresh air. Hence they are pale, dyspeptic, subject to affections of the head, and drag on a sickly existence; die before the proper end of human life, and leave a progeny like themselves."

" COMMERCIAL TRAVELLERS—have greatly the advantage of Shopkeepers; are well fed, ride from town to town, and have an employment not only more agreeable, but more conducive to health than almost any other dependant on traffic; but they destroy their constitutions by intemperance :—not generally by drunkenness, but by daily taking more liquor than nature requires. We cannot refer to such conduct except in terms of the strongest reprobation; as the Commercial Traveller is, or ought to be, better informed. Few of them bear the employ for thirty years, the majority not twenty years."

" MERCHANTS AND MASTER MANUFACTURERS—spending most of the day in the Counting House or the Mill; they are subject not only to the impure atmosphere of a large town, but occasionally to the dust or effluvium from the manufacture :— such exercise as they are accustomed to take is very inadequate to the support of good health. The way in which many men of business take their meals, is also highly injurious to health; it is far too hasty; and the nervous energy which the stomach requires for digestion, is abstracted by the mind : they *think*, when they ought to *eat;* the animal operations are sacrificed to calculation, speculation, and commercial arrangement.—But of all agents of disease and decay, the most important is *anxiety of mind.* When we walk the streets of large commercial towns, we must be struck with the hurried gait and care-worn features of the well-dressed passengers. Our muscles waste for *want* of action ; our nervous system is worn out by *excess* of action. The various disorders generally known under the name of indigestion, disorders dependant on a want of circulation of blood through the bowels, biliary derangements, constipation and head ache, are well known to be the general attendants on trade closely pursued."

———

Thus your Lordship perceives that imperfect health and short life are not confined to any class or any employment; but that the same principle which calls for legal interference and for the regulation of one trade, one class, or one age, demands it for all, and not only for the *poor*, but for the *rich*.

Your Lordship may now tell me, that these work-people of mine, who, I have endeavoured to shew you, are enjoying a considerable degree of comfort, have nevertheless signed a petition for your bill, which, you know, provides for my imprisonment. This certainly appears very strange, and does not speak favourably as to their estimation either of me, or of their own condition. As your Lordship has perhaps never visited the manufacturing districts, you may not be aware of the peculiarly excitable feelings of our working population. I may therefore inform your Lordship, that there are in every town, a number of idle, unemployed persons, who may not inaptly be termed agitators, and who live upon the contributions they obtain from those, who are more industrious than themselves. These people sometimes contrive to create strife betwixt masters and workmen, on the question of wages; at another time, they take it into their heads to agitate a time bill; and if neither of these subjects be sufficiently popular, to raise to them all the funds they wish, they again ply their wits upon some other mischief, and under one plea or other, delude the workmen of their earnings. In this way, my Lord, you may account for the general outcry, which has been raised up latterly throughout the kingdom against all master manufactures, without discrimination.

They insinuate amongst the work-people the attractive idea, that they will obtain the same amount of wages for ten hours' labour, as they now get for twelve; inferring that a diminished production will cause a necessity for the erection of new mills, and a more extensive demand for labour.

I inquired from my workmen who had signed the petition, if they really wished to work ten hours instead of twelve hours; for if that was their desire, they need not petition Parliament about it; they ought to try to arrange it with me. They replied, they did not wish it, unless it was *general* measure. I inquired if they had considered the effect it would have upon wages;— this they asserted they had not; but stated that they were induced to sign the petition because they understood it would be *good for the trade.*

I presume your Lordship is aware, that the laws against combinations, were repealed some years ago ;—and that masters or work-people are allowed to combine for the purpose of altering, increasing, or diminishing the rate of wages, or the *hours* of working. But although the agitators, to whom I have before alluded, and the work-people, have from time to time availed themselves of the provisions of this indulgent act, for the purpose of altering or increasing the rate of wages, I have never heard of a single attempt to combine for the purpose of *altering* or *diminishing* the hours of working; and although they have frequently had long protracted struggles on the question of *wages*, yet they have never made any stipulations with regard to the *hours of labour*.

With respect to the safety, in a commercial point of view, of diminishing the hours of labour in cotton mills, I beg to refer your Lordship to the calculations of several gentlemen of ability, who have taken up the pecuniary consideration of this important question, most of which have, I presume, been submitted to you. The export of cotton goods and yarns is computed by them at more than two-thirds of our whole manufacture ; a trifling increase, therefore, in our cost of production, by reason of your Bill, will deprive us eventually of our foreign customers, and throw out of employment those of our work-people who are now maintained by them.

I confidently assert, that by the operation of the Bill, as it now stands, that event would be rendered certain, and the loss incurred would not be of a temporary character, but entirely irrecoverable. Our self-inflicted ruin, would be a two-fold source of *prosperity* to our rivals ; first, by giving them the monopoly of the foreign markets ; and, secondly, by the depression of our manufacture affording them a timely and efficient supply of our most enterprising and valuable overlookers, managers, and other artisans, who would thus be induced to emigrate, and greatly assist in the extension of foreign establishments ; and of their experience and services, no ultimate encouragement in this country could ever again dispossess them. Nor could your Lordship complain, if British capital as well as skill, should find its way to other states, which are now anxious to receive it, and where its free and legitimate use would be fostered, and less exposed to dangerous legislation.*

Your Lordship, no doubt, is considerably surprised, that a measure fraught with such peril as your Bill, does not greatly alarm all the master manufacturers, and rouse them to vigorous opposition. If the master manufacturers of this country seem apathetic, as in this case it would appear, it is perhaps

---

* Some of the advocates of the ten hours' bill are reluctant to admit any extent of danger to our cotton manufacture, from foreign competition.—By the following data it will be seen, that although our own manufacture has continued rapidly to extend, we are by no means in a condition to be trifling with the abilities of our rivals, if we wish it to be understood that we value our export trade.

It appears that in the year 1821, the exportation of raw cotton from the United States of America, to France and the European continent, was somewhat more than *one-sixth* of the quantity sent to Great Britain ; and last year it amounted to more than *one-half*.

In 1831, France produced 63,000,000lbs. of cotton yarn, which will have required a consumption of nearly 80 millions lbs. of the raw material. In the same year, the *export* of Cotton Goods from that country, amounted to £2,192,240. sterling.

In Switzerland, the consumption of cotton, in 1831, amounted to 19,000,000 lbs. Only a few years have elapsed, since that country received the greatest part of her supplies of yarns from England ; she now not only receives very little below number 70, but has herself become an exporter to other countries.

The manufacture of cotton is rapidly increasing in Prussia—throughout the Rhenish Provinces—in Silesia—in Saxony, and in both the German and Italian Provinces belonging to the Crown of Austria.

Attempts, in fact, are being made, in every country which offers any prospect of success, to introduce the manufacture of cotton ; and to such an extent is this zeal manifested, that amongst the establishments in the kingdom of Naples, is one, in which the power applied, is created by the use of horses.

From information obtained on the spot, or replies to questions which were sent to manufacturers on the Continent, it appears that they can compete, successfully, with England, in coarse numbers, some say as high as 40's; others, as high as 70's or 80's —It must be kept in mind, that the quantity of yarn spun in England, above number 80's. is very small, about the proportion of 100 or 120 lbs. of coarse, for one pound of fine.

The wages paid per week, for England and on the Continent, are as follows :

For Spinners	20s. to 35s.		8s. to 10s.
Piecers	4s.	8s.	2s.	3s.
Card-room hands	6s.	14s.	4s.	5s.
Reelers	7s.	13s.	4s.	6s.

There is no Cotton Twist of low numbers now exported from this country to France, or to Switzerland. Last year there were several orders came for our yarns from Germany, restricted to a certain price, but stating that this fixed price was what it could be spun for in that country ; these prices were ¼d. per lb. lower than we could possibly produce them.

because they think your Bill is possessed of a sufficient amount
of absurdity to insure their safety in its own suicidal provisions;
they are also jaded with the continual applications for factory
legislation, all of which enactments they have been able to evade.

From the tenor of my language to you, my Lord, you may
probably think that I am against any reduction of the hours of
labour, or perhaps against all Bills for legislating on labour; this
is not the case, my Lord, although, in *principle*, there are serious
objections to this description of legislation; yet, as the principle
has been broken through, and laws passed, (although ineffective,)
it may perhaps be expedient that they should still exist. Let us,
therefore, endeavour so to arrange the details, as to make them
honoured in the observance, instead of being (as they are represented to have been) evaded without scruple.

We know that the rate-payers of every parish and township
are accountable for the support of their own poor, whenever they
become necessitous. We may therefore fairly infer, that they,
and not the common informers, ought to be charged with the
guardianship of the energies of their poor.—We know also, that
these places are invested with their own local jurisdiction, and
the appointment of their own officers. I would, therefore, re-
commend,—

1. That every parish or township where mills are situated,
shall annually appoint their own officer as mill-warden,* when

---

Besides the continental manufacturers, we have also our American rivals extensively engaged, whose abilities we must not underrate.

The official report of the Committee of the New York Convention, shews a
consumption in 1831, of 77,516,316 lbs. of Cotton, which equals the quantity
consumed in this country, twenty years ago. American fabrics are rapidly
superseding those of this country in Mexico, the Brazils, and in fact throughout all the markets of the South American Continent, and have been brought,
this year, in much larger quantities than heretofore, into the ports of the Me-
diterranean, which can only be accounted for, by the success which has attended their previous transactions.

It will also be kept in mind, that two very important items in the cost of a
piece of cotton cloth, are raw cotton and food. How much greater, therefore,
must be the advantages of our rivals, who obtain both these articles free from
taxation,—pay no poor rates,—and negotiate for manufacturing labour, free
from Time Bills.

* Some Mill owners, in excuse for their own overworking, have unblush-
ingly acknowledged, that they began the practice in self-defence; because
they had not the power of restricting the individual, who first set the example,

they appoint their overseer of the poor, churchwarden, &c. who shall, from time to time, make the necessary reports.

2. That the local authority be empowered to fine, or compelled to prosecute mill-owners for over-working; one half of the penalties to go to the poor fund, the other half to be expended in bedding and clothing, and to be distributed once a year amongst the *resident* poor of the township.

3. That the mill-owner have the power of appeal to the Magisterial Bench.

4. That *no person* should be allowed to work in a mill more than   hours in a day, or   hours in a week.

5. That no child, under eleven or twelve years of age, should be allowed to work more than *six hours a day*.

6. That night-working in mills, should be entirely abolished.

You will probably be impatient to ascertain, whether I have any thing to propose relative to the diminution of the hours of labour.—You will perceive, my Lord, that I have already proposed to diminish the hardships of the young children;—and if the indulgences, hereafter suggested, were granted to the trade, I think we may fairly calculate, that, could we meet the views of the advocates of your Bill, by a reduction of the hours of working to eleven hours a day, and eight or nine on Saturdays, we might perhaps successfully maintain our ground in the arduous struggle against foreign competition, supported as it is, by cheaper food, unrestricted labour, and no parochial assessments.

I would, therefore, beg leave to propose, that your Lordship should unite with the general body of the Cotton Manufacturers, in obtaining a repeal of the Duty upon Raw Cotton,* which amounts to about £700,000 a year; and as a large proportion of it is again exported in yarns and piece goods, it becomes a charge, hereafter to be obtained from our foreign customers, to the amount of about £500,000.

---

without *descending to employ an informer.*—Had they, as rate-payers, been in possession of a local officer as mill-warden, they could have prevented or punished any offence against the law, without incurring personal animosity.

* The Duty charged upon Raw Cotton, amounts to upwards of £4,000 a year, for the consumption of some establishments.

Having given the trade the benefit of your services in obtaining the repeal of this duty, your Lordship, I trust, will not allow your zealous interest on behalf of the *working classes* to abate, but apply, with the urgency of a demand for the immediate repeal of the Corn Laws, which press so heavily upon them. I need not remind you it is a great hardship that a working-man in this country, should pay 55s. for as much corn as his competitors, the French, can obtain for 33s. This, your Lordship will acknowledge, ought not to be overlooked in our endeavour to improve their condition.

You may possibly find, that the gentlemen of the landed interest will manifest a little acrimonious feeling towards your Lordship's proposals upon this subject, and they may perhaps tell you not only, that they *must* be protected, but that they are *our* best customers. Will your Lordship be so good as to state to them, that a correspondent of your's has informed you that the contrary is the fact, with respect to the cotton trade ; and that the foreigners are our customers to more than twice the extent. Hence they must, eventually, see the necessity of protecting and promoting British Industry and Commerce.

In offering these remarks to your Lordship, allow me to say, that I do not question the benevolence of your Lordship's design, nor undervalue the philanthropy of your advisers ; but I have an earnest desire that the proposed benefit should not be defeated by misguided zeal, nor those important considerations of this question overlooked, which your friends in the infirmity of an over-ardent benevolence, may lead you to imagine, are only intended to impede their object. I believe it is very possible, to promote the physical advantage and intellectual improvement of of the working classes without seriously endangering our manufactures, but I am convinced that this cannot be done by a statute, which will involve their employers in labyrinths of litigation, in ruinous penalties which they cannot avoid, and in punishments of the most degrading character ;—such a law will either become a dead letter, or, if enforced, will powerfully promote the extension of manufacturing abroad, and bring upon the work-people a

E

succession of hardships terminating in the eventual loss of their present means of subsistence.

Allow me to hope that my zealous feeling may not have led me to manifest any want of courtesy to your Lordship, in the freedom with which I have ventured to remark on your bill.

I have the honor to be,

My Lord,

Your Lordship's most obedient humble Servant,

A LANCASHIRE COTTON SPINNER.

APPENDIX.

ABSTRACT OF LORD ASHLEY'S FACTORY BILL.

The preamble sets forth that it has been the practice in many mills and factories to employ a great number of children an unreasonable length of time, to the manifest injury of their health and morals, for remedy whereof it is enacted:—

1. That from and after the 1st of July, 1833, no person under the age of 21 years shall be allowed to work in or during the night, that is, between seven o'clock in the evening, and six in the morning, except as hereinafter provided, in or about any cotton, woollen, worsted, hemp, flax, tow, linen, lace, or silk mill or factory, wherein steam or water, or any other power is used to work the machinery.

2. That no person under the age of 18 years be allowed to work in any such mill more than ten hours in any one day, or more than eight hours on a Saturday, exclusive of the time allowed for meals and refreshment. This provision not to extend to the fulling of woollen cloth, or to any apprentice, or other person employed therein.

3. That there shall be allowed to every child or young person employed in any factory, two full hours a day for meals: that is, half an hour for breakfast, one hour for dinner, and half an hour for afternoon refreshment daily, except on the Saturdays, when the last half hour interval for refreshment shall not be allowed.

---

4. That in case the occupier or occupiers of any factory, and the parents of the children employed therein, shall deem it more expedient that their employment shall terminate half an hour earlier than the aforesaid regulations, the half hour for the afternoon meal or refreshment may be given up.

5. That for the purpose of avoiding the inconvenience and injury of working by gas and other artificial lights in the mornings of the winter season, the children may breakfast at home in the months of Nov., Dec., Jan., and Feb. in each year, in which case no interval is to take place for breakfast between the commencement of their labour and the dinner hour, and return home in the evening at the time agreed upon, without the half hour's refreshment in the afternoon, so that the period of their labour, from its commencement to its conclusion, including the dinner hour shall not exceed eleven hours in any one day, nor nine hours on the Saturday.

6. That the time fixed upon for the meals of the children shall be the same for all the young persons so employed.

7. That the labour of children from the commencement in the morning to the termination in the evening shall be continuous, except during meal times, and shall not in any case exceed twelve hours including three meals, or $11\frac{1}{2}$ hours, including two meals, or eleven hours, including one meal.

8. That the hours may be varied in case of floods or other impediments.

9. That no time lost by interruption, or in consequence of stoppage from the breaking of machinery, shall be made up.

10. That no children under nine years of age shall employed in any factory.

11. That occupiers of mills are not liable to penalties for employing children contrary to the act, if they have a certificate for so doing.

12. That if notice in writing be delivered to any occupier that any child in his employment is under age, he shall enquire into it.

13. That machinery shall not be cleaned on a Sunday.

14. That parents or guardians giving false certificates of age, shall be liable to a penalty not exceeding £5., and not less than £

15. That any mill owner convicted of procuring false certificates of age, shall be liable to a penalty of £100.

16 That the whole of the interior walls of the mill shall be white-washed at least once a year, except such parts as are painted.

17. That after the passing of this act, the rooms in each mill to be built shall be ten feet high, under an annual penalty of—

18. That no justice, being a proprietor or occupier of a factory, shall act as a justice of the peace in the execution of this act.

19. That when all the justices in the division are disqualified, those in the next may act.

20. That it is not necessary to set forth the name of each partner in law proceedings under this act.

21. That the service of any process on any occupier, his principal clerk or manager, shall be considered a sufficient service.

22. Informations to be brought within thirty days subsequent to any offence, except such as shall be laid in consequence of any inspection of the time-book, which information may then be laid any time not later than three months.

23. That the regulations shall be hung up in the factories, signed by the occupier or occupiers, regarding the earliest age at which children are employed therein, the hour in the morning of each day at which they are to commence their work, and the time in the evening when they shall be dismissed, and also the time fixed upon for their meals and refreshment.

24. That a time book shall be kept in each mill, in which the occupier or occupiers shall cause to be entered each and every day, a true and correct account of the time at which the steam-engine or water-wheel, and other machinery in the factory shall have been in operation during such day,—such time-book to be signed weekly by the master, or by some person appointed by him to sign the same, and that the said book, or a copy thereof, shall be produced for inspection before any justice of the peace, before whom any information or informations regarding any offence against the provisions of this act shall be laid, and that the said book shall be delivered quarterly to the clerk of the peace, in such county, borough, or town, in which the factory is situated, and shall be open to inspection and examination to any person demanding to see the same, on payment of one shilling for such inspection.

25. That any occupier or occupiers of such mill, making or causing to be made false entries in such book, shall forfeit any sum not exceeding £100, and not less than £50; and any person making such false entry, not being the occupier, shall forfeit any sum not exceeding £20, nor less than £5.

26. That a certificate from the time-book shall be transmitted to the clerk of the peace quarterly, signed by the occupier or occupiers, with a declaration which shall have the force and validity of an oath, that the provisions of the act have been adhered to.

27. That the penalty for not delivering such certificates shall be £100, and not less than £50.

28. That a regular clock shall be kept in the factory, to be regulated by the nearest principal public clock of the parish, and the hours of labour shall be constantly regulated by one clock

only, which clock shall be named in the regulations hung up in the factories.

29. That the principal upright, or horizontal, or other shafts, commonly called the millwright work or going gear, as well as other dangerous parts of the machinery, which commonly are, and ought always to be guarded, fenced, or boxed off, and to which the children and young persons employed in the factories would be otherwise exposed, shall be so fenced or boxed off. And in case of death ensuing from any accident happening in the factory from neglect thereof, the coroner shall summon a jury, upon which no owner or occupier of any mill or factory, or the father, son, or brother of any such occupier shall be qualified to sit; which coroner and jury are to inspect the mill and machinery where the accident happened, and if the verdict of the coroner's jury shall be " Accidental death by the culpable neglect of the occupier or occupiers of the said mill or factory, in not properly guarding, fencing, or boxing off the machinery therein," or words to that effect, the occupier or occupiers shall, by warrant under the coroner's hand and seal, be forthwith committed to take his or their trial at the assizes ensuing for the county where such offence has been committed.

30. That in case of any accident happening to any child, in consequence of the machinery in any factory not being properly guarded or boxed off, which shall not occasion death, but grievous injury in body or limb, so as to render it difficult or impossible for the sufferer to earn his or her maintenance in after life, it shall be lawful for the parent or guardian of such child to make complaint before a justice, who is empowered to summon the parties before the petty sessions, and to convict the occupiers of such factories, in which such grievous injuries occur by wilful neglect, in a penalty not exceeding £200, and not less than £50, for every such accident, which shall be paid to the sufferer, if 21 years of age, and, if under, deposited in the nearest savings' bank, in his or her name; the interest to be paid half-yearly to the parent or guardian until the sufferer attain 21 years.

31. That in case the steam-engine or other propelling power or machinery in a factory be at work before half-past five in the morning, and after seven in the evening, except in case of interruption of work before named, then it shall be lawful for justices to convict the parties complained against, unless it shall be proved by two or more witnesses, that no children or persons have been employed in any time or manner contrary to the provisions of this act, on the day mentioned in the information.

32. That no appeal shall be allowed against conviction, nor such conviction be removed by certiorari into any court, except where the persons convicted would suffer imprisonment, or where the penalty exceeds £20.

33. That it shall be lawful for any justice, before whom complaint is made, to summon persons as witnesses before him, and if such persons do not appear, or refuse to give evidence, then it shall be lawful, on proof of service of such summons twenty-four hours before the time appointed for appearance, to commit the defaulters to prison, for any period not exceeding three months, nor less than one month, or until such persons submit to give evidence.

34. That any occupier or person employed in any such factory, who shall act contrary to any of the provisions of this act, for which offence penalties are not provided, shall, on conviction, pay at the discretion of the justice, any sum not exceeding £20, nor less than £5, which shall be doubled for the second, and trebled for the third offence, and the offenders be imprisoned for not more than twelve nor less than three calendar months.

35. That any occupier or person employed as aforesaid, who shall be convicted a second time, shall forfeit double the penalty of the first conviction, and for the third offence, treble the penalty, and also be imprisoned not more than twelve nor less than three months.

36. No female so offending shall be imprisoned, except for neglecting or refusing to pay any penalty under this act; but for every third and subsequent offence such female offender shall pay twice the amount of the penalty in lieu of the imprisonment.

37. That only one penalty for any offence against the same provision shall be recoverable in any one day, if the offender, after conviction, prove that the offence is and no longer will be committed. And also that the justices shall be empowered, when they see just cause, to deduct the costs before the penalties shall be divided; and that it shall not be necessary for the complainant to name in any summons or information the particular township in which the offence was committed, but it shall be sufficient to set forth the name of the parish.

38. That all informations may be heard before two or more justices not disqualified as aforesaid, and all penalties and costs shall be levied by distress of the offenders' goods, by warrant of two justices, rendering the overplus, if any, to the party offending; and in case such distress cannot be found, and the penalties and costs shall not be forthwith paid, the justices may commit the offender for any time not more than six months, nor less than one month.

39. That for the six months after the 1st of July, 1833, the duration of the daily labour of children and young persons, may be lengthened beyond the term of ten hours in any day, and eight hours on the Saturday, by one hour and a half, and for the next three months by one hour, and for the three months thence ensuing, by half an hour beyond the said term; and in case any oc

cupier shall, during the time between the passing of this act and its coming into operation, continue the labour of children beyond the time limited, and the additional periods allowed during the three successive periods of six months, three months, and three months, or in any other way offend against the provisions of this act, he shall be liable for every offence to the penalty imposed for the same, as if this act had already come into full operation.

40. That the expenses incurred by any complainant or witness, or other person employed in carrying any regulations of this act into execution, may be ordered to be paid by the offender convicted and allowed by the justice or justices.

41. That the words " mill " or " factory," used in this act, shall be deemed to comprehend all buildings and premises used in any manufactures comprehended in this act.

HENRY SMITH, PRINTER.

PROTEST

AGAINST THE

SECRET PROCEEDINGS

OF

THE FACTORY COMMISSION,

IN LEEDS.

PUBLISHED AT THE REQUEST OF THE SHORT TIME COMMITTEE.

BY MICHAEL THOMAS SADLER, F.R.S.

"THEY LOVE DARKNESS RATHER THAN LIGHT."

LEEDS:

PRINTED BY F. E. BINGLEY AND CO., TIMES OFFICE.

1833.

ADVERTISEMENT.

THE following letter is not meant to be, in any degree, an exposition of the Factory-System; but of the mode in which the Commission now sent among us, thinks fit to act, and, it is understood, has acted, throughout its Inquiry, so called. It is printed as it was sent, with some slight additions, and published at the request of the Ten Hours' Bill Committee. Whatever difference of opinion might have been entertained in some quarters as to the original appointment of the Commission, it is conceived there can be none respecting the nature of its proceedings. After all the anxiety, expense, and suffering, which the operatives have so long undergone in their efforts to rescue their offspring labouring in mills and factories from their degraded condition, to appoint at the instance of the *adverse party*, a Commission notoriously ignorant of the whole question, was no very gracious proceeding; but for that Commission to erect itself into a *secret tribunal*, from which the people and the press are wholly excluded; and (in communication with the opposing party) to subject the witnesses for the operatives to a rigorous cross-examination from the verbatim report of their evidence (delivered a year ago), and still to refuse a similar report of the evidence of the witnesses against them, who will, therefore, be protected from the possibility of a like scrutiny, is probably one of the grossest proceedings on record, at least in this country. It required no little ingenuity to invent such a course of proceeding, and not less resolution in acting upon it; but the Commission may rest satisfied that the public is not in a temper to be thus duped and insulted at the same moment. It may be assured that its whole proceedings, whatever part of them it may please to publish, and at whatever conclusions it may, in its wisdom, think fit to arrive, are perfectly useless — And God forbid they should be otherwise, it were far better that the whole expenses of the summer tour of the several parties it forms were utterly thrown away, than that a precedent of so dangerous and unconstitutional a character should be ever treated in England but with the feelings it deserves. The operatives of Great Britain would once more have braved all the discouragements and injuries they have hitherto suffered by such investigations, and have gone before any tribunal from which the press and the people of England should not have been excluded ; though they are well aware that such a course could even then have answered no purpose but that of stopping the mouths of their adversaries. As well might an aquatic excursion of a few Junior Lords, in the Admiralty barge, be dignified by the name of a Naval Inquiry, as the summer tour of these parties be regarded as affording the possibility of a full, fair, and satisfactory examination of this most important and deeply interesting Question.

TO

MESSRS. DRINKWATER, POWER & DR. LOUDEN,

COMMISSIONERS, &c.

GENTLEMEN,

I have just been told that you have expected an answer from me to a paper which you sent to myself and several others, entitled " *Memorandum of the proposed method of taking down the evidence in Leeds, under the Factory Commission.*" I thought I had expressed myself so decidedly averse from the proposals which that document contains, and also that the two friends with whom I came to your meeting, Messrs. Hall and Osburn, had so fully explained to you that evening, the determination of the committee of operatives upon the subject, that any further communication with me was neither expected nor desired. I have not however the slightest objection to re-state, in a more formal manner, the propositions with which we were entrusted, being fully persuaded that they will be sanctioned by the public as just and necessary; though, according to the private and settled regulations of the Factory Commission, as referred to by you, they were rejected as totally inadmissible.

Much then, and justly as the operatives object to the Commission on many important grounds, yet fearing nothing but injustice and secrecy, they instructed us, before they became voluntary parties to the inquiry, to demand on their behalf; first,

THAT THE PROCEEDINGS SHOULD BE OPEN AND PUBLIC.

I had thought that few arguments would have been necessary to have recommended this course, especially on the present occasion. If ever there was an investigation where on every account the utmost degree of publicity ought to have been courted, and secrecy carefully avoided, it is the present one. The interests, feelings, and veracity of the numerous body seeking redress, demanded at least this guarantee; and still more I think the character of the

Commission itself, labouring under a suspicion from which nothing else would have been so likely to have purged it, at least if its proceedings were calculated to bear the light. To the character of even our most ancient and venerated institutions, our courts of justice, publicity is essential. It is not held sufficient that the judges should be totally unconnected with the cause or parties at issue : that the jury should be indiscriminately chosen and subject to the challenge : that the proceedings should be conducted according to established rules, they must likewise be OPEN, or the whole would become a solemn mockery of justice, and be deemed an insult upon the people ; how much more then, in the present case, ought the public to be admitted, where *you* are at once the judges and the jurors ; actually nominated at the instance of, and by, the adverse party ; and not liable to be challenged by those whose cause you have to determine ; that public which always stands the vigilant guard of the weaker and oppressed party. Gentlemen, I was astonished at your decision to the contrary, but I found you so decidedly averse to the open course, that it was useless long to press it. I have since heard that it has positively been denied that the proposition was even made. I assert that it was made and rejected, as my two friends will witness. Any dispute or difference upon this point shews, therefore, in limine, the necessity of the second proposition : namely

THAT THE EVIDENCE SHOULD BE TAKEN DOWN IN FULL BY A SHORT HAND WRITER, APPOINTED BY MUTUAL CONSENT, AND SWORN BEFORE YOU.

This proposal you peremptorily rejected ; even refusing to take it into your further consideration. You declared that the Commissioners had as a body determined that the evidence should not be so recorded. You claim, therefore, to deal with the evidence (which is public property) as well as to dictate the proceedings just as you please, and, as it appears to me, in a manner as inconsistent with the ends of justice, as with the established usages of the British constitution ; and yet I find that the Secretary of the central committee in London, Mr. James Wilson, has ventured to utter a tirade against the representatives of the Lancashire committees, now in town, as though in objecting to appear before this secret tribunal, the operatives feared to present themselves before one impartially chosen, and whose

proceedings should be public. Though their case, it might
have been hoped, demanded no evidence, but the prompt and
indignant feelings of every human heart, still they have
constantly, and often to their permanent detriment, gone with the
utmost readiness before committees of both houses of Parliament, and, when before the Lords' committees, delivered themselves, of course, upon oath. But let me remark that the committees of the highest court in the empire, the House of Lords,
(whose personal respectability, about which so much was said the
other day, is, I should conceive, as high as that of the Commissioners) absolutely provide for that which you positively refuse ;
namely, the introduction of a short hand writer, for the purpose
of publishing every iota of the evidence given before them. As to
commissions of this nature, I ventured to remark that the constitution of England regards them with no peculiar degree of
favour, not extending to them the power of courts which can compel the attendance of witnesses, which I only mention to remind
you of your answer to me—that you were assured (I presume by
the ministry) that parliament would pass a short bill, compelling
the attendance of witnesses, were it necessary. But I venture to
ask you, whether you think that any parliament of this country
would pass 'a short bill,' compelling the attendance of the hum-
blest subject in the empire to give evidence before you, without
affording him the privilege, or as I should call it, the right, of
being heard in public, and the indispensable security that all he
should utter upon oath might be fully and faithfully recorded.
You stated, indeed, the practice of the judges in taking down
notes would be your model, but I confess that I have heard of no
judges who follow the course which you prescribe, but those,
perhaps, of the Inquisition. The notes taken of judicial evidence
are often short, because they are principally for the purpose of
assisting the memory of the judge, or for occasional reference
afterwards ; but, different to your's, their correctness is guaran-
teed by both the press and the public. But the reports of your
proceedings should have been made in full, as their object
ought to have been the satisfaction of parliament and the people
at large And it was quite essential that the interrogatories
should have been also given verbatim, so as to have shewn the
nature and animus of the whole inquiry.

But I perceive that the notes which you propose to take, were to be open to the inspection of one or two gentlemen on behalf of the operatives, and as many factory owners, whom you would allow to be present during a *certain part* of your proceedings. This one (or two) gentlemen might take his or their own notes, " for the purpose of assisting him or them in sifting the evidence, " or suggesting further topics of inquiry: with the understanding, " however, that till the Commission is concluded, no other further " publication of such notes shall be made than those purposes " require:"—as if any one would think for a moment of publishing such notes, necessarily meagre, and utterly valueless, as being wholly private and unauthorised,—at any period or for any purpose. I beg to refer to any one who has had the conduct of, or actively assisted in, any public inquiry, whether his whole time and his utmost attention have not been required in order to the full discharge of his duty, without undertaking the somewhat arduous additional one of a short hand writer, with a view to a full publication of the proceedings.

I would also remark, that your method, independently of other considerations, is most objectionable as being different to that of the select committee of the House of Commons. The minuteness with which the evidence of the operatives was taken down and published, has exposed them to the most rigorous scrutinies ; and doubtless abundance of trifling discrepancies will be eagerly sought for in the voluminous report now before the public, though I have not hitherto heard of a single misrepresentation of the slighest importance having been brought home to any of the witnesses : the operatives of England are no liars. But this inquiry, instituted by the opposing party, and conducted upon such different principles, is most unfair in this particular, that by refusing to allow the opportunity of publishing a report equally minute and accurate, you absolutely protect the evidence of the mill owners from the very ordeal to which you are at this moment rigorously subjecting that of the poor operatives.

Waiving for the present any further remarks upon this topic, there is one which I wish to make on the terminating proposition in your memorandum, and which I cannot but regard as the climax of the regulations of this pro-factory inquiry After having refused to admit the public in any case whatever during the whole investigation, and rejected the only means of publishing any full and authentic record of the whole proceedings, you go on to state, that even the privilege you proferred of one or two of the friends of the Ten Hour Bill being present and permitted to take such notes as you describe, and limited to the purposes you explain, shall only be extended to certain parts of the inquiry, intimating that there are others which you have hitherto found effectual, or may consider to be desirable; these, therefore, you propose to conduct in perfect privacy, allowing, however, certain of us to see what you may have thought proper to put down as the result of this kind of investigation ! It must be at once obvious that a reservation of this large and indefinite character renders your preceding propositions (guarded and scanty as are the advantages they offer to the operatives) almost wholly nugatory, and makes it ten-fold more imperative upon their friends to demand on their behalf, that ALL proceedings had on this most momentous subject should be OPEN, RECORDED and PUBLISHED.

I will here just remark, though perhaps somewhat out of place, upon an argument of yours (and the only one I heard advanced) against admitting an official reporter, which I think yourselves, when you reconsider it, will hardly deny is one of the strongest possible reasons in favour of such a course. You objected to a short-hand writer though impartially chosen, or appointed by yourselves, and duly sworn; because his report might possibly differ from your notes. Now this possibility I admit, but I think that it amounts to a reason why such a person should be appointed to report, and that you should not have that duty also imposed upon you, or in other words that your proceedings should be assimilated to those of committees of Inquiry of both Houses of Parliament, whose regulations are usually held as good precedents for the conduct of all inferior ones of a similar nature throughout the empire.

But I confess that you argued little, but dealt copiously in persuasives grounded upon your avowed candour and personal respectability in order to induce us to accede to your scheme of proceeding. The claim which you made of confidence I confess I cannot answer with sincerity. Your individual respectability I readily admit, but private respectability and public confidence are held to be very distinct things in this, and, I believe, in most other countries. And you claim our confidence under circumstances which are totally inconsistent with such a feeling. Our confidence in the Judges of the land, and of the Juries who assist in the administration of Justice, is all but unbounded, but it would be instantly withdrawn, nor could it be restored, were they determined to conduct their proceedings as you do, in secret, and utterly refuse the means by which they could be fully made known to the public.

Allow me to add that there are other circumstances connected with the Commission of which you form a part, which render, in my judgment, publicity in all its proceedings more than ordinarily necessary; such as the following—The Commission was issued in virtue of almost the very smallest majority that ever, perhaps, carried any important question, and one which would have been a minority but for what I deem a very unfortunate accident.—That majority was made up in no inconsiderable degree by individuals personally interested in the question, who, I think, ought not in any such circumstances to have voted at all, and who are excluded from so doing in many Committees of the House—And that majority, small as it was, and constituted as I have said, was obtained, if the speech of the mover had any effect, on the strength of some of the grossest misrepresentations ever uttered within the privileged walls of Parliament, as one of the gentlemen who accompanied me to your meeting, and whose authority I am sure you will respect, is ready to make oath; as others have already done in respect of some of the most flagrant of his charges.—You appear to be quite ignorant of the subject of the inquiry, which to its due examination demands habits, talents, and experience far different from those requisite for mere legal investigations : and you come at a time of the year when the Factories, which you propose to examine, are usually in the best state ; and after full notice of your approach, and abundance of time given to prepare for your reception. It is the winter season in which the condition of the children is the most distressing ; roused hours before day light, and whatever be the weather, hail, rain or snow, they proceed to their daily toil, continued in many cases (till lately) with only one short intermission and sometimes with none, sweating in a heated, or inhaling a fibrous and dusty atmosphere, in certain processes almost seethed in hot water, and drenched in steam and spray; and hours after "the beast has laid down in his lair," still toiling by the glare and stench of gas, till exhausted nature has to be roused by the thong or the billy roller, when the loud and frequent shriek of infancy is heard above the roar of revolving wheels; till after such a day's labour as this (if such protracted hours are to be called a day!) the little victims of oppression, if they be not " night workers," are dismissed, when they plunge into the cold air, hurry shivering home and to their bed, from which they have again to be roused at an untimely hour to pursue the same unhappy course, which sends multitudes of them to their long home, and to their final rest, in the very blossom of their life. I say, gentlemen, *that* were the season—and before the present measure of relief was agitated—was the time when your personal visit might have been of some use, but under the present circumstances IT IS DELUSIVE. You would then probably have arrived more easily at the conclusion, that Ten Hours' labour a day are sufficient, which, let me remind you, are in effect TWELVE HOURS, except the poor child is, like the boat-horse, to work and eat at the same time, as they have been too often compelled to do—and that these Twelve hours must become at least thirteen, except they could be at once miraculously transported from their beds to the Mill. Gentlemen, remember that the *Ten Hours' Bill* is in effect a *Thirteen Hours' Bill.* I have received a letter from a poor boy this very evening on this subject, in which he says, (but under the strictest injunctions of secrecy,) " if Lord M——; (meaning his master) were made to work one day in my room, he would think Ten Hours quite enough!" I dwell upon this subject because I fear I comprehend too well the ultimate object of this Commission, and could have divined its results even before it had commenced its operations. But at whatever time you had come, you could not in the period to which your tour is, I understand, to be limited, have made yourselves at all acquainted with the subject. Your central secretary, I think, dwells upon the advantage of your inquiry being pursued upon the spot,—but I will venture to assert that your observations, however conducted, can produce nothing at all equal in correctness, copiousness or value, to those

made also upon " the spot" by men whose talents for such investigations are not likely to be soon surpassed, whose disinter-
estedness was most conspicuous; who practised in the very focus
of the factory system, with which they were personally and pro-
fessionally conversant, for a greater number of years than, probably, (I mean no offence by adverting to the fact) the oldest of
you gentlemen have lived; and who directed the energies of
their capacious and benevolent minds to this important subject.
I mean such men as Drs. Percival, Aikin, Ferrier, Symmonds,
and many, many others. After their deliberate and recorded judgment upon this subject, the repeated inquiries which have been
instituted regarding it, especially the present, have been a shame-
ful waste of the public money and a wicked insult upon public
feeling. They have been instituted however for one and the
same object, and alas! they have invariably succeeded. " Forty
years long" has the inquiry been continued; thirty and upwards
has it from time to time, and sometimes for years together, been
under the consideration of Committees, and you are now here on
the same subject. To make it a question whether the children
of the poor, should be laboured more than twelve hours a day,
including meals, excites in my mind inexpressible disgust, and is
enough to make every parent worthy of the name shudder. The
difficulty I should conceive is how to reconcile that term with
the health and life of numbers of the rising generation, to say
nothing of their recreation or mental and moral improvement.
The Commission, had they intended to take the best evidence
on the subject, or at least known how to have done it, needed
not to have travelled far, or separated. The mortuary registers
of England are now collected, these they might have consulted
and they would then have seen whether they did not respond to
the unanimous opinion of the ablest medical men of this or any
country, as to the cruel, destructive, and mortal effects of the present system. As however you are here, I venture to hint that the
Sexton of Holbeck, for instance, is a properer person to consult,
as to the state of health or the mean duration of human existence, for the last five years in that spinning place, than the
newly appointed surgeon or physician of any Factory. In such
records is it that the victims of this system " being dead yet
speak," and with a voice that fills every feeling mind with the
deepest emotion and enters into the ears of God himself. One

more objection might be fairly urged against your proceeding. In examining witnesses upon the spot, it is hardly likely that the operatives under the immediate eye and controul of their employers should venture to speak out, much less dare to contradict the evidence of their masters. Indeed you expressed yourselves as being well aware of this great difficulty, and of the risk to which the operatives would be subjected of losing their employment and their bread, as many of them had done, by appearing and speaking the whole truth. But you confessed that you were not prepared with any offer of indemnity for those who might thus be undone. Notwithstanding, therefore, the observation of the central secretary, I think that this is *not* the preferable course, at least if truth be the sole object of the inquiry ; on the contrary, I would ask whether any method could be much better calculated to overawe and intimidate the witnesses for the measure, or tend more certainly and completely to defeat the ends of truth and justice. Since you have appeared I have continued to receive abundance of communications from both parents and children upon the subject, and many of them most important, but they have mostly been given under the seal of the strictest secrecy, and are consequently useless.

But I will dwell no longer upon my objections to your proceedings. I need not remind you that your whole plan met with the entire and indeed enthusiastic approbation of the Mill Owners. You heard from them expressions of the most unbounded confidence, and the warmest compliments to yourselves. But on the contrary, you saw how myself and friends were treated, and will probably recollect the terms in which the whole body of Evidence of the Select Committee, and the character of the witnesses were assailed. They quite concurred, with I think one exception, in your plan of excluding both the public and any short-hand writer, or other reporter from the whole of your proceedings.

It is only justice to you to acknowledge that your propositions were as unanimously hailed on the one side as they were rejected by the other. But it is interesting to remark that the side by whom they were rejected was that of the poor and the oppressed ; and still more so, that their ground of objection was not that they asked for PRIVACY, but that they demanded PUBLICITY.

They only asked that which has seldom been denied in this country, at least in a just cause, *a fair stage and no favor*. Objecting as we did to many of your proceedings and regulations, we contented ourselves with simply demanding that the public should be a party to these proceedings in a cause in which the public has taken so generous an interest—and admitted personally, or at least through the medium of the press, to this inquiry.

Without this guarantee I told you that I should take no voluntary part in the proceedings, though well aware of the disadvantages to which I may be subject in consequence of this resolution. But I have used no influence to keep those witnesses from appearing before you, whom you have summoned and who have referred to me on the occasion. They are aware of the unfairness of the course you are pursuing, but I have only urged upon them to speak the truth, and (notwithstanding the disadvantageous circumstances under which they are, this second time, as witnesses, placed,) the whole truth.

I do not know whether you are sufficiently acquainted with the history of the subject to be aware that, from the first, whatever has been the degree of limitation proposed to Parliament in favour of the factory children, whether twelve, or eleven and a half, or eleven hours, it has constantly met with a continued and vehement opposition on the part of the master manufacturers, as a body. Now, however, the question has happily made so large a progress in the public mind, that what it was a little while ago thought ' madness' to propose, it would be now deemed ' madness' altogether to resist. Hence we are assured that the opponents of the measure would agree to an eleven hour bill, provided always that its clauses were made palatable. And you are probably aware that the same party who were a short time ago addressing themselves, as they hoped, to the selfishness of parents, stating that the wages of the poor children would, by a natural and irreversible rule, be always exactly correspondent to the length of their labour (and therefore, that just as this was abridged those must be lowered), is now promising, that if they will consent to an eleven hours' bill, they shall nevertheless still receive twelve hours' wages. In what sort of attitude, then, does this proposition exhibit the past conduct of such to their poor and helpless dependents ? Will it not be naturally asked,

whether they have not been taking one hour a day more from
these children than they have paid for ? I hope not ; otherwise
the secret of the immense and rapidly accumulated fortunes
made in many instances would indeed be most disgracefully sol-
ved. But what becomes of the arithmetic of these professed political economists ? If one hour's diminution of work is to occasion no diminution in wages, what will two hours' diminution
occasion ? — One sixth diminution, they answer ! But this
reasoning is too absurd to notice, and I only mention it to introduce my final appeal to you.

The operatives fear that this parade of inquiry, which, as you
explained it, is to extend to all ages, and to so many branches
of industry, is only to usher in an eleven hours' bill. But God
forbid that you should be accessary to this intention ! Insigni-
ficant and short as seems the difference of an hour a day to the
idle or the wealthy, this hour is of incalculable importance to
the child,—" he is poor, and setteth his heart upon it !" On
this remission will depend the life itself, in many cases, the
health and strength in more, of the exhausted little labourer,
who could work within a certain limit with, perhaps, comparative impunity, but beyond that would, like the labouring brute,
sink and fail at once. That utmost limit is already defined by
the unanimous voice of the heads of the medical profession.
But even could it be transgressed without the most deplorable
effects, which, however, we utterly deny,—still beware how
you deprive the childhood of poverty of the privileges of nature.
This hour is to become the daily term of domestic enjoyment,
of parental endearment and affection—the hour of innocent sport
and relaxation—the hour of moral and mental improvement—
the hour, I trust, of devotion and of rest. And after all, how
few, though precious, will be the minutes wrested from the grasp
of avarice and oppression ! still the term of infantile and youthful toil will stretch to Twelve long hours, including meals ;
abundantly sufficient (as you perhaps think in your present en-
gagement) for human exertion for a continuance, at any age, or
in any employment.

In conclusion allow me to say that however much I may have
been insulted or opposed for the part I have taken, I have never
in all I have spoken or written upon this exciting topic, any more
than at the present moment, dealt in indiscriminate censures.

Among the Mill-Owners of this country are many most estimable and benevolent men ; numbers of these are with us, and many others who act contrary to us on this occasion, do so I am persuaded more under the influence of an *esprit-de-corps*, than from any personal or improper motives. My own conduct has been dictated by no hostility, open or disguised, to the manufacturing interests of the country, but from an earnest wish to reconcile them to the feelings and principles of humanity. Nay I am fully persuaded that the Bill I have had the honor to propose, and which I have to the best of my power supported, through evil report and good report, would, if carried into effect, confer an invaluable boon upon humane and honourable employers, as well as become a blessing to those whom they employ, and to the nation at large. God forbid that we should for one moment entertain the absurd and disgraceful idea that our boasted manufacturing and commercial advantages rest upon the abhorrent foundation of infantile cruelty and oppression. On examining this subject with the most careful attention, I have satisfied myself to the contrary, and am fully persuaded, that in this, as well as in all other instances, to do justly and love mercy is the surest ground of national as well as individual prosperity.

Though I have extended this address to you to so great a length ; when I sat down to write, it was merely my intention shortly to state to you the reasons why I could not act with you on behalf of the operatives, which, in conclusion I beg to repeat,— namely, because YOU REFUSED TO CONDUCT THE PROCEEDINGS OPENLY, OR ALLOW THEM TO BE RECORDED FULLY ; and I have only to add, that if I had determined otherwise, I should have forfeited their confidence, with the consciousness of having deserved it.

Personally, permit me to express for you feelings of much respect and consideration.

I have the honor to be,

Gentlemen,

Your most humble Servant,

MICHAEL THOMAS SADLER.

Leeds, *May* 20th, 1833.

F. E. BINGLEY AND CO., PRINTERS, TIMES OFFICE, LEEDS.

REPLIES

TO

MR. M. T. SADLER'S

PROTEST

AGAINST

THE FACTORY COMMISSION.

BY

JOHN ELLIOT DRINKWATER, Esq.,

AND

ALFRED POWER, Esq.

LEEDS:

PRINTED FOR BAINES AND NEWSOME.

1833.

REPLIES,
&c.

Scarborough's Hotel, Leeds, 25th May, 1833.

SIR,

IF you had not thought proper to publish your address to my colleagues and myself, I should not have considered any reply necessary on our part, either collectively or individually; but I feel compelled now, however reluctant, to deprive you of any pretext for advancing that the statements of that address have remained uncontradicted.

It is foreign to my temper lightly to charge any one with intentional misrepresentation; and in this case, I am spared that pain, by observing that you appear to act and write under the influence of a highly excited imagination, which disqualifies you at present from rightly estimating either our conduct or your own.

The two principal points of your letter, of which I deny the accuracy, are—

1st. That you represented yourself, at our interview, as a delegate on behalf of the working classes, or appeared there in any other character than that alone in which we invited you to be present, as an individual who had taken a prominent part in the previous inquiry.

2d. That either on your own behalf, or as the representative of any person or party, you stipulated as the price of your assistance, that our proceedings should be *open* and *public* in a greater degree than we proposed to make them so

In order to avoid farther mistake, it is right to add, that if you had made such a stipulation, we should not have acceded to it; and we should have said so in our written proposition, in the same distinct manner in which we negatived the only proposal you did make, the presence of a short-hand writer. You must remember that the words "*and cannot be acceded to*" were added by me to the expression of our opinion on that point, at your own suggestion "to show (as you said) that the proposition had been made the subject of discussion."

For the present, I wish merely to place on record my individual view of the statements of your letter; I beg leave to decline entering in detail into the discussion of it, unless you shall call upon me to do so, when my time is again my own; the business of the Commission affords us sufficient employment, without allowing our attention to be diverted towards controversies only remotely affecting the subject of our inquiries.

You are pleased to convey to us the assurance of your personal respect and consideration; but I confess that I am at a loss to reconcile that declaration with the opinions you profess on the nature and object of the Commission we have accepted. I frankly own that if I could believe you capable of undertaking any office with the sinister motives you have not scrupled to attribute to us, I could neither esteem you as a statesman, nor respect you as a gentleman.

I have the honour to be,

Sir,

Your obedient Servant,

JOHN ELLIOT DRINKWATER.

Michael Thomas Sadler, Esq., &c. &c. &c.

Scarborough's Hotel, Leeds, 25th May, 1833.

SIR,

YOUR letter to us of the 20th instant, had it remained unpublished, would, I believe, have received no answer or notice of any kind from my colleagues or myself, our time being too much occupied at present, to notice individual opinions and conclusions respecting ourselves and our proceedings, if expressed within those exact limits, that just verge of courtesy, which I must allow that you have preserved on this occasion. The publication, however, of that letter demands, from the respect I owe to myself, some inquiry into the grounds both of the statements and conclusions, contained in it; and as these have for the most part a personal application, it has appeared necessary that any reply to that letter should proceed upon mere personal grounds.

Before proceeding to question the propriety of your convictions ,respecting ourselves and our proceedings, allow me to bring in review before you, very briefly, your own conduct and your present position, with reference to the question of Factory Regulation, and the inquiries which have been made, and are now making, into this subject; so as to press upon your consciousness, as distinctly as may be done without offence, a very reasonable distrust of your own judgment and the temper of mind in which you have hazarded certain observations.

In the course of a long and zealous advocacy of a measure now identified with the Bill, called Lord Ashley's Bill, you, it is well known, opposed yourself in the first instance, to the institution of any public inquiry into the questions involved. It is not for me to say whether you were properly or improperly driven from that position; it is enough that the principle of public inquiry was ultimately conceded. The result of an inquiry, conducted under your auspices, as Chairman of a Select Committee of the House of Commons, is well known. The minutes of the evidence then taken having been laid before the House of Commons, that body refused to legislate upon the evidence so taken ; and a Commission has been appointed for the purpose of obtaining farther information. No doubt, Sir, you, to whom that evidence might appear satisfactory and sufficient, you, who were anxious to legislate in the first instance without any public inquiry whatever, must be at a loss to conjecture the grounds upon which the House of Commons came to that determination ; but the question between us here is, whether, making every allowance for that uncertainty of mind in you, your conduct since the appointment of this Commission is justified by the feelings which may be supposed to have promoted it.

A part of the Commission appointed by Government to pursue the inquiry arrives at Leeds, where you are residing; they receive a deputation from the operatives of the Short Time Committee ; the Commissioners state to them their intended method of proceeding, as afterwards propounded to yourself ; the operatives are disposed to consider it satisfactory to themselves ; they abandon their preconceived prejudices against the Commission; they deliberate upon the question of giving the Commission their assistance and co-operation, and come to a unanimous decision in the affirmative.

This took place on the Tuesday night, the evening after our arrival in Leeds. On the Wednesday morning, Sir, when you attended us as a private individual at our request, not one word transpired of your being *entrusted*, as you now represent, with *two* propositions. By whom entrusted does not even now appear; but being so entrusted, allow me to say that your diplomacy on that occasion was not very creditable to you : for, distinctly as your first proposition, " that the proceedings should be open and public," now appears upon paper,

I believe that no person in the room, with the exception of yourself, was aware that it was for one moment in contemplation. The only point which I understood you then to make, as the condition of your lending facility on your own part to our inquiries, was the presence of a short-hand writer; and that you certainly contended for with considerable zeal. You say, properly, that we rejected that proposal, and even refused to deliberate upon it; but you omit to mention that you yourself distinctly disclaimed, in the first place, the design of the publication of such notes during the progress of the inquiry; and, in the second place, any distrust of the accuracy of those notes, which we stated, as a matter of necessity already determined on in London, we must take ourselves for the convenience of the inquiry. I do not remember, Sir, that you suggested, in this deficiency, any other ground of argument for the presence of a short-hand writer.

Our propositions were, at your request, put into writing, and forwarded to you on the understanding, that you would consider them, and acquaint us with your determination in the evening. Remember, Sir, you were acting in our eyes (and you knew that) as a private individual. We received no communication from you, until, after the expiration of a week, you sent us the letter now published. The interval, however, was not an idle one, as we are well informed. You met the Short Time Committee the day you left us; you denounced our proposed method of proceeding as involving secresy and mystery; and by your influence with the operatives, aided by that of Mr. Oastler, you induced them to depart from the determination they had previously formed of assisting us in our investigations.

You are better aware, perhaps, even than ourselves, how much this course was disapproved by many of your most zealous and respectable partizans; and let me ask

you, Sir,—can you or do you for one moment doubt
the sincerity of those gentlemen of your party in Leeds,
or their attachment to that cause which you also are
believed to have at heart, who all, without exception,
have determined to act separately from you; preferring
disunion among the friends of the Ten Hours Bill, to
co-operation with you in the course you have chosen
to adopt ? You also know that some of the most sensible and well-disposed of the operatives themselves
have renounced your guidance as the leader of their
party, and consider your present conduct as injurious
to their cause; and that, notwithstanding the excitement
by which it has been attempted to encumber the proceedings of the Commissioners here, they are prosecuting
their labours steadily, and with effect, and receiving
every assistance from all quarters, and from all parties,
excepting that immediately connected with yourself.

Under these circumstances, Sir, I can understand and
make allowance for those feelings which dictated the
tone of your recent letter; the whole burthen of which,
as applicable to us and our conduct, lies in your affecting to distrust our minutes of the evidence which we
are now collecting. This has formed the only tangible
ground of your opposition to our inquiries from the
first : it has been the topic of your harangues to the
operatives about us; and it was worse than idle in you
to disclaim it on your interview with us at Scarborough's
Hotel. Now, Sir, on what ground you insinuate the
probability of unfairness in me, I claim individually
to know. On what ground or by what right do you
describe me as " nominated by an adverse party ?"
Adverse to whom ? and to what? Am I, in the discharge of a public office of which the essence is impartiality, and the whole scope investigation, to be
denounced as the nominee of a party, merely because
you do not relish the appointment of the Commission ?

or are you in possession of any other ground for such a statement ? If so, you would do better to bring it forward, than make empty allegations of this nature. The imputation of accepting such a trust to serve a particular party should not be lightly made.

I cannot follow you through a dissertation, which should have formed the staple of a speech within the walls of Parliament against the appointment of this Commission. The youth and inexperience you are pleased to impute to us, and the many difficulties arising from the season of the year, the short period of our labours, and the arts and influence of the master manufacturers, are just so many reasons why you should have afforded, rather than have withheld from us your assistance in our struggles after truth. But when you speak of the proceedings of the Commissioners as " not only inconsistent with the ends of justice, but with the established usages of the British constitution," allow me to say that either your ideas on that subject are very confused, or they belong altogether to a previous and foregone question, namely, the appointment of this Commission. You do not appear to know that a Commission, constituted like the present, has no authority to hold an open Court, and is not expected to open its proceedings to the public ; were that so, it would, of course, be intrusted with the powers of necessity incidental to every open Court. But this, Sir, you know very well, that had we understood you to make the proposition which you state yourself to have made, and had we in compliance with it (as we certainly should not) opened our proceedings to the public in Leeds, you know, Sir, that that course must inevitably have had the effect of defeating all inquiry here. To bring this difficulty home to you by an illustration,—What power, let me put it to yourself, less than that of committal to the House of Correction, during pleasure, could have protected our open Court against the demeanour of your chief partizans, Mr. Cavie Richardson and Mr. Richard Oastler ?

That we proposed to open our proceedings at all was, we acknowledge, as much from considerations of personal convenience to ourselves, as of mutual satisfaction to the parties prominently interested ; yet much as we should have coveted the presence of some of the more calm and dispassionate advocates of the Ten Hours Bill, we cannot on the whole, and from recent experience, regret the absence of others less candid and less discreet, or believe that our inquiries will be less usefully conducted on that account.

You do not in any part, Sir, of your long letter, point out the expediency or necessity of the presence of a shorthand writer, otherwise than by the covert suggestion of grounds which in our presence you most distinctly disclaimed.

To pass from the body of your letter to the short summary at the conclusion, of the reasons why you " could not act with us on behalf of the operatives," I beg leave to state as shortly, that the two reasons recounted do not appear to me to touch your conclusion at all.

As to the first, we have *not* refused to conduct the proceedings openly—as openly as every mind, except your own (if indeed that forms such an exception) deems practicable.

As regards the second,—it does not appear, and never has, that the evidence so taken, as was proposed by us, would not have been recorded *fully*.

I have the honour to be,
Sir,
Your obedient humble servant,
ALFRED POWER.

M. T. Sadler, Esq.

APPENDIX.

MEMORANDUM

Of the proposed method of taking the evidence in Leeds, under the Factory Commission, as submitted to the Gentlemen who met the Commissioners at Scarborough's Hotel, on Wednesday, 15th May, 1833 :—

" The witnesses shall be examined by the Commissioners in the presence of one or two gentlemen on the part both of the promoters and opposers of the Ten Hours Bill, and the notes of evidence taken down by the Commissioners shall be at all times open to the inspection of those gentlemen.

" It will be of course at the option of any gentleman present to take his own notes of the proceedings, for the purpose of assisting him in sifting the evidence ; or suggesting further topics of inquiry ; with the understanding that until the business of the Commission is concluded, no other or further publication of these notes be made than these purposes require.

" If desired, the notes of each witness's evidence shall be read over to him.

" The presence of a short-hand writer does not appear to the Commissioners desirable, and cannot be acceded to.

" This plan applies solely to those examinations in which the Commissioners receive direct assistance from either

party ; as the Commissioners do not wish to be precluded
from continuing any mode of conducting other inquiries
than those above specified, which they have found
hitherto effectual, or may consider desirable ; but they
pledge themselves to communicate the information which
they so collect in the same manner as that which is taken
down in the more formal manner above detailed."

EDWARD BAINES AND SON, PRINTERS, LEEDS.

ADDRESS

TO THE

FRIENDS OF JUSTICE AND HUMANITY,

IN THE WEST RIDING OF YORK,

FROM THE

MEETING OF DELEGATES

OF THE

SHORT TIME COMMITTEES,

ESTABLISHED TO PROMOTE THE LEGISLATIVE ADOPTION
OF THE TEN HOUR FACTORY BILL,

Assembled at the Yew Tree Inn, Birstall,

OCTOBER 28TH, 1833.

Friends and Countrymen,

We feel it to be our duty once more to claim your attention to the important question of Factory Regulation by Law.

This question we need not say has never been made by its advocates a *party* question. We have always founded it upon the plainest precepts of Christianity, and have called upon all who loved the Bible, who respected the Labouring Classes, and who pitied oppressed Infancy and Youth, to come to our aid.

Every attempt of its enemies to invest it with a *party* character has failed; and we can now as always hitherto, confidently appeal to our fellow countrymen for the consistency of our conduct, and to our God for the uprightness of our motives. Since this question was closely pressed upon public attention, an important and equally lamentable step has been adopted by the legislature, which has been followed by the silence of grief and disgust, and which our enemies have mistaken for *despair*.

It would be manifestly unjustifiable in us, and in those numerous bodies of Operatives for whom we act to remain silent any longer. Assisted by your zealous and self-denying exertions, the Short Time Committees have been enabled to support the Parliamentary Advocates of the Ten Hours Factory Bill, with a measure and degree of popular suffrage and feeling, seldom equalled and never exceeded in this country. For this we ought at least to express our sincere gratitude, and we are sure that you will not fail to render the same kind sympathy and assistance, as long as we can shew sufficient causes to call them forth.

It is known to you all, that by the influence of the Factory Masters, who opposed us, and that of their friends in the House of Commons, in the late session, the Ten Hour Bill was thrown out, and Lord Althorpe procured an Act to be passed in its stead.

By some it may be supposed that the question is now settled, and that the supporters of the Ten Hour Bill ought now to be content, or ought at least to give the Act of Lord Althorpe "*a fair trial*," before they proceed again to agitate the public mind on the question. But we feel assured, that upon a more accurate and complete view of the case, every sincere friend of the Factory Workers, will discover greater cause than ever for strenuous exertions, by which the victims of an heartless system may be delivered from thraldom, ignorance, and destruction, *now legalized* in a Christian land.

The questions before us are these:—

WAS OUR CLAIM FOR THE TEN HOUR BILL FOUNDED IN JUSTICE, AND HAS LORD ALTHORPE'S ACT SATISFIED THAT DEMAND?

To the first of these questions we boldly answer " Yes," and to the second we as firmly reply " No," and we are quite sure we can justify such answers by facts and by truth.

WAS OUR CLAIM FOR THE TEN HOUR BILL FOUNDED IN JUSTICE?

It had been proved that children of very tender years had been subjected to Factory Labour, and we demanded that none under nine years should be allowed to work at all in those establishments—this demand has been granted, except in the case of lace and silk mills. But when we have acknowledged thus much, we have declared all that is of any material value in Lord Althorpe's Act. What remains of it is for the most part either deceptions or unjust we shall hereafter engage to prove.

To return to the Ten Hour Bill—It had been *proved*, that

the greatest irregularity existed in the hours of factory labour —that the ordinary hours in the greater number of factories were about 12, but that in cases of *brisk* trade and *urgent* orders from merchants, which certain rich mill-owners had an interest in monopolizing, those hours were extended to an almost incredible degree, that 14, 16, and even 18 hours labour out of the 24, had been exacted to suit the profit and convenience of the masters. Nay, cases are upon record and established by the Factory Commissioners themselves, where Factory Labour has been performed by the same set of Children, as well as Adults, without cessation except for meals for *Forty-five Hours!!* And who shall declare the beatings, the kickings, the hangings, (Note 1,) the suicides, (Note 2,) of the Factory Children—and the mangled limbs, and the lifeless corpses, and the wasted forms of the Factory Youth. But of these we cannot now treat—the Day of Judgment will declare it all. And as a necessary consequence of this irregularity and monopoly, it had been further shewn, that seasons often of considerable duration occurred, when the greater number of mills worked but half days, and many stood entirely still. And in connexion with this view of the irregularity occasioned by monopoly and avarice in consequence of which the Factory Labourers were liable to be *worked to death* one while, and *pined to death* another, it was clearly ascertained, that the time actually required and (taking the average of mills in seven years) the time actually *employed* to supply the *marketable demand*, did not exceed Ten Hours a day.

Thus far then, even good *policy*, and the just interests of *honest* men engaged in the Factory System, fully justified our demand—it being sufficiently obvious, that the Great Capitalists investing their property in this System, were prone like the voracious Shark, to devour their smaller but equally industrious and more honest neighbours.

It was also plainly shewn that the time of human occupation among the generality of the productive and laborious Classes did not often reach Ten Hours a day, and that the System of our boasted mechanical improvement, which ought to have left man a good surplus of Time for rational and religious enjoyments, was calculated to engross almost every moment of his existence, which was not demanded for sleep, and to make him into a mere machine—less esteemed than the iron and wood upon which he was requested to attend.

These evils appeared to be immensely aggravated when it was considered the young, and more particularly the female sex constitute the the great majority of the Factory Workers. Thus we beheld the morning of life turned into "a day of darkness and of gloominess"—that which should have been the *spring time* of existence, converted by frigid Avarice into its winter—the season designed by Nature, and by Nature's God for instruction overclouded with ignorance, and the little ones denied the healthful gambols of infancy. Here too we saw the seeds of *social* dissolution—Children and youth estranged from parental influence all the day, and (awful to contemplate) a race of parents springing up, who by early habit, have ceased to regard such a separation *as an evil*, and who, hardened by the cruelties and hardships *they* have endured, can without a pang, doom their miserable offspring to even greater calamities and deprivations. We saw (and facts *have* proved it, and will prove it no illusion) in this boasted system of mechanical improvement, unless strongly reined in by the law, the nuccleus of a nation's degradation and ruin—a system which with one hand was casting thousands down into a premature grave, and rearing with the other an ignorant, vicious, unsocial, and hardened race, to spread the moral pest of their spirit and example far and wide. We saw in fact the cold and calculating selfish principle which inspires the Manufacturing Adventurer, rapidly insinuating itself amongst the Operative Population, even robbing the maternal breast of tenderness, and stifling the fondest affections of infancy and youth. Nor could it escape the most cursory observer, that religion was chiefly involved among the objects of this rapid desolation, and that the leprosy which infected the *Hearth* had polluted and saturated the *Altar* itself. And we not only beheld these evils as spectators, most of ourselves have tasted these "bitter waters" in our youth, and now live to behold our offspring subjected to the same unchristian system, to which inexorable necessity obliges us to submit them.

Who that saw this could be silent, except some votary of Mammon, personally interested, or some sycophant, more despicable than he, who was sheltered by the folds of his blood-stained garments. We lifted up our voices, and not in vain—Our Appeal was heard and felt—the justice of our demand was admitted. It was no unreasonable nor exorbitant plea that we urged. Many complained that our demand was less than justice could accept, nor could we deny it—We did but require that those who were created in the image of God, should have time for religious, social, and moral duties, and rational enjoyments. And when a demand so reasonable could no longer be withheld, we have been constantly met with the cry, from either *interested* or *ignorant* men—" You have not proved your case." Thus when Mr. Sadler appealed to the Legislature and the Country in 1831, and supported his appeal by the learned and voluminous Evidence already obtained by Sir Robert Peel's Committees on this question, he was drowned with a call for a Select Committee *to prove his case.* He yielded reluctantly to the demand—and surely if ever a case was abundantly substantiated, it was by that Committee. England read its Report and blushed—it fired her with indignation, and she cried "At once and for ever wipe this foul blot away." Then was a clamour raised for "*further enquiry,*" which Lord Ashley resisted in vain; and an expensive and unconstitutional Commission was appointed. That Commission made its Report—confirming all the material and even the minute points of the Evidence of Mr. Sadler's Committee, and, if possible, exposing the dark cavern of Tyranny still further than before. Partial as was that Commission, even upon the evidence of one of its own body, and contradictory and dishonest as was the Report which the Central Board professed to found upon the Evidence, it added on the whole to the weight of Evidence upon which we demanded the Ten Hours Bill.

The expectations of the Nation were now raised to an unprecedented height—the honest and benevolent Owners of Manufacturing Machinery were sanguine of obtaining protection from their overwhelming Competitors, and some freedom from the thraldom of their own system, which they deeply felt. *Parents* without number, who still retained their natural affection, panted with hope, that the hour of their children's deliverance was at hand, and were ready to evince their sincerity by a partial sacrifice of their wages if required.

The songs of the *Children and Youth* of the Factory Districts were heard to drown the noise of those rumbling wheels on which they attended, as they joyfully anticipated a speedy remission of their deadly toil, and an allowance of those manifold privileges of which they had been so long and unjustly deprived. Yes, expectation was wound up to her highest pitch, when at last, an interested party in the House of Commons, bartering their political influence to the ministry of the day, for their own sordid ends, were suffered to prevail over the *truth* and the *right*, and partly by a plausible pretence of greater humanity to the younger part of the Factory Workers, and partly by an alarm of danger to our commercial interests, the people of Great Britain suddenly found themselves cajoled by a deceptious and oppressive measure, which makes the last state of the Factory Workers worse than the first. That this is the character of Lord Althorpe's Act the following brief examination will abundantly prove.

The Act of Lord Althorpe, or more properly of his Lordship's Factory Commissioners, is obviously impracticable, and can afford no real Relief to the Factory Labourers.

Instead of—it has, for a time, injured their cause, by throwing around them *the mere semblance* of *protection* without any reality; whilst by hushing the voice and blinding the eye of public sympathy, it has deprived them in a great measure of the only protection they have hitherto possessed.

This Act, from the moment of its birth in the Chambers of the Central Board of Factory Commissioners, (at which Mr. Poulett Thompson assisted) to that of its passing the Houses of Parliament, has been entirely under the care and direction of a few great Mill Owners; and their whole aim has been, to establish a 12 Hour Bill—to throw dust in the eyes of the public by a proposition of EIGHT HOURS labour for those under 14 years, and establishing a System of *Relays* or *two sets* of these junior workers in a day, to keep time with the 12 hour workers. This scheme was calculated to gratify the public, who were *not able to see through the delusion*, as being *more humane* than the Ten Hour Bill: but the Patrons of the Relay System knew well that it was *impracticable*. As this Relay System is a principal feature of Lord Althorpe's Act, we shall now shew its impracticable character, from most independent and satisfactory testimony. It will be proper first to state that about the time when the Central Board of Factory Commissioners made their Report, one of the District Commissioners for Scotland, Mr. STUART, held a most extraordinary correspondence with his brethren of the Central Board, which he published in the London Papers, addressing his letters to Mr. Wilson, the Secretary of the Central Board.

In this correspondence he loudly and justly complains of "palpable omissions" of important Evidence sent from the Country by himself and other Commissioners, as well as from some of the greatest Manufacturers. We shall quote several instructive passages from this correspondence.

Mr. Stuart writes July 20, 1833.

" There have been material omissions in selecting for the press the Documentary Evidence, formerly transmitted by me. I do not know, never until now having been at all consulted on the subject of those Reports, why the answers of the mill-owners of the United Kingdom to the circular queries of the Central Board, as printed on pages 88, 89, and 90, of their first Report were not engrossed in it. A tabular view at least of those answers might, I conceive, have been very easily prepared, and could not fail to have afforded very valuable information, most of all in pointing out, as it appears to me, the absolute *impracticability*, every where except in the great towns, and even there, the manifest inconvenience and risk of limiting the hours of labour for children, until the commencement of their fourteenth year, *to eight hours ;* above all, the answers to the query relative to the employment of *relays of children*, ought to have been printed, as affording the best information which the Commissioners of the Central Board had obtained on the subject of the chief recommendation in their Report; I allude, of course, to the regulation requiring the employment of relays of children under fourteen years of age. I saw enough of the answers of the mill-owners, which I, from time to time, on our journey, forwarded to you, and of the state of the population of the factories which we visited in Scotland, very many of which, especially of the flax factories, are situated on rivers and rivulets, altogether remote from towns, to be thoroughly satisfied that any legislative enactment, rendering the employment of relays of children necessary, *cannot be enforced*, and that its only effect will be to stop the mills altogether."

Mr. Stuart supports his view of the impracticable character of the *two sets*, or *relay* system, on the authority of Mr. Buchanan, "the oldest Cotton Spinner in Scotland," "educated with Sir Richard Arkwright," and managing partner of "the Catrine Works," the largest in Scotland.

Mr. Buchanan states—

That " a double set of hands could not be collected, and sufficiently trained for a series of years; that supposing a relay of hands under twenty-one years of age could be got, the adults could not be supposed to work above *fourteen hours* in the day, *allowing the least possible time for meals and refresh-ment*, which would only give seven hours for those under twenty-one, **and** the produce in that time could not afford more than *half the present wages to the younger hands*, which would be found totally inadequate to afford the means of support and comforts which that class now enjoys, and that, since, *all his work-people are paid by the piece*, he does not see the possibility of distinguishing the produce belonging to each, so as to pay for their individual exertions."

Mr. Stuart also quotes Mr. Houston, a large manufacturer, at Johnstone, Renfrewshire.

" *He is of opinion that any such regulation could not possibly be carried into effect*, so far as respects the children engaged in the *throstle spinning* here, because the *requisite number of children could not be pro-cured in this neighbourhood*, and at all events the children could not be procured for *the half of the wages* they have at present."

Mr. Stuart again cites Messrs. W. & J. Brown, and Messrs. Baxter, Brothers & Co. of Dundee.

" I saw them separately, but they entirely agreed in thinking any regulation to obtain *the work of young workers for half days, and by relays, imprac-ticable ; the parents could not afford to support them if they only got half wages, which was all that the mill-owners could give, supposing them only to work for half of the working hours.*"

These important testimonies, as well as others of similar tendency from Lancashire, Mr. Stuart complains have been *kept back.* He adds—

Mr. COWELL told me the other day, that he, who was one of the Commis-sioners in Lancashire and Manchester, was *certain* that the plan of the Central Board could not be carried into effect in that district."

And he declares also, that the delay of the publication of the answers to certain printed Lists of Queries from the Mill Owners, was among the " PALPABLE OMISSIONS."

He is sure that had these returns been before Parliament they would not have sanctioned the Relay System—they would have seen it to be " *impracticable.*"

He accuses them of giving a prominence to the few testimonies which appeared to favour their scheme, and of keeping back, or at least not introducing into their Report, (the only document likely to be read by Members of Parlia-ment) the vast mass of opposite tendency. Mr. Wilson on behalf of the Central Board, defends or apologizes as well as he can : declares that there was no *intention* to omit, and by way of lessening the importance of those Returns to the printed Queries sent to all the Mills in the Kingdom, he tells Mr. Stuart—" These Returns are replies to *their own* queries." Upon this, Mr. Stuart observes in his answer of August 3rd, "I do not understand the meaning of your remark that the return of the mill-owners are replies to *their own* queries." But if Mr. Stuart would have read the second page of the First Report of the Commissioners, he would have seen it broadly hinted, that "Several of *the principal Manufacturers,* and of the Representatives of Manufacturing Districts," had no small share in "framing the queries," and this evidently what " *our beloved* John Wilson " means by stating that "they answered *their own* queries!! " Mr. Stuart, however, with all his Scotch perseverance could not succeed. He complains in his letter of July 31, "The Central Board do therefore, even now, maintain their *right* to withhold, *until after the period had expired,* during which they had reason to expect it was to be of any use, what I maintain to be *the most material evidence* which they could procure on the subject of their own recommendation." And further on he states—

"I know well how difficult it is to convince *those, who in the closet have adopted a theoretical notion, in accordance with their general and preconceived views, that it is at variance with facts, and with the evidence afforded by the senses.*"

In one part of his defence of the Central Board, Mr. Wilson tells Brother Stuart, that the Relay System " *had received the acquiescence of the principal Manufacturers now in Town, as Deputies from their respective Districts,*" and encloses to him a printed copy of "*Resolutions entered into at a Meeting of the Deputies from the principal seats of the Cotton Manufacture.*" To this information Mr. Stuart replies—

"I do not attach, I am bound to say, the slightest value to the minutes of a meeting of deputies " from the principal seats of the cotton manufacture," held at Palace-yard on the 16th instant, and of which you have sent me a printed copy. I do not know how many manufacturers attended this meeting of the thousands in the United Kingdom, but I have reason to believe, that only one manufacturer from Scotland, *(except the gentlemen in parliament,)* was present, viz. Mr. HOLDSWORTH, *of Glasgow,* and that gentleman had no authority to act for the manufacturers of Scotland. That gentleman was decidedly opposed to *the system of relays of children,* when I was at Glasgow last month, as all the other eminent manufacturers there, or whom I saw in Scotland. *But he has told me since the meeting of the 16th of July, that he now gave his approval to the measure, because he knew it to be impracticable, as the inspectors to be appointed would report within the first year. But if you are to be influenced by the opinions of the master spin-*

B

ners assembled at Palace-yard, you should, I apprehend, give fair notice of your intention, that the population of the factories, and especially the younger population, may have their representatives at this bit of a parliament, to whose wishes you are now paying so much deference. Many of the great master spinners are said to be anxious to put down the small establishments in the country. Your recommendation, if carried into effect, would, of course, be attended with this to them beneficial result. And so far they, or some of them, may give it their approbation."

We have thought it important to quote largely from this Extraordinary Correspondence, because it is calculated not only to shew THE GROSSLY PARTIAL CHARACTER OF THE COMMISSIONING SYSTEM GENERALLY, but in the present case especially, where the interests of many poor helpless children, and many indigent but industrious families were to be weighed against the wealth and the pride of a few tyrannical and selfish men, it is calculated to illustrate THE CRUEL TRIUMPH OF MIGHT OVER RIGHT.

What a piece of sheer mockery was this Commission! Here were three Government Hirelings and their Secretary with most philosophical coolness, sitting in judgment upon a cruel murderous system—the criminal party whispering in their ears, and guiding their pens all the while. Considered as a Commission, if it had been conducted with any thing like fairness, some good might have resulted, but as it is, we have only unmingled evil in its product, namely, Lord Althorpe's impracticable and unjust Act to legalize the Slavery of the Factory System.

Hear Mr. Stuart once more, on the unfair dealings of the Central Board.

"There was quite enough of time, after our return, for the Commissioners, who had seen the state of the factories, and of the population throughout the manufacturing districts of this country, to have had a meeting, and to have agreed on a general report, after perusing the *whole* evidence."

Why was not this counsel, so just and reasonable, pursued? Had the Medical Commission been admitted to pour a little Humanity into the scale, against the Political Economy and Self-interest of this Congress—a little common justice, such as the brute creation itself obtains at the hand of man, the poor Factory Workers might have been in some measure relieved; but as it is, their last state is worse than the first.

This then (as children would say of " the House that Jack

built") this is the Central Board that listened to the interested
Mill-owners—that promised Lord Althorpe their political
influence: this is the Lord Althorpe that professed such
tender humanity to the children—such anxiety to meet the
just expectations of the Public—such delicacy towards the
refined susceptibilities of the Manufacturers—such apprehen-
sions for the safety and productiveness of the Capital invested
in Machinery—and the prosperity of *"our Foreign Trade."*
Yes, and this is the Noble Lord who has cajoled the humane
people of England by his professions, and left the Factory
Children and Youth worse than he found them. And this
too is the famous Factory Commission—moved for by Mr.
Wilson Patten, the Patentee of the Copper Roller, and who
depends on the great Cotton Manufacturers for his custom
and the value of his patent—And this is the Commission that
has cost the country so many thousands, and by whose most
impartial and elaborate Report, Lord Althorpe's Bill was
framed and adopted.

But let us hear what Mr. Stuart, himself one of the Commissioners, says of the results of its labours.

*"The Report of the Factory Commissioners is no more the report of the
twelve persons appointed to see things with their own eyes, and to report
their observations on them, than of any twelve gentlemen whom one may
by chance meet in St. Paul's Church-yard. It is the report of three
gentlemen residing in London, who, for aught that appears in the Report,
never visited a cotton factory, nor a flax factory, in their lives."*

" If your views shall be carried *by the force of the Government*, the consequences will inevitably be to convert a considerable part of the population
called into existence by the establishment of our manufactures into paupers,
and to do irretrievable mischief by depriving great numbers of families of the
means of support."

And let us hear too what the same Mr. Stuart says of its
adoption by Parliament.

" *It is possible, however, that such a measure as you advise may be
carried in a thin House towards the close of the Session.* And I therefore
still feel it to be my duty, from the conviction I sincerely entertain of its danger, to do all in my power, by availing myself of the opportunity afforded me
by this correspondence, to advertise you of the fatal consequences to be
apprehended from success."

And now, fellow countrymen, we leave you to reflect
upon the imposition which has been played off upon you, at
the expense of so many thousands of pounds, and above all
at the cost of so much increased misery to the wretched

Factory Workers. Here is your "impracticable" Bill—an Act which Mr. Holdsworth, of Glasgow, and his Fellow "Deputies" only sanctioned "*because they knew it would be impracticable.*"

Have we not then still a claim upon your attention? Without going one step further we now appeal to you—"HAS LORD ALTHORPE'S ACT ANSWERED THE JUST DEMAND OF THE FACTORY WORKERS FOR LEGAL PROTECTION?" You will answer "No," and conclude with us that it has *aggravated* and *not relieved* their case. May we not reasonably *agitate* again for the Ten Hour Bill? By the help of God we will, and not cease, till it be adopted. And we hope for your aid, and may HE who has all hearts in his hand incline you to render it!

Here then let us take leave of the contrivers of Lord Althorpe's Act, "three *gentlemen* residing in London, who never visited a factory in their lives," and who when making their Report carefully excluded from their counsels those who *had* "seen with their own eyes." These worthies, guilty as they were (see Mr. Stuarts letter of August 3rd,) of "*great, extensive, and palpable omissions,*" have been allowed to perpetuate and to legalize the Slavery of the Factories, and to gratify the larger Manufacturers by handing over the Factory Youth to their cruel cupidity, and the *small* mill-owners to their malice. (See quotation from Mr. S's letter of July 31, at page 10.) These are the *just* and *impartial* men, who would not attempt to provide against the destructive effects of the "*wet*-spinning of *flax*, and the *web*-dressing in power loom factories—employments obviously attended with imminent danger to the young people." And yet, Mr. Stuart wrote to them from Greenock—

"*I witnessed a more painful sight* again and again *in beholding the miserable, unhealthy-looking beings, in the wet-spinning and web-dressing apartments.*"

O how long shall the clammy hand of Avarice be allowed to press down Poverty to the dust!

In further proof that Lord Althorpe's Act is impracticable, we may refer to the clauses 11 to 16, which regard THE OBTAINING CERTIFICATES OF AGE FROM MEDICAL MEN, which are to be countersigned by the Magistrates, and if any Magistrate refuse to countersign he must state his reason in writing, and application MAY be made to the Quarter Sessions by the Parents of Children, in such case.

Let any man who knows the manufacturin g districts, say if this scheme be *practicable?* Have not surgeons and magistrates enough employment already, with the crimes, vices, and misfortunes of the Factory Workers? Take Manchester, Leeds, or Glasgow. Consider the immense number of young workers who from time to time will become of age and apply for work, and of others who are weekly DYING OFF, and the consequent influx of fresh hands. What number of Magistrates will be required then to attend to this constantly recurring business of Certificates. And as to the Medical Men, they are not after all *obliged* to give their valuable time and attention to such matters, and may decline to take any such trouble upon them. Who is to pay their charge, if they choose to make one? Let it be further considered what loss of time must thus be occasioned to parents, and to children. Who that spends five minutes thought on this part of the Act, does not see that it is morally impracticable—that if there were 50 Magistrates where now there is but one, it would fully occupy them, *to the exclusion* of other business, and that the result must be, that Factory Masters will be under the necessity of employing children illegally, and Magistrates cannot punish the offence.

Again, we call attention to the 35th clause of this Act, and which we may call THE GRAND NULLIFYING CLAUSE. "And be it further enacted, that all *complaints* for offences against this Act, shall be preferred at or before the time of the Visit, *duly notified,* of any Inspector, next after the commission of such offence; and *written* notice of the intention to prefer the complaint for such offence, shall, by the complainant be given, within 14 days after the commission of such offence, to the party or parties complained against: provided always, that no more than one penalty for a repetition of the same offence shall be recoverable, except after the service of the written notice as aforesaid."

By this it is plain, that if the most enormous offences are committed against this Act, there can be no redress until the "*duly notified* visit" of the Inspector takes place. He may visit without duly notifying it, to dine with the masters, to feast upon those luxurious viands which the labour of the poor children procures; but if the visit has not been "DULY NOTIFIED" it would be very rude to disturb the banquettings of such well-bred gentlemen, with poor children's wrongs. But supposing *duly notified* visits to take place. There are but four Inspectors for the whole kingdom, and its thousands of mills, and its hundreds of thousands of factory workers: how *can* they, although they should work *twice* 12 hours a day themselves, how can they, if they were forty in number rather than four, "inspect" a tithe of those crowded districts, or "hear and determine" a tithe of the "duly notified" complaints.

But who can read this clause, that knows the harsh discipline of factories, and the slavish spirit which the system has imposed upon the majority of the Factory Workers, and will not immediately see, that the clause was evidently *meant* to *stifle and prevent all complaints?* There must be notice in *writing* —then why not give all the Factory Workers *time* to learn to write, and to write grammatically—and to study and know those laws which they so often break ignorantly? And as to the giving *notice* of complaint, would not, in many cases, the bread of a whole family be forfeited by such an act, and then, perhaps he would have to deal with his most honourable master (that *was*) either as the Overseer of the Poor, or else as a Justice of the Peace. In fact, the whole clause implies an energy and independence of character which the Factory Workers in general do not possess, and which the system is well calculated to put down. There can be no doubt that there are many vast establishments, which would require one Inspector to devote his whole time to them, and where constant and "duly notified" visits are very requisite.

Consider the bearing of this clause upon the educational part of the scheme. How are the "School Certificates" to be *authenticated,* and by whom? How is it to be *proved* that the same child has not been driven, by dire necessity, to work at two different mills in one day? Does not the inadequate remuneration, of which Messrs. Holdsworth, Baxter, Ashworth, and others, have testified, render such a breach of the law morally certain in many cases--and who is to detect it? The " duly notified visit" may be far distant, and the poor victim may be in her grave when the visit actually occurs.

In fact to work this blundering Act, instead of four Inspectors for the whole kingdom, there is scarcely a large manufacturing town where more than four might not find full employment. How many hundreds then are required? On the whole the "palpable omissions" of the Central Board, (as Mr. Stuart would say) have resulted in a most "palpable" *cheat,* and that a most *expensive* one too.

We now proceed to shew, that this Factory Act is also POSITIVELY UNJUST in the greater part of its provisions.

And first of all, consider the hours of actual labour assigned to young persons above 13 and under 18 years. *Twelve hours* of actual labour, added to 1½ for meals, and to the time of going, returning, and preparations, will constitute generally fifteen hours of occupation. *Fifteen hours* occupation ! This is involved in Lord Althorpe's Bill, and this is his *tender mercy* for all young people in factories between thirteen and eighteen years ! And is then, the Medical Evidence before the three Parliamentary Committees to be all cast away? And all that, too, of the Medical Men on the Factory Commission ? And is common sense to be outraged by telling us that young people of the age of thirteen and between that and eighteen, are in no danger of physical injury, from this *degree* and this *kind* of labour, when every mother knows the fact to be otherwise, and that there is not a more precarious stage of human existence than this very stage? When do young people *more* require the watchful care of both parents than during these years, whether it regards their health or their morals ? And is not *this* the eventful stage of existence, when for the most part the character is formed for life—unalterably fixed. Is not this, too, the period when the mind most expands, when instruction is most requisite as well as most serviceable, and yet this is Lord Althorpe's chosen season, virtually to exclude the youth of his country, employed in manufactures, from almost every chance of moral improvement, and rational enjoyment, and to doom them from thirteen years old to eighteen, and often to the end of their earthly race, to the sickening alternations of " bed and mill."

" O but (say our opponents) only consider our *foreign trade*—shall we ruin our foreign trade?" To which we reply, " Cursed is the trade foreign or domestic, that dooms our youth to an apprenticeship of brute labour, and pagan ignorance. Cursed is the trade that dooms a whole population to alternate exhaustion and excitement. Cursed to any country is the system, which, for the sake of enriching a few by the aid of the boasted mechanical *improvements* of the day, robs industry of its reward, and leaves an honest man to his choice—of the poor-house, or, what is worse, of being sustained by the deadly toil of his own children!"

Here we beg our countrymen to observe that the *legalizing* of this 12 hour system, under the mere hollow pretence of protecting childhood and youth, is virtually, the adoption of a system of more than 12 hours *actual* labour, and 15 hours occupation for *Adult* Operatives too. The Children *go before, in the team* of mechanical labour, and the Adults, both those who work *in* factories, and those who get work *from* factories (such as Combers and Weavers) must at least keep up to the pace of the "fore horse."

We appeal to a Christian country, professing to revere and to distribute the Bible—We appeal to those who bring it to our cottage doors, and kindly ask us to subscribe for it—We ask them "*What is the Bible-day of Labour.*" "Are there not 12 hours in which *men* ought to work?" And would the Saviour of mankind deny time for meals out of the 12 ? We are sure he would not. He spake of *Men* too, and not of Women, and of Children and Youth. These he called to sit at his feet and hear his word, and the children he embraced in his arms and clasped to his bosom. But in the year of *our Lord* 1833, *his professed* disciples, have found out an "improvement" system, which takes the woman from her cottage, dooms the youth to toil and ignorance, and divides manhood into two parties, one party condemned to perform the labour which should employ the whole, and the other party condemned to stand by " all the day idle," and all the day hungry, and to think themselves happy, if they in their turn may be allowed to *work* themselves to death, instead of being *pined* to death.

The Bible-day is from six to six, or from sunrise, in an Eastern country, to sunset, which was often less than twelve hours of our time—but Lord Althorpe's day, and that of a Reformed Parliament, is in some cases ordered *by law* to extend from half-past five to half-past eight, and in others from five to nine! (See the first and third clauses of the Act.) Surely "the tender mercies of the wicked are cruel." And does not this plainly argue, that man is considered by such legislators as merely made for brute labour, that his whole existence is to be employed to enrich a few adventurers, and to impoverish and exhaust himself? Where then shall we look for greater *injustice?*

We also point at the PARTIALITY of this unjust measure—LACE MILLS ARE UTTERLY EXCLUDED FROM IT. And why? Is there some spell at the threshhold of a Lace Mill, which will not allow Avarice to enter? What though Lace Mills, just now, may be ever so faultless, (which we do not admit) yet competition and avarice may soon make them as bad as any. And why are Silk Mills also excepted, with regard to employing children under 13 more than the 48 hours per week? The work is cleaner, and the atmosphere is purer, but *the human machine has a mind to teach as well as a body to tire,* and why should the silk manufacturer be allowed by clauses 7 and 8. to take a child of four years or five and work it ten hours a day, for in these mills there is to be no restriction of age in this respect. Is this an adherence to *principle*—is this right and *just?*

Again, we observe that THERE IS NOTHING IN THIS ACT TO PREVENT A MAGISTRATE FROM ACTING IN HIS OWN CASE, OR THAT OF A RELATIVE. The great Mill-owners have of late, been very ambitious for a seat on the magisterial bench, and a vast proportion of the Magistrates in the manufacturing districts are either mill-owners, or " interwoven " with them.—How can a just administration of this Act be expected under these circumstances? Is *this* the liberty of which we hear such boast? Is *this* the *independance* of our Judges?"

Again, we perceive that in this Act THERE IS NO TIME WHATEVER ALLOWED FOR MEALS, TO THOSE WORKERS WHO ARE RECOGNIZED AS INFANTS. For those under thirteen no meal hours are provided, and they may be *lawfully* worked nine hours without stopping! Will it then be said, that they cannot work when the other workers stop? In many cases this may hold true, but scheming, screwing, Avarice, may soon invent some " improvement," by which a part of the work at least may *go on* during the meal hours of the older workers, and be attended by the infants, and there is reason to believe that this will be the case. And why did not Lord Althorpe, that kind Patron of Infants, provide against this. What! no *rest*, no *play*, no *meal times* for those under thirteen? They may be worked nine hours incessantly *by law*, and this is Justice and this is Humanity!!!

But what shall we say to *those clauses which* ALLOW THE WORKING-UP OF LOST TIME IN ALL MILLS? A strong plea *was* made for water mills, on the score that their *power* depended on many precarious causes, and in some cases even on Providence. But it seems now, that to all such pleas a deaf ear should be turned. *Providence is kind, but man is cruel.* Let the owners of water mill *power* get legal protection from the owners of steam *power*, but let not infancy and youth be deprived of the care of a kind Providence and a just law. When the mighty Steam Leviathan engages to " *work up time*" for the sickly infants, or worn down youth, it will be time enough to admit, that the exhausted *human* machine ought to " work up time" for the steam engine or its proprietor. " One good turn deserves another."

But where shall we find a parrallel, the cruelty and *injustice* of REFUSING as the House of Commons did, TO OBLIGE MASTERS TO FENCE OFF DANGEROUS MACHINERY? When this clause was discussed in the Legislature of Great Britain, we were told that the "common law" afforded a sufficient protection. And yet this " common law " is so *uncommonly* expensive that poor labouring people cannot get at it. And if they could, how would it avail to restore mangled limbs, or to raise to life an indistinguishable mass of human flesh, blood and bones, just untwined and still shivering from an unguarded shaft or wheel? Or how shall the tears of the Fatherless, of the Childless, or the Widow, be wiped away by Mr. Poulett Thompson's " common law"? Well had it been if the cause of the Factory Child had been tried before a Sanhedrim of Jews, THEY would, with greater humanity, have legislated in the spirit of their own law, as found in Deuteronomy, xxii, 8. "When thou buildest a new house then thou shalt make a battlement for thy roof, *that thou bring not blood upon thy house*, if any man fall from thence." Regardless however of human life, or of "bringing blood" upon his machinery or his profits, the mill-owner in these Christian days is to be put to no inconvenience, not even to the expense of five shillings, though it were to save a soul from death or to hide a multitude of sins. *O Temple of Moloch, how doth the blood of the poor ooze from the crevices of thy lofty walls!* What can more fully illustrate *the spirit* of those who framed this Act and " drove it through a thin House at the close of a Session," (as Mr. Stuart, the Factory Commissioner alledges) than this refusal to guard off dangerous machinery? Thus too has that *salutary provision* of the Ten Hour Bill been *omitted*, which *regulated the height of rooms* of future mills, with a view to proper ventilation. The character of the whole concern is expressed in a few words —"*Capitalists* shall flourish and reign, although the people perish."

In good keeping with this sentiment is the *rejection of that clause in the Ten Hour Bill, which enacted that a sufferer from unguarded machinery should be provided for by its owner*, after proper investigation before a jury as in the case of Coroner's Inquests. Our Saviour once asked—" Is not the *life* more than meat, and the body than raiment?" Had he asked these proud and reckless men the question in *this* form and said " Is not the *life* of even a poor child, more valuable than all your iron, and wood, and steam—Is not the body of one of my creatures more valuable than all your profits?" These audacious men would have answered with a contemptuous " No."

THE PENALTIES OF THIS ACT ARE UNJUST, BEING SO DISPROPORTION-ATE TO THE " PROFITS " WHICH MAY BE OBTAINED BY BREAKING IT.

The highest penalty is £20., and the Inspector or Magistrate has a power even when a breach of the law has been proved, to discharge the criminal without penalty, " if it shall appear to such Inspector or Justice that such offence was not *wilful* or *grossly* negligent." (Clause 31.) It appears not at all unlikely that when a complaint of the breach of the Act comes before a Mill-owner Magistrate, or one of his "interwoven" friends, it will *most clearly* " appear to such Justice, that such offence was not wilful or grossly negligent." How natural for men to "support their own order!" Now, as to the *highest* penalty (£20.) in a few days or nights at *certain* seasons of trade, large mill-owners may make or save twice or five times £20. How shall a law be kept when it is more profitable to break it than to keep it?

It is not so with the keeper of an illicit *still*, or the vendor of a pint of illicit beer, or the smuggler. Heavy fines are provided for them, and finally imprisonment for audacious and persevering offenders. Nay, even among us, whose labour produces the country's wealth, if a poor weaver should be found who does not finish his master's work in due time, or who damages, or purloins the material, a very heavy fine would by *law* be imposed, and the inability of a poor man to pay it, would ensure him a *prison* instead. Of this we are not now complaining. Let the working man be tied fast to his duty. Let it not be in his power to hurt his employer with impunity; but let the law extend its other hand over the employer too, and LET OUR LAWS BE EQUAL THAT THEY MAY BE OBEYED. *Let* the rich man go to prison, if he *will* teach the poor man by his example to break the law; and let the poor man's life and limbs, and his children's life and limbs, and their happiness, and moral as well as religious good, be at least *as precious*, in the eye of the law, as a rich manufacturer's *warp and weft*. For the imprisonment of wilful and persevering offenders without regard to rank in society we will yet plead, inasmuch as the fear and dread of a disgraceful incarceration is the least consideration, that will keep the unprincipled adventurer to the law—that will adequately protect the poor man and his child, or that will allow an honest master to come without ruinous disadvantage into the market.

There is one most novel, as well as most unjust, feature in this Act, which is, that IT LAYS A TAX OF MORE THAN 8 ℔ CENT UPON THE WAGES OF FACTORY INFANTS TO PROVIDE FOR THEIR EDUCATION.

When a proposition was lately made to tax *rich* men's property, the greatest alarm seemed to prevail at the very mention of it. Indignation reddened almost every face, and certain ruin was predicted if such a shocking proposal should be adopted. But " *the rich have many friends*," and thus have they demanded "the poor man's ewe lamb," as a sacrifice and a feast in the *sacred*

c

temple of Lord Althorpe's Humanity, whilst *his own stalled oxen* are lowing for want of appetite, and their own well fleeced thousands are whitening the plain. Poor Factory Child! There was none to plead thy cause! Thou wast dumb before thy *shearers*, who were showering down *crocodile's tears* over thy ignorance, and yet laughing inwardly at their own cunning! "ONE PENNY IN EVERY SHILLING TO PAY FOR SCHOOLING" says this matchless Act. (Clause 20) O what will the great nations of the earth say when they read it? This Queen of Commerce, *Great* Britain, which sways her mighty sceptre so far and so wide—whose merchants are princes, and whose fleets and armies have awed the world—this second Rome for empire, this second Carthage for commerce, assembled her hoary senators in solemn conclave, to decree that Factory Infants shall pay "*One Penny in every Shilling for Schooling! ! !*" Besides this, it is herein decreed, that in certain cases "the township shall pay out of the Poor Rates" what the "one penny in every shilling" fund, does not supply for the *sufficient* maintenance of a school master, and thus are the little tradesmen and the public to be still further taxed, first to educate the producers of the mill master's wealth, then when worn down to maintain; and lastly, when dead, to bury the victims of this "glorious system!"

Let us now notice the office of INSPECTORS appointed under this Act, and the MOST UNCONSTITUTIONAL AND UNJUST POWERS INVESTED IN THEM.

Had *we*, and the friends of the Ten Hour Bill generally, proposed *virtually* to place the Factory System *under the police*, and to appoint over it Police Magistrates like these, possessed of such despotic powers, what condemnation would not have been heaped upon us! As it is, the murmuring is *very low* though *very sincere*—at least amongst those who have "dug a pit for others and are fallen into the midst of it themselves." Under former Acts, applicable exclusively to *Cotton* Mills, certain persons had been appointed as *Visitors*, who from their station in society, and their locality, might in many cases possess the confidence of the poor and the respect of the rich, and be able to moderate the rigour of this system of youthful imprisonment. Now, however, it is found *expedient* to have four men well paid out of the national purse, who it seems are entirely unacquainted with the factory system. However incompetent they are for their task, they are at least amply provided with most unconstitutional means of annoyance and mischief, where they may be inclined to employ them. By clauses 17, 18, &c., of this Act, they have the following powers.

1. To enter any factory, or mill, or school attached thereto, at all hours, day and night, when the same is working, and to examine on oath, any person on the spot or elsewhere.

2. They, or any of them, have power *to make* all such rules, orders, and regulations, as may be necessary for enforcing the Act; and these rules, after being published for two weeks in a newspaper, are to be as binding as an Act of Parliament, and, in fact, they are to become the *Laws of the Land.*

3. They are to have complete controul over the schools to which children under 13 years are sent, and although in clause 20, it is said to be "some school chosen by the parents or guardians of the child," yet in clause 23, the Inspector is empowered to withhold *the pay* from any school-master, or mistress, "if he shall be of opinion that they are incompetent, or *in any way* unfit" for their office. Where now is the "choice" of the parents? Is it not evident from this, that the religious and moral instruction of the younger Factory Children, is thus placed under the control of the Inspectors, who

have it in their power to give what character they please to that instruction, and either to educate them as Christians, or to make them "Jews, Turks, Infidels, or Heretics," as may please them, to the entire exclusion of all interference either from parents or employers.

4. The Inspectors are to have the whole body of Police under their control, when necessary. Any one obstructing them is to be fined *not less* than £10. And in every case *one* Inspector, or one Justice may act—*two* Magistrates are *not* required.

5. They are empowered by clause 38 to summon whom they please "*forthwith to appear*" by day or by night, with notice or without notice, and if any one so summoned does not " appear," or " submit," or if he " resists " they may commit him to prison for two months.

Now we appeal to the Public whether it is not fair to presume, that an Act framed by three Commissioners, (or more properly " Omissioners," who were appointed, superintended, and guided, as Mr. Stuart asserts, by " *a bit of a Parliament*" of large Mill-owners throughout, is it not fair to presume, that *such* an Act will bear lightly on "the Order " who procured it? And further, that those who got the *Act* adopted, have influenced the appointment and will control the conduct of the four Inspectors? But it will be best seen in its own working. We, however, who know the Factory System and its innate tyranny, have no need of the gift of prophecy to anticipate what its effects will be. It allows of *instantaneous* summonses, which are found exceedingly convenient in Inquisitions: so will they be in Factories, and the effect will be, *intimidation*, involuntary contradiction, defective evidence, and for transgressors—ESCAPE: and then we shall learn " from high authority " that the Law is effective—and in proof of it, there have been few, if any, *convictions !*

To crown all this arbitrary scheme there is no appeal allowed to any court from the decision of the Inspectors, who are allowed to MAKE, to INTERPRET, and to ENFORCE thus much of the Laws of Great Britain. If we go on thus, we shall soon be able to do without that " Bit of a Parliament " which meets at Westminster—for it can only be " a bit" of one, when a briefless Lawyer—a broken-down Merchant—a poor Aristocrat—and " an intimate friend of Lieut. Drummond," are allowed to exercise the same powers in the Country.

We shall only add to these notices, that many valuable provisions of the Ten Hour Bill are omitted.

That of discontinuing work two hours sooner on Saturdays, to enable the people to make their markets, and to prepare for the Sabbath, as well as to ameliorate the toil of the latter day of the week. Under this Act the factories may go on ordinarily till half-past seven, and in some cases till nine o'clock on a Saturday night. There is no exception in favour of this day. This needs no comment.

By the Ten Hour Bill, persons below 21 years were not allowed to perform *night*-work—that most demoralizing season for factory labour: by this Act those who are 18 years old may be worked in the night.

Again by the Ten Hour Bill, provision was made for *preventing* the mending or cleaning of machinery on the Lord's Day—and also to correct that cheating system for screwing some hours of extra labour out of the workers by means of what are called " speed clocks," but which have a sad trick of travelling some what slower than *Old Time*, being attached to the moving power or engine. Also, by the Ten Hour Bill, the factory youth were not allowed to be wronged out of their meal hours, by being set then to clean the machinery. This is also omitted.

Having given, as we hope, a sufficient exposure of this IMPRACTICABLE and UNJUST Act, we now appeal to every rank and class among our fellow-countrymen. We appeal to the NOBILITY and GENTRY of the land. By the exaltation of their rank, and by the bravery of their ancestors, we call upon them to stand in the gap for the poor and helpless. "*The head cannot say to the foot I have no need of thee*," and if this system goes on unrestrained, it will soon lead to events, which the more elevated classes must endure with ourselves. When the foundations of society are crushed by the *maul* of Oppression, and made to crumble under the keen frost of Avarice, "the cloud capt towers" have no room to boast—soon they must totter in their turn.

We implore the MINISTERS OF CHRIST to help us. With deference we would say, that a few blasts from their gospel trumpets (unless they give "an *uncertain* sound") would bring down the proud walls of Tyranny to the ground. The poor can bear their sharpest rebukes, if they see the ambassadors of God *impartial* and fearless. We implore you to plead our cause.

We appeal to the FACTORY PROPRIETORS. Why should they be thus indignant because their system is assailed? We do not censure *them indiscriminately*—we are proud to say that some of them are our friends. We are sure they can never be prosperous as a body, as long as the present system goes on.

"The *small* Mill-owners" as Mr. Wilson, the Secretary of the Central Board, calls them, have generally taken up a very mistaken position on this question. They have very erroneously supposed, that a Ten Hour Bill would annihilate them entirely, not considering, that whatever curbs monopoly, favours humble and honest industry, A Ten Hour Bill would prevent the great capitalists from *gormandizing* as they do, all the large and profitable orders—they would be obliged to allow their smaller neighbours a share. But it is stated by Mr. Stuart, in his letter to Mr. Wilson of July 31, already quoted, "that many of the *great* Master Spinners are said to be anxious to put down the smaller establishments in the country." We can tell Mr. Stuart, that this is not only "said to be" but also *known* to be the case, and e're long it will not be doubted by the *small* men themselves, however they may be deceived at present. That such has been the design of the framers of this Act, and that such will be its operation time will prove. But to the whole body of Manufacturers we would say, Let justice triumph—let discord be destroyed—let youth be protected—let domestic intercourse be re-established. And to such of the Manufacturers as are religious men by profession, we would most forcibly appeal, that they ought either to disprove the facts and arguments we have adduced, or else to renounce all pretensions to religion, if they continue their opposition: and we pledge ourselves that if we can avail any thing, such men shall either cast off their piety or their tyranny.

And what shall we say to the PARENTS OF FACTORY CHILDREN? Had they a due sense of the evils to which their offspring are exposed, they themselves could and would in one day apply the remedy, by refusing any longer to allow their youth to work under such a system. But in too many cases, a disgraceful indifference prevails. O! let parents arise and help us, for God will otherwise require their children's wrongs at their hands.

Can SUNDAY SCHOOL TEACHERS refuse their aid? Surely they can never sanction the wickedness, the *sacrilege*, of making the valuable system of Sunday Schools, which many factory masters warmly support, a pretext or excuse for long, tedious, and destructive hours of labour, and social deprivation, and all "for filthy lucre's sake." O No! Such conduct would bespeak a deep-dyed malignity, not to say hypocrisy, which we will not impute to them.

To the YOUNG FACTORY WORKERS we would address ourselves with the most tender kindness and affection. You, shall still have our best exertions ; let *us* have your frequent and fervent prayers ! Pour them out before a God of boundless compassion, and forget not to pray, especially, for those who employ you, that God may soften and turn their hearts. If they oppress *you*, still, be *you* faithful to *them*. And thus may you hope, that by God's blessing your cause shall prevail. And when it does succeed, let it be your *care* to improve your spare time to the honour of your God, and in learning those things which are useful, and let your parents and friends thus see, that you value your privilege, and love your duty. Again we say, night and morning, pray to God to bless your friends, and to prosper their exertions on your behalf.

We appeal to ALL CLASSES for pecuniary support, to enable us still to persevere in this conflict, by means of the press, and by such other methods of discussion as may be most approved. We invite all classes to join the FACTORY REFORMATION SOCIETIES. We have *now*, no source of pecuniary support but such as the Public at large may be inclined to afford, and we trust we shall not ask their assistance in vain. It would ill become Britons, who contribute hundreds of thousands of pounds yearly for foreign objects of benevolence, to leave the Young Factory Workers of their own country to perish, And here let our countrymen, once for all, understand that the evils of Lord Althorpe's Bill are not chargeable upon us. Already we are charged with the blame of those manifold annoyances and impracticabilities which are found in it.

To the OPERATIVES OF GREAT BRITAIN we finally appeal.

You have never sanctioned or approved, or wished in any way to promote this oppressive and delusive Act. *You* had nothing to do with that "Bit of a Parliament" which got it passed, and procured the Ten Hour Bill to be thrown out. We may thank Mr. Stuart for pointing out and holding up to scorn, this "Bit of a Parliament." How prodigiously ridiculous have they made themselves ! There was the *Bit of a House of Commons*, sitting in awful state, in Palace-yard. Mr. *Holland Hoole* being *Mr. Speaker !* And there was the *Bit of an Upper House*—the "three gentlemen who never entered a factory in their lives" at the Factory Commission Office, with "our beloved *Edwin Chadwick*, one of the petty Editors of a Ministerial Journal, on the woolsack ! And there were Messrs. Poulett Thompson & Co. *behind the throne*, prompting these *Bits of Lordlings*, Why, brother Operatives, we poor *ignorant* fellows could make as grand a "Bit of a Parliament" as this ! At all events Mr. Stuart encourages us to try our hand at it. (See page 10 of this work.) FELLOW OPERATIVES *and Countrymen*, our labour is our property, and we have a right to dispose of it as we please, or else we are slaves not freemen. We have shewn that the old Bible-day has never exceeded 12 hours *occupation* and 10 hours *labour*. But in as much as there have been such SPLENDID IMPROVEMENTS IN MACHINERY, surely we might with propriety claim at least two hours further abatement of labour on that score; or else what good have these *improvements* effected, and what is become of the promise of *less labour for man*, with which the introduction of Arkwright's invention was attended ? Consult among yourselves, and what you do—do quickly. Let all your proceedings be guided by the principles of Justice,

Liberty, Subordination, and above all Christianity. You will then *have* the sympathies of your fellow subjects, and the blessing of your God.

Signed on behalf of the Meeting of Delegates from the Short Time Committees of the West Riding of York.

Yew Tree Inn, Birstall,
Oct. 28, 1833.

JAMES BEDFORD, *Chairman*,
S. GLENDENNING, *Secretary.*

P. S. We beg to call attention to the following edifying Speech of Mr. CHARLES WOOD, M. P. for Halifax, and WHIPPER-IN of the House of Commons, at a Public Dinner at Halifax, on November 1st, 1833. Surely, Britain will now see how the Factory Bill was obtained.

"Another bill of considerable interest to this part of the country, and which was supported by Government, was the Bill for the Regulation of Factory Labour. On this subject Government was placed under circumstances of extreme difficulty. At the beginning of the session a large majority of the House, I believe, would have carried what was called the Ten Hours Bill, which would have been injurious to the interest both of master and workmen. With some difficulty, and by a very narrow majority, we were able to send down a commission of enquiry, but we could do it only on pledging ourselves that a bill should be passed. On receiving the report of that commission, Government was left in a minority in the House of Commons, but afterwards, *in consequence, I must say, of the exertions of the representatives from the newly enfranchised towns, we were able to carry a Bill.* Whether that Bill be good or not I cannot say, but I can say it was the only course Government had in its power to pursue to avoid a much greater evil."

NOTES.

NOTE 1, page 3.—Particular reference is made to the case of a boy, named Tomlinson, of Leeds, whose Overlooker has been committed by a Coroner's warrant to York Castle, to be tried for manslaughter. It was given in evidence that he repeatedly and cruelly beat his victim. The instruments used were a heavy brush handle, on one occasion a ladder, and frequently his hands: the whole being consummated by *hanging* the poor wretch with a rope till he was nearly dead!

Hanging, by a rope under the arms for a considerable space of time, was practised upon a Factory Boy at Huddersfield. whose case Mr. Oastler published. And daily poor children are now very shamefully beaten, seized by the hair and thrown down on the floor by the Overlookers. One poor child, who died some time since, near Bradford, had received, as her parents stated, a serious internal injury by a heavy blow in the side, from the *fist* of her Overlooker. Shortly before her death she exclaimed in an agony of pain, lifting up her little withered arms, "Oh if there be a hell —— —— will go there, for he has killed me!" Volumes might be filled with such tales of sorrow. How can it be expected that nature can, in many cases, endure the protracted toil of the factory without coercion? In order to dispense with the whip in the West Indies, the hours of adult labour have been reduced to 45, for which term of labour the Negro is to "*receive clothing, lodging, and every other necessary.*" And Mr. Charles Wood, M. P., adds in his late speech at Halifax, "*More than this, I am confident that this term* (45 hours a week) *will be abridged by the interest of the Master, in those Islands.* HE WILL FIND IT FOR HIS OWN INTEREST TO SHORTEN THE PERIOD." (See Leeds Mercury's Report, Nov. 2.) Let the same period of 45 hours labour be adopted for all the Factory Workers, and then you may abolish the strap, and the belt, and the stick, and the screw key; all of which are frequently used to drive the young workers up to their tasks.

NOTE 2, page 3.—Suicides have occurred, which have been traced to insufferable Factory Labour. A boy, named *Giles Gledhill*, at Holme, near Huddersfield, had been worked, for nearly *six* months in a woollen mill, two or three nights in a week, in addition to his day labour. He had been heard to say, that before he would he worked so he would hang himself. He had received no extra wage for these nights that he worked, but the Manager had promised to give his mother "*something*" additional. Upon the strength of this the mother went to Huddersfield to purchase him some new shirts. On her return she met a stranger, who asked her if she had heard what had happened at Smithy Mill? She answered, "No." "A boy, said the man, has hanged himself." "What boy?" enquired she eagerly. He answered, "they call him Giles Gledhill." The poor mother spake no more, she swooned, and was carried home in a state of insensibility. The week before his death, he had been three days and three nights without leaving the premises, or going home. He took every opportunity to sleep when the Overlooker was absent.

Another and similar case occurred at Halifax. A young girl, about seventeen, entreated her parents to allow her to leave factory work, and promised to work for her living at ANY occupation they could get for her. This they would not do, alleging that they should lose her wages, and could not find her other work. At last she grew desperate, and on her way home, one evening, purchased poison and destroyed herself.

Although these may be cases of rare occurrence, yet they shew the necessity of a very strict and extensive restriction of a system, in the operation of which cupidity or necessity give an impetus to competition, wherein competition occasions loss and not gain, and inflicts upon the worker wretchedness and poverty, and a degree of labour which destroys the body and brutalizes the mind.

MINUTES AND RESOLUTIONS

Of a Meeting of Delegates from the Short Time Committees of the West Riding of Yorkshire, established to promote the Legislative Adoption of the Ten Hour Factory Bill, assembled at the Yew Tree Inn, Birstall, October 28th, 1833.

That the Principles of the Ten Hour Factory Bill, introduced by Lord Ashley into Parliament during the last Session, are those of Justice and Humanity; and that it deserves the Support of every Friend of his Country—but that it is capable of some Amendments in detail, to render it more binding and effective, which call for serious consideration.

That the Act of Lord Althorpe, called the "Factories' Regulation Act," makes the last state of Factory Workers worse than the first—that multitudes are deluded by the jugglery of this deceptious and oppressive Measure—and that it is manifestly the duty of those who have so solemnly and repeatedly pledged themselves to so sacred a Cause to undeceive the Public as to Lord Althorpe's Act, and still to claim for the Factory Workers the Ten Hour Bill.

That the friends of the Ten Hour Bill be earnestly recommended to organize themselves after the usual manner of Benevolent and Religious Institutions, and that *a Society be now established*, to be called "THE FACTORY REFORMATION SOCIETY," the objects of which shall be—1st. the promotion in the first instance of the Legislative Adoption of the Ten Hour Factory Bill for all under *Twenty-one Years of Age*—2nd. the Protection and Benefit of all Persons engaged in Factory Labour, or connected with the Factory System.

That the Friends of this Cause be earnestly invited to form Branch Societies in every Town, and Associations in the Villages, as extensively as possible; and that every such Society shall be established, and the Committees of the same appointed, at Public Meetings.

That Quarterly Meetings of the Branch Societies shall be regularly held on the Full Moon Weeks, and similar Meetings shall be held in the Villages; and that at all the Public Meetings, the Magistrates, Medical Men, and Mill Owners, either by Notes, or public Advertisement, shall be respectfully and invariably invited to attend, on every such Occasion.

That the Committee of every Society shall present to its Constituents at the Quarterly Public Meetings, a Quarterly Report of its Proceedings: and that an Account of all Contributions which have been received or disbursed, shall be audited by the Committee every Quarter, and published at least every Year.

That Subscriptions be solicited among all Classes, for the purpose of printing and circulating Information, and otherwise promoting the objects above expressed—especially the Legal Defence of the Injured and Oppressed, as far as it can be effected—but that on no occasion shall Music or Banners be provided from the General Funds.

That a Central Committee shall be formed from the Branch Societies, (each Committee sending one Member,)—that the Central Committee shall meet Annually, or oftner if necessary, and the Local or Branch Committees Monthly, or oftner, as circumstances may require.

That the Central Committee shall be empowered to call General or West Riding Meetings at such time and place as they deem fit. That the Central Committee shall appoint a *Secretary for Correspondence*, who shall be empowered to assemble the Central Committee when he deems it necessary, provided he has the concurrence of at least five Members in so doing. It shall also be his duty to assemble the Central Committee at any time, upon the Requisition of at least *five* of its Members—That as this is emphatically the Operatives' Cause, some Operative duly qualified, would be most suitable for the Office, and that he ought to be remunerated for his Services.

That the Secretaries of Branch Societies shall pay all Letters and Parcels sent by them to the Central or Local Committees. That the Local Committees shall give Notice of special or important Business in Writing to each Member. That due Notice shall be given to the Secretaries when any important proposition is to be made, but that no Resolution already sanctioned shall be nullified by this provision, and that every Branch Secretary shall keep up a regular communication with, and make known all important circumstances to the Secretary of Correspondence.

That it will be advisable either to solicit Lord Ashley to start the Ten Hour Bill in the House of Commons early in the next Session, or to avail ourselves of Lord Kenyon's proffered aid in the House of Lords—but that when the Societies, as a body, have given pledge of their support to any Patron of the Bill, it shall be upon the express condition that such Patron shall engage not to diverge from the course originally marked out, without the consent of the Societies.

That being deeply sensible of the inefficacy of all Human Exertions without the Divine Aid and blessing, it is earnestly recommended that Periodical Meetings be held, solemnly to petition the Throne of Grace for that Justice and that Help which has been hitherto refused to the Youth of the Factory Districts, by covetous, unreasonable, and interested Men.

THE FOLLOWING STATEMENT OF PRINCIPLES WAS SANCTIONED BY THE MEETING.

" That we expect and *demand* in a Country which professedly submits to the Laws of the Divine Redeemer of Mankind, the fulfilment of his *Golden Rule*—

'*Whatsoever ye would that men should do to you do ye even so to them !* '

and that with an especial reference to those who are peculiarly unable to help and defend themelves.

We demand Equal Laws both as respects protection and punishment, and without regard to poverty or wealth. And whereas *Young Persons of Property* are protected against the Usurer, and in some cases against their own parents, up to 21 years, so we demand that the Law should protect *the Children and Youth of the Productive and Industrious Classes* from rapacity, cruelty and imposition, by reason of demoralizing, destructive, and protracted *labour* during *their* minority, or up to 21 years.

We are fully assured that no System of Trade or Commerce can prosper without the blessing of the most High God, and equally certain that he never will smile upon that System, or that Country, which (in allusion to the present Factory System, even under Lord Althorpe's Act,) deprives his accountable Creatures, in the Morning of Life especially, of TIME to learn their Duty to God and their Neighbour—a System which in many cases destroys, curtails, or embitters their Lives, and deprives them of the Enjoyment of that Rational Existence which Divine Goodness has been pleased to bestow.

ERRATA.
Page 3 line 8 for ' cases are' read 'a case is'   Page 4 line 2 for ' requested ' read ' required '
3   27   exceed   amount to   6   22 after ' of '   this
Page 6 line 22 after ' of ' read ' this '

Atkinson, Printer, Bridge Street, Bradford.

NATIONAL REGENERATION.

Which Letters contain a development of all the principles and all the views connected with this important contemplated change in the Manufacturing affairs of the country.

LONDON:

PUBLISHED AT 11, BOLT-COURT, FLEET-STREET;

AND MAY BE HAD OF ALL BOOKSELLERS.

1834.

London : Printed by William Cobbett,
Johnson's-court, Fleet-street.

NATIONAL REGENERATION.

MR. FITTON TO MR. FIELDEN.

Royton, Dec. 11, 1833.

My DEAR SIR,—In a conversation which I had about ten days ago with Mr. Milne and Mr. W. Taylor, I promised them to submit to you my opinions in writing on the subject of the national-regeneration scheme in which you are now engaged. A variety of circumstances, the detail of which could be of no possible interest to you, have hitherto prevented me fulfilling that promise. I am rather the more particular in stating this, as I observe that some of the Manchester papers are attacking your project, and I wish you distinctly to understand, that as my opinions were formed before, they cannot at all have been influenced by these attacks.

From this you will infer that I have a feeling against your project. I feel desirous, however, that you should know that I am as anxious as even you can be, to see some such arrangement as that contemplated by you carried into effect; but so strong, so decided is my opinion, of its utter impracticability in the present, or perhaps in any other condition of society, that I must candidly, but with the highest possible degree of respect, confess to you that I would rather not have seen your name connected with it.

In my mind the project is founded altogether on an erroneous idea of the great principles of human action. As far as my humble powers of observation have ever enabled me to form a judgment, the great incitements to exertion have been, primarily, the fear of want and secondarily, the hope of reward. These two motives, I take it, operating on every individual to a less or greater extent, produce that active spirit of competition so universally diffused through society. This is nothing but what you of course know quite as well as I, and perhaps you may tell me that the evils of this universal spirit of competition being so clear, it is your object, by means of this new arrangement, to check it. Your design in so doing would be laudable, that I readily grant, but I am also as fully satisfied of the entire inadequacy of your means to your proposed end. In order to effect that object, it would be necessary to get rid of individual selfishness, or to convince every individual that no advantage was to be obtained by it. One requires a much higher elevation of moral sentiment, and the other a much greater degree of understanding, than either now does, ever did, or, as I think, ever will, exist in the world. I am the more warranted in this opinion because your present project, although new in name and form, is not so in principle. It has been attempted, on a pretty large scale, in ancient times, and in other countries, and partially, in more modern times, even in our own country. The agrarian law of the Romans, the laws of Lycurgus, and some others, might be mentioned as instances of the former. The Utopia of Sir Thomas More, the Oceana of Harrington, and the attempted Millennium in the time of the Commonwealth, by at that time a powerful party in the state, may be cited as so many instances of the latter. All these furnish so many proofs of the positive inefficacy of any effort to subdue the spirit of individual selfishness, by arbitrary regulations, however plausibly devised, or by whatever authority supported. As to the idea of mankind becoming wiser, and consequently more liberal and disinterested, however agreeable it may be to the wild vagaries of the well-meaning, benevolent, but, as I think, mistaken Robert Owen, it is in my humble judgment one of those opinions which daily and hourly experience contradicts. You will see, therefore, that I have not the slightest hope of the cause in which you are engaged being successful.

You will perhaps say, that my opposition to your scheme is not very gracious, unless I could submit something better in its stead. I have nothing to submit but this : the party to which you

and I may be said to belong, have generally contended, that in proportion, as taxation has increased, the distress of the labouring classes has been augmented ; from which position we have necessarily adopted the conclusion that a great reduction of taxation was necessary, in order to effect their relief ; hence our consistency in favour of Reform as a means of reducing taxation. Now, my dear sir, I wish to submit to you whether the wisest course would not have been that of unitedly and steadily persevering to effect this object, instead of a part of our strength being wasted on a project which I cannot but believe, that you yourself regard as being of very questionable practicability. If, after having effected this object, any arbitrary regulations. for the restraint of human labour should appear to be necessary, the subject could then be considered more freed from complexity, and with much less prejudice than it can be now. Though even in that case, if any thing was to be done, what it might be, is a question surrounded with so many matters for consideration, arising from the amount of population, the demand for labour, the quantity and kind of money in circulation, &c. &c., that at present it is quite impossible rationally to discuss it.

I have now taken the liberty of freely and candidly stating to you my opinions on this subject. Had I not known that your mind was so well and liberally constituted as it is, I might not, in all probability, have been quite so unreserved ; I do know, however, that you would at all times much rather any person who differs in opinion with you, would frankly state that difference, than keep it concealed ; and I know, therefore, that I shall not suffer in your estimation in consequence of the plainness with which I have now expressed myself. If, in the course of the foregoing remarks, any expression should have dropped from me at all calculated to hurt your feelings, I sincerely beg you to ascribe it to inadvertence and not to intention ; for I can truly assure you, although I differ so decidedly with you on this particular subject, that no one has a higher opinion of your judgment in general, nor of the universal feeling of benevolence which actuates the whole of your conduct. Believe me to be, my dear Sir, most respectfully,

W. FITTON.

MR. FIELDEN'S ANSWER.

MY DEAR SIR,—Your excellent letter of the 11. I received on the 14. instant, and I embrace the first opportunity I have since had of replying to it.

Knowing that it is not your practice to adopt opinions on trust, nor to sanction proceedings emanating from any quarter, without being first thoroughly convinced of the truth of the one, and of the propriety and practicability of the other, I feel no surprise that the measures recommended by the National Regeneration Society, of which I am proud tó be a member, should have called forth the objections so ably set forth in your letter.

The proposal submitted to the productive classes, recommending them to lessen their productions, in some articles one-third, in order that they may improve their condition, is so novel and unprecedented in its character, and at first appears so much opposed to accomplish its end, that I should have felt some astonishment if it had not called forth the opposition of thinking men, who are not in possession of the facts which demonstrate the necessity there is for the productive classes to adopt such a course ; so far, therefore, from feeling any uneasiness at your conduct in condemning the proposed plan of eight hours' work for the present full day's wages, I feel grateful for the opportunity you have given me of defending the measure, and answering your objections.

You denounce the plan as utterly impracticable, it being founded on an erroneous idea of the great principles of human action; which principles, you say, cause incitements to exertion — primarily, from the *fear of want*, and, secondarily, from the *hope of reward*. These two motives operating on every individual, produce competition, so universally diffused through society. You admit the design to check competition to be laudable, but the means proposed are inadequate to the end ; to effect it, you say it is necessary to get rid of individual selfishness, or to convince every individual that no advantage is to be obtained by it ; that to do one requires a higher degree of moral sentiment, and the other a much greater degree of understanding, than either does, or ever will, exist in the world.

Now, my dear sir, I infer, that the prevalence of this fear of want, of this hope of reward, and of this individual selfishness, constitute in your mind the great obstacles to the practicability of the plan of " eight hours' work for the present full day's wages ;" and if I can show that the fear of want would be abated, the hope of reward strengthened, and individual selfishness gratified by the general adoption of the plan among the productive classes, your reasons for assuming it to be impracticable will lose their force. By this course, too, we shall avoid going to the question, whether projects similar in principle have been before tried and failed, either in ancient or modern times ; and which question, I think, may with propriety be dismissed, because no such attempts have ever been made by any people having the powers of production which this country possesses ; and we are in many other respects very differently circumstanced, so much so, that the times when such failures took place, bear no analogy to the present times, and consequently this reasoning, applicable in one case, would be altogether inapplicable in the other.

I agree with you that a reduction of taxation to the extent the people are justly entitled to, would be a cure for the sufferings under which they groan. Since, however, the Reformed Parliament has disappointed the productive classes of the hopes they cherished, that such a reduction would be made, the safety of society requires that they should, by a plan of mutual protection, upon the principle recommended by the National Regeneration Society, endeavour to lessen its pressure on those who produce, and thereby cause it to fall with greater weight on those who do not produce. And such a course would, in my opinion, not divide the people in their efforts to get a reduction of taxes, but its tendency would be in exactly the opposite direction.

Having thus briefly adverted to the principal points in your letter, I will now endeavour to show, that the regulation of "eight hours' work for the present full day's wages," proposed for adoption by the National Regeneration Society, would be advantageous to the productive classes, both masters and workmen, and that they possess the power of legally and peaceably carrying it into effect.

In agricultural labour, in the dockyards, and the public works, and I believe in many other branches of manual labour, the average time of work, the year round, does not now exceed forty-eight hours per week ; and, therefore, no alteration of the time of labour for those so employed is suggested. It is in our manufacturing establishments, where the time for labour is fixed and determined by the master, in opposition to the wishes of the work-people, that the grievance arising from long confinement and excessive toil, is the most loudly complained of, and if a corrective be applied to this, it will soon extend its beneficial influence to all other trades and occupations ; the persons engaged in which will, for their own protection, adopt such regulations as the alterations of the time of work in our manufactories may render necessary. For the sake of distinctness, and without any departure from the principle, "that eight hours' labour per day is enough for any human being," I will confine my observations to the bearing the plan would have on those engaged in the manufacture of wool, of silk, of cotton, and of flax—the four branches of industry embraced in the Factory Bill of last session ; all which branches have undergone a similar increase per cent. or nearly so, since 1815, the close of the war ; and as a natural consequence, the employers and employed, in these branches of manufacture, taking a series of years, must have been in a similar position as respects profits and wages. From official returns now before me I find that in cotton imported, and entered for home consumption, and on which duty was paid, there was in the six years, beginning with 1826 and ending with 1831, an increase of 42 per cent., as compared with the six years, beginning with 1820 and ending with 1825. In flax for the same periods, the increase was $38\frac{8}{10}$ per cent.; and in silk for the like periods, the increase was $34\frac{1}{2}$ per cent. Wool, used in manufacture, being in part an article of home production, its consumption cannot be obtained with the same accuracy : but the import of wool, entered for home consumption for the same periods, shows an increase of 30 per cent. : and as the pressure arising from increased taxation in *things* must have operated pretty nearly equally on all these branches of industry, urging on those engaged in them to a corresponding increase of production, there can be no rational doubt as to their being relatively circumstanced, taking a series of years with regard to profits and wages.

Believing this to be true, I shall now show what have been the effects of this increase of production on those engaged in the cotton trade, the business with which I am conversant, and in articles which are a fair criterion of the state of the trade, and of which I have been a manufacturer myself ; and I shall show that the effects of the increase of production have not been such as to abate the fear of want, encourage the hope of reward, or gratify *laudable* individual selfishness, but to increase the fear, disappoint the hope, and prevent the gratification ; and that the manufacturers, if they would secure for themselves and their work-people better profits and better wages, better education and more enjoyment, must retrace their steps, lessen the supply of their productions, and adopt the regulation proposed.

To illustrate the truth of what I have advanced, by figures and facts which I know to be correct, or as nearly so as the case admits of being made out, I beg, sir, to call your attention to the following tables :

TABLE No. I.

An Account of the Cost, &c. of one piece of third 74s Calico, from 1815 *to* 1832 *inclusive.*

REFERENCES TO THE COLUMNS IN THE TABLE.

No. 1. Shows the number of lbs. weight of cotton required to make a piece of third 74*s* calico.

2. The average price of the cotton per pound in each year.

3. The average cost of cotton required to make one piece in each year.

4. The average price of such calico in the Manchester market.

5. The average sum the manufacturer had for labour, expenses, and profit, in every year, from 1815 to 1832, both years inclusive.

6. The sum per cent. less the manufacturer had for labour, expenses, and profit in each year than he had in 1815, the close of the war.

7. The sum per cent. more the manufacturer had in 1815, for labour, expenses, and profit, than in each succeeding year respectively.

8. The sum the manufacturer would require for one piece of such calico for labour, expenses, and profit, when 50 per cent. is added to what he had in 1832, to give him and his work-people the same sum of money to cover the increased cost of production that would accrue from a diminution of one-third of the quantity manufactured.

9. The sum the manufacturer had for labour, expenses, and profit, in 1824, when the quantity manufactured was one-third less than in 1832.

10. The sum per piece, and per cent., the manufacturer would gain by reducing his production one-third, after allowing 50 per cent. more than he had in 1832, for labour, expenses, and profit, when he again obtains, as he would do on the diminished production, the sum he had in 1824, for labour, expenses, and profit.

11. The number of pieces of third 74*s*, the money price of which would buy 300lbs. of upland cotton at the average price it sold for in each year, exclusive of duty.

12. The number of pieces a fixed income of 3*l.* would buy in every year from 1815 to 1832.

13. Average price of a quarter of wheat and a quarter of oats in each year, from official returns.

14. Wages paid to the hand-loom weaver for weaving one piece of third 74*s* calico.

Year.	1	2	3		4		5		6	7	8	9	10	11	12	13				14	
									Less per cent.	More per cent.				Pcs.	Pcs.	Wheat per qr.		Oats per qr.		Hand-loom Weaving per piece.	
	lbs.	d.	s.	d.	s.	d.	s.	d.								s.	d.	s.	d	s.	d.
1815	4 3/10	19½	7	0	18	0	11	0						24	3⅓	63	8	22	11	4	6
1816	4do	18½	6	7½	16	0	9	4½	14¾	17				25½	3⅔	76	2	22	6		
1817	4do	20	7	2	15	3	8	1	26½	36				29	4	94	0	31	6		
1818	4do	20	7	2	16	0	8	10	19¾	24				28	3⅔	83	8	31	6		
1819	4do	13½	4	10	13	0	9	2	16¾	20				24½	4⅔	72	3	27	4		
1820	4do	12	4	3	11	6	7	3	34	51				24½	5⅓	65	10	23	6		
1821	4do	9 7/16	3	4½	10	6	7	1½	35¼	53				21½	5⅔	54	5	18	11		
1822	4do	8⅛	2	11	10	0	7	1	35½	55				19	6	43	3	17	7		
1823	4do	8 3/16	2	11	9	6	6	7	41¼	67				20¼	6⅓	51	9	22	3		
1824	4do	8½	3	0	9	0	6	0	45½	83				22¼	6⅔	62	0	24	1	2	3
1825	4do	12¼	4	4½	9	9	5	4½	51	104				29½	6	66	6	24	11		
1826	4do	6¾	2	5	7	2	4	9	56¾	131				22	8⅓	56	11	25	11		
1827	4do	6¼	2	3	6	5	4	2	62¼	164				22¾	9⅓	56	9	27	4		
1828	4do	6⅛	2	2½	6	3	4	0½	63¼	172				23	9⅔	60	5	22	6		
1829	4do	5⅝	2	0	5	7	3	7	67½	206			Per pie.	23½	10⅔	66	3	22	9		
1830	4do	6⅝	2	4½	6	3	3	10½	65	183			1*s.* 2¼*d.*,	25	9⅔	64	3	24	5		
1831	4do	5⅝	2	0	5	9	3	9	66	193			or per cent	22¾	10⅛	66	0	25	4		
1832	4do	6⅜	2	3½	5	6	3	2½	71¾	242	4 9¾	6 0	24½	26	10⅔	61	0	24	0	1	6
													18)	433							
														24	pieces, average of 18 yrs						

TABLE No. II.

72s Calico made by Power Loom.

Year.	1 lbs. of cotton for one piece.	2 Price of cotton per lb.	3 Cost of cotton for one piece.		4 Value of one piece.		5 Sum for labour, expens. & profit.		6 Less per cent. than in 1815.	7 More per cent. in 1815.	Sum for labour, expenses, and profit, when 50 per cent. is added to the sum received in 1832.		Sum for labour, expenses, and profit in 1824, when one-third less was done than in 1832.		Gain to the manufacturer by working 8 hours instead of 12 hours per day.
		d.	*s.*	*d.*	*s.*	*d.*	*s.*	*d.*							
1815	$5\frac{1}{3}$	$19\frac{1}{2}$	8	8	27	0	18	4							Per piece
1824	$5\frac{1}{3}$	$8\frac{1}{2}$	3	9	13	6	9	9	$46\frac{3}{4}$	89					1*s.* $7\frac{1}{2}$*d.*,
1831	$5\frac{1}{3}$	$5\frac{5}{8}$	2	6	8	3	5	9	$68\frac{1}{2}$	218	*s.*	*d.*	*s.*	*d.*	or per
1832	$5\frac{1}{3}$	$6\frac{3}{8}$	2	10	8	3	5	5	$70\frac{1}{2}$	238	8	$1\frac{1}{2}$	9	9	cent. 20.

HALF-ELL VELVETEENS—20 lbs. Weight.

		d.	*s.*	*d.*	*s.*	*d.*	*s.*	*d.*							
1815	$21\frac{1}{8}$	$19\frac{1}{2}$	34	8	100	0	65	4							Per piece
1824	$21\frac{1}{8}$	$8\frac{1}{2}$	15	7	51	8	36	1	$44\frac{3}{4}$	81					8*s.* 1*d*,
1831	$21\frac{1}{8}$	$5\frac{5}{8}$	10	0	33	4	23	4	63	180	*s.*	*d.*	*s.*	*d.*	or per
1832	$21\frac{1}{8}$	$6\frac{3}{8}$	11	4	30	0	18	8	$71\frac{1}{2}$	250	28	0	36	1	cent. $28\frac{3}{4}$

30 HANKS WATER TWIST.

	Cotton required for 1lb. twist.	Price of cotton per lb.	Cost of cotton for 1lb. twist.		Value of 1lb. of twist.		Sum for labour, expens. & profit,		*Less* per cent. than in 1815.	*More* per cent. in 1815.					
		d.	*s.*	*d.*	*s.*	*d.*	*s.*	*d.*							
1815	$1\frac{1}{7}$	$19\frac{1}{2}$	1	$10\frac{1}{4}$	3	3	1	$4\frac{3}{4}$							Per lb.
1824	$1\frac{1}{7}$	$8\frac{1}{2}$	0	$9\frac{3}{4}$	1	8	0	$10\frac{1}{4}$	$38\frac{3}{4}$	65					$2\frac{3}{8}$, or
1831	$1\frac{1}{7}$	$5\frac{5}{8}$	0	$6\frac{1}{2}$	1	0	0	$5\frac{1}{2}$	67	204	*s.*	*d.*	*s.*	*d.*	per cent.
1832	$1\frac{1}{7}$	$6\frac{3}{8}$	0	$7\frac{1}{4}$	1	$0\frac{1}{2}$	0	$5\frac{1}{4}$	$68\frac{1}{2}$	219	0	$7\frac{7}{8}$	0	$10\frac{1}{4}$	30

TABLE No. III.

An account of the number of Bags of Cotton (of 300lbs. each) consumed per week in the years 1815, 1824, 1831, and 1832, and the sum per annum the manufacturer had for labour, expenses, and profit, supposing the whole of the Cotton consumed in each year respectively had been worked up into any of the four leading articles of manufacture in the Cotton trade, referred to in this account, and the sum he would have had for working up the whole of the Cotton consumed, into these four leading articles in equal proportions.

Four Leading Articles of Cotton Manufacture.	6500 Bags per week in 1815.	11,500 Bags per week in 1824.	16,300 Bags per week in 1831.	17,300 Bags per week in 1832.
Third 74s Calico	13,070,700	12,483,250	11,098,262	10,542,188
Power Loom 72s Calico	17,334,540	16,250,650	13,619,873	13,612,073
Half-ell Velveteen	15,439,500	15,273,916	13,817,645	11,722,913
Water Twist, 30 hanks per lb.......	6,186,375	6,727,500	5,165,062	5,130,531
4)	52,031,115	50,735,316	43,700,842	41,007,705
Average of the four articles worked up in equal proportions..........	13,007,778	12,683,829	10,925,210	10,251,926
Sum for working up 6500 Bags in each year..........................	13,007,778	7,169,120	4,356,678	3,851,301
Decline per Cent. from 1815		44	66	70½
Sum per Cent. *more* in 1815 than in each succeeding year referred to..		81	196	237
Sum which would have been received for the quantities worked up at the rate paid in 1815	13,007,778	23,013,761	32,311,812	34,620,701

TABLE No. IV.

Account of the number of pounds of cotton that would be required to make one piece of the three first articles, and one pound weight of the last, of these four leading articles in the cotton trade; the price of cotton per lb. duty paid; the cost of cotton for one of each articles; the sum the manufacturer would require for labour, expenses, and profit, on each article, for producing one-third less, to obtain the same sum of money he did in 1832; the value of each article when such sum is allowed; and the number of each articles (say the same as the last eighteen years) that the cotton-grower would get for 300lbs. of upland cotton, cotton and goods being at the prices in the Table.

	lbs. of cotton for one article.	Price of cotton per lb., duty paid.	Cost of cotton for one of each articles.		Sum for labour, expenses, and profit.		Value of each article.		Number of any of these articles the cotton-grower would get for 300lbs. of upland cotton.
	lbs.	d.	s.	d.	s.	d.	s.	d.	
Third seventy-four calico	4 3/10	7½	2	8¼	4	9¾	7	6	24
Power-loom seventy-two calico ..	5⅓	7½	3	4	8	1½	11	5½	15⅔
Half-ell velveteen 20lbs. weight ..	21⅓	7½	13	4	28	0	41	4	4⅓
Water-twist 30 hanks per lb.	1 1/7	7½	0	8½	0	7⅞	1	4⅜	131

These tables present a history of the works of those engaged in the cotton trade, for the eighteen years ending 1832; and I have no hesitation in saying, that history presents no parallel to a like increase of production, or to a like increase in the taking away from the producers, for the use of those who do not produce. Industry is deprived of its just reward, and in the midst of unexampled plenty, those who labour and toil, and that more effectually than any other people, are not allowed to have what is necessary to supply their wants. The fear of want increases, the hope of reward is blighted, and laudable individual selfishness is disappointed, amongst those who toil in more than the ratio of increase of production; in fact, the harder they labour, the more they produce, the less they have.

Whether we look to the products of manual labour, as instanced in the case of the hand-loom weaver, or of manual labour aided by the most improved machinery employed in the cotton trade, we find that, for a nearly three-fold quantity produced in 1832, the manufacturers and their work-people had a much less command over the first necessary of life, than they had in 1815, for little more than one-third of the quantity. Truly, it may be said, we labour for that which is not bread, and spend our strength for nought; while those who tax us, and those who live on fixed-money incomes, get an additional increase of the fruits of our labour, more than correspondent with the increase of our production, and for which we receive no equivalent whatever. And can this course of proceeding continue? No, it cannot. The manufacturers cannot go on in this course much further, however disposed they might be to do so : seventy parts out of one hundred, constituting the whole for labour, expenses, and profits, have departed, between 1815 and 1832, both years inclusive, and many parts more will be found to have fled in 1833; and there is no possibility of preventing the mass engaged in this business from being involved in one common ruin, unless they retrace their steps. They are contending against nature. Providence designed that the gifts she has bestowed on man, for increasing his supply of the necessaries and comforts of life (by the invention and aid of machinery, or otherwise), should not be abused; and so surely as we take *improperly* from those who labour, and give it to those who do not labour, so surely will a day of retribution and vengeance overtake the oppressors.

The evils of our manufacturing system have long been complained of, and remedies proposed, which have, however, been disregarded by the manufacturers. Since I commenced writing this letter, I have received one from a respectable gentleman in Manchester, Mr. David Holt, who has been engaged in the trade upwards of forty years. His account of the misery and dissatisfaction existing in the minds of the work-people, effects of the unkind and improper conduct of many of the masters, is not, I believe, at all overcharged. I annex you a copy of his letter,* and I sincerely wish with him that the manufacturers would change their course, and observe the golden rule of doing unto others as they would like to be done unto; and, instead of making further reductions in wages, as I hear some have already done, and others intend doing, that they would shorten the time of labour, lessen their production, which would give better prices and better profits, and enable them to continue, at least, the present wages, and to restore satisfaction and contentment to their work-people.

If any arguments were wanting to show the necessity for, and the advantages to be derived from, the adoption of the regulation of " eight hours' work for the present full day's wages," the tables I have given indisputably furnish them.

In these tables, the cotton manufactured into the four leading articles referred to, is assumed to be American uplands, and the bags to weigh 300 lbs. each; and although there are many other sorts of cotton, the price of which,

* See Appendix, No. I.

and the weight of the bags of which, differ from what is here stated, and also many descriptions of cotton goods manufactured, besides the four sorts mentioned in the tables; yet, as those not mentioned bear a relative value to tho $\frac{5}{6}$ there mentioned, the argument to be deduced from these tables is not affected by the difference in these respects, of weight, of price, or of manufacture.

The number of bags of cotton consumed per week, is taken from the annual statements of the cotton-brokers, and the prices of cotton are the average prices I and my partners have paid for American uplands in each year. In reference to columns No. 5, tables 1 and 2, you will see, that in 1815, when the consumption of cotton was 6,500 bags per week, the manufacturer had for labour, expenses, and profit, 11s.,18s.4d.,65s.4d., and 1s. 4¾d. for each article respectively; in 1824, when the consumption was 11,500 bags per week, he had 6s., 9s. 9d., 36s., and 10¼d.; and in 1832, when the consumption was 17,300 bags per week, he had only 3s. 2½d., 5s. 5d., 18s. 8d. and 5¼d., for labour, expenses, and profits, on each of the said articles respectively. And table No. 3 shows, that taking the average of the four articles, and supposing the whole quantity of cotton consumed in the respective years to have been worked up into these four leading articles in the cotton trade, in equal proportions, the manufacturer had 44 per cent. less in 1824, and 70½ per cent. less in 1832, for the manufacturing of four of these articles than he had in 1815; and that for the whole quantity the cotton would make that was consumed in 1815, say 6,500 bags per week, he had 13,007,778l., whereas, in 1832, when the consumption of cotton was 17,000 bags per week, he had only 10,251,926l., although the latter quantity, if it had been paid for at the rate the manufacturer was paid in 1815, would have commanded 34,620,701l., that is, 237 per cent. more than the manufacturer got in 1832 !

When nearly three times the quantity manufactured in 1832, was paid for with less money by two millions three quarters at thirteen millions, than little more

than one third of the quantity commanded in 1815, and to manufacture which increased quantity in 1832, more than double the number of persons were employed, can you wonder, sir, at the strange anomaly of increased production being accompanied by increased and increasing distress among the manufacturers and their workmen? I am sure you cannot. No: let those who conduct the Whig press make good their assertions so often repeated, if they can, viz., that the productive classes in Lancashire have a greater command over the necessaries and comforts of life now, than they ever had at any former period. I should like to know in what they make the necessaries and comforts of life to consist; if they say, in cotton goods, and in cotton goods only, then they are right; for never, at any former period, could the workman buy so many of these articles with the wages he received as he can now; even the poor hand-loom weaver, whose destitute condition is admitted by all, could buy a greater proportion of the third 74s calico he wove up in 1832, than he could in 1815, although his wages were, as shown in column 14, table No. 1, 4s. 6d. per piece in 1815, and only 1s. 6d. in 1832.

But let us see what corn these manufacturers and their work-people could get in return for their labour. To show this, I have, from official returns, given in table No. 1, the average prices of wheat and oats in every year from 1815 to 1831, both years inclusive; and from the Mark-lane corn letter, the average prices of 1832. If you take the average of the first nine years, you will find the quarter of wheat to be 67s. 2d., and of oats, 24s. 2d.; and the average of the last nine years, you will find wheat to be 62s. 2d, and oats 24s. 7d.; while the average price the manufacturer had for labour, expenses, and profit, was 8s. 3d. per piece, in the first nine years, and only 4s. 3d. in the last nine years to which the table refers. The manufacturer, therefore, has had to make, during the latter nine years, very nearly two pieces for the same quantity of wheat, and more than two pieces for the same quantity of oats, that the manufacture of one piece would procure for him in the first nine years to which the table refers; and if we take the two first years, 1815 and 1816, and the two last years, 1831 and 1832, we find the price of wheat to have been nearly as high, and the price of oats full as high, in the latter two years as in the first two years; while the sum the manufacturers had for manufacturing one piece, the first two years, was 10s. 2d., and in the last two years, 1831 and 1832, only 3s. 6d.: so that in the last two years, the manufacturer had to make very nearly three pieces, for the same quantity of wheat that he could get for making one piece, in the first two years.

Look here, sir, what manifest injustice the manufacturers inflict upon themselves and their work-people, by deteriorating the value of their labour, through over-production, which has sunk its relative value nearly two-thirds in eighteen years, as compared with the first necessary of life, and in the purchase of which pretty nearly three-fourths of the working people's wages must be expended. And what folly it is to make our manufactures so cheap, that those who make them cannot live by their labour, but have, in thousands of instances, to submit to the degradation of seeking relief from the parish, and that, too, when they are in full employment.

I shall be told, sir, that this reasoning makes out a strong case for the repeal of the Corn Bill. I admit it; but such repeal ought to be preceded by a large reduction of taxes; and, if the landed interest will not cause such reduction of taxes to be made, they must have the Corn Bill wrested from them, and take the consequences. The taxes press so severely on those engaged in agriculture, that notwithstanding they get the little clothing they can purchase so much cheaper, all the evidence taken on the subject tends to show that they are in a condition which it is frightful to contemplate. They give at least three quarters of wheat for the same amount of taxes, that could be paid with two quarters during the war; and this, with

corn at the present price, I do not believe they can do much longer.

But how do the taxes affect the manufacturer, with his increase of production? This is shown in table No. 1, column 12, in which you will see, that all living upon fixed-money incomes, have experienced a progressive increase in the command a given sum of money has afforded them over manufactured articles since 1815; that 3l., at that period, would only buy 3⅓ pieces, whereas, in 1832, the same sum would purchase 10⅔ pieces, an increase of 220 per cent. drained out of the labour of the manufacturer. For though the cotton, to make these pieces of, was lower in money price in 1832 than in 1815, yet it did not cost the manufacturer less in reality; for, in 1815, he got 300 lbs. of cotton, exclusive of duty, for 24 pieces of calico, and that was just the average number of pieces paid for 300 lbs. of cotton, during the whole eighteen years, table No. 1 embraces, as shown in column No. 11: for the cotton, exclusive of duty, that would make 70 pieces of these calicoes, the manufacturer has, during the whole time, given an average of 24 pieces.

Now, sir, what has the owner of vested interests, as they are called, done to merit this increase of from 3⅓ pieces to 10⅔ pieces, for an annuity of three pounds; while there are hundreds of thousands of weavers in the kingdom, toiling and sweating all the day long, whose command over wheat and oats in return for their labour, has been reduced in the proportion of nearly 10 to 3? This is an important question, and one deserving of the attention of all who are interested in the security of property, and the safety and well-being of society. The owners of *fixed*-money incomes, however, could have no right to complain of the manufactures, if they reduced their manufactures two-thirds, instead of one-third, as is proposed by the Regenerating Society, and thus make their labour of the relative value it bore to money in 1815, the close of the war, and since which time no loans have been contracted by Government. But the reduction of time of labour to eight hours per day, would not place the owner of vested interests in a worse position than that in which he stood in 1824, with regard to his command over manufactures; that is, as you will see in table No. 1, column 11, year 1824, he would get at least 6⅔ pieces, just double 3⅓ pieces he had in 1815; and, on the supposition too, that the price of cotton should exceed 8d. per lb., and the sum for labour, expenses, and profit, for one piece, should be 6s., the same as both were in 1824. But as cotton, if the new regulation be adopted, would certainly fall to the prices of 1832, and may fall much lower, you will see, that with 2s. 3½d. for cotton (its price in 1832), for one piece, and 4s. 9¾d. for labour, expenses, and profit, as put down in column 8, say 3s. 2½d., and half that sum (or 50 per cent. added, to give the same money for two-thirds, as is now obtained for the whole quantity produced), the price of the piece would then only be 7s. 1¾d ; whereas, in 1824, it was 9s., and gave the manufacturer 6s., as shown in column 9, for labour, expenses, and profit. This 6s., when it is again obtained (and I have every reason to suppose it would be), would give the manufacturer 1s. 2¼d. per piece, or 24½ per cent., as put down in column 10, table No. 1, more than he now gets, besides the 50 per cent. for the increased cost of production, to give him the same money for making two-thirds of the quantity as he now has for making the whole; and the price of the calico would then be 8s. 3d. instead of 9s., as in 1824.

In like manner I have shown in table No. 2, that the manufacturer would get 1s. 7½d. per piece more, for 72s calico made by power-looms; 8s. 1d. per piece more for half-ell velveteens; and 2⅜d. per lb. more for thirty hanks water twist.

As the price of cotton, in 1832, would be too low to command twenty-four pieces for every 300lbs. of cotton, and which proportion it will ultimately command (although some years may be required to effect it, and during which time the manufacturer would have the advantage in his favour), I have shown in table No. 4, what would be the price and cost of cotton for each article, the value of each article, and the sum for labour, expenses, and profit, to give the manufacturer the same sum of money for making two-thirds the quantity, as, in 1832 he had for the whole, and the cotton grower, the average number of articles of manufacture for 300 lbs. of cotton, he has had the last eighteen years, which, by lessening his supply (as has been before observed), he will get, and then the two parties will effect an exchange of their commodities, as beneficially as they have done before. The table No. 4 shows the price of cotton at 7½d per lb., which is about its present price, and the value of a third seventy-four calico at 7s. 6d., which leaves 4s. 9¾d. for labour, expenses, and profit; but though 7½d., or perhaps a little more, is the present price of cotton, the present price of the calico is only about 6s. and consequently a rise of 25 per cent would take place, as I have lately stated in a letter to Mr. Cobbett, which letter he published in the Register.

After 50 per cent. is added for labour, expenses, and profit, and with cotton at its present price, the manufacturer will get as much corn for the lesser quantity, as he did for the larger, and forty pieces of his own manufacture, where he now gets fifty-two pieces. But three-fourths, at least, of the poor man's earnings are laid out in food, and only one-fourth in clothing, and he would consequently get a relief from toil to the amount of one-third without suffering any material diminution in his comforts as regards his command over both food and clothing, and if he chooses to employ a part of the time he will thus have left for his own use, he may make himself more comfortable than it was possible for him to be before the change proposed. His productions are so excessive, that they are now too cheap compared with other things. The hand-loom weaver is in the destitute condition I have described; and the workman manufacturing by machinery is following close on the heels of the hand-loom weaver; his work has been

14

made much harder, and his wages have been considerably reduced, since 1815; and though he can now, with his present wages, get more of the articles he makes than he could in 1815, his wages will not buy him any where near so much wheat or oats, as his wages in 1815 would.

The fact is, the manufacturers in the cotton trade (and those in flax, silk, and woollen, if not as bad, yet must be approximating to this state), have made their manufactures so plentiful by the increase of machinery, and the additional labour which they exact from their hands by the increased speed of the machinery,* that their productions *stink* in the nostrils of all to whom they are offered; and though the manufacturers are, again and again, told by their customers, that their productions are too abundant to secure a good profit, and by the economists, that the distress they so often complain of, is the result of manufacturing too much, yet, strange to say, there is the greatest unwillingness to do less, or to make their business respectable, and their work-people comfortable, by making the supply of their manufactures so limited, as not to exceed the demand.

Nothing could be more easy than this, if a good understanding were cultivated between the employers and the employed; if the masters would agree, and act upon a plan of mutual protection, instead of playing against each other at "beggar my neighbour," and also agree that the wages of their workmen should be liberal, and their time of labour moderate, say not more than forty-eight hours per week, they would find themselves all the happier from pursuing this course, and, I will add (what most seek after), all the richer too. Then there would be no occasion for factory bills, inspectors, millwardens, relays of children, and all the degrading restraints which overworking, tyranny, and oppression, engender, and which debase man, constituted lord over the creation, below the level of the brute.

* See Appendix, No. 2.

What a contemptible figure do the manufacturers cut, in the estimation of all thinking men! See them disputing with each other, what sort of a bill to restrict their liberties should be sanctioned by Parliament, and who best understands what number of hours, out of the twenty-four, is the proper number for their hands to work; and declaring that the hands (who certainly are the best judges of this matter) do not know any thing at all about it, nor what is for their good: moreover, every nation where manufacture is carried on is visited, and inquiries made, whether the hours of work are longer, or whether the screw is tightened more, in other countries, than it is in England, as if for the purpose of making the English the greatest slaves in the world.

And this, it is said, in effect is necessary, otherwise we shall lose our foreign trade. Better would it be to lose our foreign trade, and even to forbid the exercise of any mechanic art whatever, as was the case with the Spartans in the days of Lycurgus, than that those employed in factories should continue to be the slaves they now are. Would to God these factory gentlemen would look at home, and see how they have more than three articles of their manufacture taken from them now to pay the Jews, when, in 1815, they paid only one such article; and, as a consequence of the increased exaction for the Jews, made upon those who cultivate the land, the manufacturers have also three pieces of their manufacture to pay for corn, where they should only pay one piece. Much better would it be for the manufacturers (and it is their duty) to turn their attention and put a stop to such unjust and iniquitous exactions, from the productive classes of society. In doing this, their time and their talents might be much better employed, than in promoting factory regulation bills, that shall enable those, who are unfeeling enough, to extend the labour of their adult work-people to sixteen hours a day, as the bill passed in the last session of Parliament does; and, if I mistake not, such was the design of the contrivers of

y one looking to see what those
are, will find a considerable
ion consists of things scarcely
by the productive classes em-
in manufactures; and may be
among the useless things not
ur working for; and many more
ings come from other foreign
e trade with; and as regards
money to foreigners since 1815,
nish bonds, the Portuguese,
Prussian, Mexican, Brazilian,
enos-Ayrean loans, not to men-
er, will be quite sufficient. The
f money thus lent are said to
to upwards of 100 millions
! And for depreciation of
y, and alterations, against this
in the exchanges, I need only
Brazil, Buenos Ayres, and
tinople, to show the losses that
en sustained from such causes.
il, the currency has been so de-
y the substitution of paper mo-
d copper, for gold and silver
at the milrea, which at par of
e is 67½, would a few years
y remit 18d. from Rio Janeiro,
nt, 40d. is the rate of exchange
ence; but at Bahia, the present
e is only 30d. per milrea. At
Ayres, from the depreciation of
and other causes, the exchange,
was a few years ago at 44d., is
duced to 7d. per dollar; and at
tinople, fourteen piastres would
remit 1l. sterling, which nine-
iastres will now only remit.
my dear sir, what part of the
rments, two pieces, and two
of twist, the manufacturer now
ut of every three such things
d, by pursuing a system of fo-
ade, so objectionable as that I
t described, I will not stop to
because, I think such traffic
ievous, and is the consequence
sed production, unaccompanied
sponding means of a like in-
f consumption among the pro-
classes at home; or, in other
y taking improperly from those
our, and giving to those who
abour, and, when this ceases,
ectionable traffic will also cease;

and its continuance only shows our
folly, and exposes the cruelty of making
the work-people in our manufactories,
work immoderate hours for so worthless
an object.

If we inquire into foreign trade, deserving of regard, and worthy of our
encouragement; that is, the exchange
or barter (which it resolves itself into,
though effected by money) of those useful things of which we have too much,
and the foreigner too little, for those
other useful things of which the foreigner has too much, and we too little, we shall find that the quantities of
each have been nearly the same during
the last eighteen years, to which the
tables refer; and that instead of giving
them three pieces now, as Mr. Freetrader says, for *one* we gave in 1815,
there has been a uniformity preserved
in the relative value of these articles,
such as those who have not looked into
the case have little conception of; and
it shows that the relative value of these
things (years of scarcity and abundance excepted) remains unchanged, and
this foreign trade would be carried on
to any extent we may require, after
eight hours' work for the present full
day's wages, has been adopted: for
none of our foreign rivals have the
power to prevent it, as the principle of
exchange or barter applies to them as
well as to us, and will be observed after
we have made the reduction proposed
in the quantity of our manufactures,
that is for instance, for every 300 lbs.
of cotton we shall have to give twenty-
four pieces of seventy-four calico, or
15 3 pieces of seventy-two power-loom
calico, or 4⅓ pieces of half-ell velveteens, or 131 lbs. of water twist, or
some other things of the same value,
as we have done the last eighteen years;
and any other country which requires
this cotton must do the same as they
have done, or otherwise they could
not have had it during the same period; for no one country ever did, or
ever will favour another country in
this respect; and when the supply of
things is at any time too abundant
from one country, to secure an exchange equal to their intrinsic or

it.* Was it for the purpose of increasing the income of the Jews?

"Oh! no," says the supporter of
vested rights, "it was for no such pur-
"pose, there was no such design. It
"was to promote our foreign trade.
"America, France, Switzerland, and
"other countries, are now our formi-
"dable competitors, and unless we can
"produce cheaper than they, we shall
"lose the trade, and our country will
"be ruined." This appears so plausible to the manufacturers, that they
follow up the cry, and by excessive
production, commit a suicidal act, to
support the avarice of the Jews.

These factory gentlemen might not
be aware, that the competitors they
dread would try to imitate us in every
species of tyranny we may adopt, rather
than abandon their manufacturing pursuits; and that they have many advantages which we can never possess
while we continue the taxed people we
are. Look at America, with her freedom from debt, her high-protecting
tariff duties, her cheap food, and the
raw material at home; and at the continental manufacturers, with corn and
labour so much cheaper than in this
country, and then let these gentlemen
ask themselves, that, were it desirable,
which it is not, that we should force these
competitors out of the trade, is there
any rational ground for thinking that
we should be successful in any attempt
we may make to do so?

No; it cannot be: to secure a good
trade to the producers in this country,
the supply must be diminished, in order
to obtain profits; and to continue them,
the means of the productive classes at
home must be increased, in a ratio
correspondent with any augmentation
that may be made in production. This
would place the people of this country
in a state of independence and comfort,
such as can never be effected by any
increase or extension of trade with
foreigners; the tendency of which is
rather to destroy our independence than
to promote it.

Although the apprehended danger to
our foreign trade is not an objection

See Appendix, No. 3.

urged by you against the proposed regulation of "eight hours' work for
twelve hours' wages," yet as it is so
often and prominently put forward, you
will, I am sure, sir, excuse a few remarks on this point; and I might first
call on those who constantly join in
this cuckoo cry, to prove that the productive classes have benefited in any
way by the increase of foreign trade,
that has been going on the last eighteen
years: and if they will not forget that
the productive classes engaged in the
cotton trade got more by 237 per cent.
for manufacturing, in 1815, than they
got in 1832; and that the masters and
work-people together, the number of
whom must have been double in 1832,
to what it was in 1815 (and ought to
have been much more), and that the
larger number collectively had a much
less command over the necessaries and
comforts of life, for working up 17,300
bags of cotton a week, in 1832, than
the lesser number collectively had for
working up 6,500 bags a week in 1815;
if they do not forget this fact, they will
find such proof more difficult than they
are aware of; nay, they will find that it
cannot be given.

I might also ask them to inquire,
whether in 1824, the year in which the
consumption of cotton was 11,500 bags
a week, about what it would be again
if the eight hours' regulation be adopted,
and which year, although so often
boasted of, as a year of great prosperity
by those who knew nothing about it,
was the worst year, to those engaged in
the cotton manufacture, of any year between 1814 and 1824, as reference to
the sum received for labour, expenses,
and profit in table No. 1, column 5,
will show. I might ask them, if in this
year 1824, or in any other year preceding it, the foreign trade was not
better than it has ever been since, and
if the manufacturer had not better profits, the work-people better wages, and
the merchants exporting goods more
satisfactory orders, and more certain
and better returns, and for want of
which since, many respectable merchants have been reduced to bank-
ruptcy and ruin, many more have

quitted business, and the manufacturers have had to add to their own business that of a merchant, with a view to make out of both the profit they previously had on manufacturing *only*, and in securing which they have completely failed. I might ask them all this, and the answer would be in the affirmative.

I might ask them further, to show me, if they could, that as we had a better foreign trade, a better home trade, better wages for the work-people, better profits for their employers, and much more satisfaction to both, when we worked up two-thirds of the quantity of cotton we do now; I might ask them to show me, why we should not have these things again, if the time of labour in factories were reduced to eight hours a day, and the present full day's wages paid; and I challenge any of them, or any of those whose dupes the manufacturers are, to show me that such would not be the consequences, of carrying into effect the objects of the Regenerating Society.*

Foreign trade then, or no foreign trade, they have taken their eggs to a pretty market, at any rate; and seeing that their manufactures were of the same intrinsic value for the use of men in 1832, that they were in 1815, that they would make as many garments of the same sort, at one period as at the other, it would be well for them, while they are pursuing the inquiry, to put this question to themselves, who gets the two garments, two pieces, or two pounds of twist, which we now lose out of every three that we produce?

Methinks I hear some freetrader say, "The foreigner gets them to be sure, "and he'll have them too, if not from "us, our competitors in America, "France, and Switzerland, will give "them; they can produce them cheaper "than we can, because they have no "corn laws, and they have bread "cheaper and wages lower, and we "must either sell our goods as cheap as "our foreign rivals do, or we shall be "driven out of the market, our manu- "facturing population will be thrown "out of employment, the land cannot "keep them, and universal anarchy will "be the consequence."

Well then, Mr. Freetrader, I suppose, that to continue our foreign trade, and put a stop to our rival competitors abroad, and also to secure profits to our manufacturers, who say trade is in a *sound* and *healthy* state, but one and all of whom agree that there is an absence of profit, and that capital will leave the country unless profits be secured; to do this, I suppose, sir, we must work, all above eighteen years of age employed in factories, sixteen hours a day, in order that we may make the two garments, two pieces, and two pounds of twist, we now lose, and which, you say, the foreigner now gets, into three of these things, and by this course annihilate our foreign rivals at once, and thus place ourselves in the enviable situation of making the subjects of Great Britain manufacture all the clothing, that is necessary to supply the whole world. "Oh! no, no, no," says he, "we must have the corn laws off, "bread cheaper, and wages lower, and "then our foreign rivals will grow "corn, instead of going on with ma- "nufactures, and they wil give us *their* "corn in return for *our* manufactures, "and we shall never look behind us "again."

I am afraid this is something like the twaddle which is talked among the manufacturers, and by which their minds are blinded, and a view of their situation, utterly at variance with the truth, is entertained.

Now, let us see how the case stands. Foreign trade, deserving of our encouragement, consists in this country's exchanging its surplus produce or manufactures for such surplus produce or manufacture of any other country, as may be exchanged without endangering the safety and well-being of the productive classes in this country. But if the surplus wealth created by the industrious classes in this country, be exchanged or given away for foreign productions, of little or no value whatever to those who created the wealth (and a great many almost useless

* See Appendix, No. 4.

articles of luxury, imported into this country, in return for our manufactures, are of this description), no justification can be set up for continuing a system of over-working those who produce the wealth in this country, to foster and uphold a trade so pernicious as this.

And, on the other hand, to place ourselves in a state of dependance on foreigners for articles of the first necessity, such as corn, to the injury of the home grower, and without any permanent advantage to the manufacturer, who by such a course would only exchange his home customer for a foreign customer; and as the former is more certain, and in every sense more to be relied on than the latter, to distress those engaged in agriculture and manufactures in this country, by an increase of such foreign trade to accomplish such an object, is to be guilty of the grossest folly imaginable. Look at the situation, this country is now in, as stated by Mr. Jacob, in his evidence before the Committee on Agriculture in the last session,* and I am sure, you will require nothing more to convince you of the imminent danger to be apprehended, by placing ourselves in a state of dependance on foreigners for supply of corn, instead of encouraging and securing a sufficient supply at home.

Besides the two objectionable branches of foreign trade I have alluded to, there is another altogether unworthy of our pursuit, and which is the result of excessive supply of the articles we produce; I mean what is paid for with money borrowed by foreigners from capitalists (as they are called) in this country, or foreign loans. The people of this country have first to work hard to raise the means to lend this money, and then they have to labour, perhaps still harder, to get the amount back again from the foreign country, which borrowed it from this. An immense sum has been lent in this way by the Jews in this country, since the close of the war; and I cannot see that any advantage has been derived by our productive classes, from foreign trade thus created, exceeding what they

would have had, if the[...] tured, sent out, and[...] way, had been sunk in[...] see, that loans to forei[...] our foreign trade, by su[...] dreaded competitors w[...] up manufacturing est[...] thereby promote the[...] trade, our manufacture[...] anxiety to preserve.

The supply of Brit[...] foreign markets, has[...] too, for some years[...] stocks have almost co[...] in those markets, on[...] mense losses have be[...] British merchants, fr[...] that has been going[...] greater losses still,[...] of foreign money, ex[...] alterations in the exc[...] of all which evils ha[...] the manufacturer, a[...] his excessive prod[...] forcing a supply ou[...] long-continued toil[...] for which there is[...] and for which ov[...] the foreigners cann[...] of such useful prod[...] have; and, for the[...] because they have[...] fore remit us, in p[...] our working for.[...] of the Jews in thi[...] their income fro[...] people in this co[...] part; and to ma[...] which the value o[...] we get from th[...] to balance the[...] had to a syster[...] depreciation of[...] fall in the exchan[...] having thus sett[...] to see what fools[...] thus cheated our[...] is m[...] duced and sent[...] nufactures, than[...] to pay us for.

In support of[...] to observe that[...] the Cape of[...] China, we im[...] amount of nea[...]

* See Appendix, No. 5.

relative value, as measured in the things of another country of the same intrinsic or relative value, and for which they were sent to be exchanged, the country sending too much reduces the supply, until the relative or intrinsic value is restored. And this applies to all descriptions of *useful* produce or manufactures, exchanged by one country with another, years of abundance and scarcity, and which nearly balance each other, being always excepted. On turning to table No. 1, you will see that 24 pieces of calico, the make referred to, have commanded 300lbs. of upland cotton during the last eighteen years; in which period, three years have commanded considerably more, and three other years considerably less; but, taken together, the excess in the three years nearly balances the deficiency in the three other years, and the other twelve years approximate so nearly to the standard, as confirms the truth of this statement, and that, too, notwithstanding the great difference in the money value of such articles, in this country, during the eighteen years referred to.

Many more articles of import might be referred to, to show the same uniformity of exchange; but there is no necessity for it, because the principle of proportion and relative value arises out of the necessity of the case, and is observed in despite of any efforts that may be made to destroy it.

We see middle men, as they are frequently called, from their being a kind of go-between in the buying and selling of the articles, step in, and, with their *surplus capital*, derange the order of exchange for those things, for a time, as has been the case this year in cotton; a scarcity was first asserted, speculation ensued, and I find that for this year (1833), the manufacturer of the cloth in table No. 1, will have had exacted from him, by this interference between him and the cotton-grower, 30½ pieces, for 300 lbs. of upland cotton; and this interference has so deranged the circumstances of many virtuous tradesmen, that ruin will follow, and misery and suffering result to them and their work-people, which is now beginning to manifest itself, in a reduction of wages.

The evils, sir, are so numerous, arising out of the system of working too long, and producing too much, and the benefits that would accrue to the manufacturers and their work-people so palpably apparent, that I will not tire you by pursuing the subject further, relative to the advantages to be derived from the adoption of " eight hours' work for the present full days' wages"; and now for a few words as to how the plan may be carried into effect.

The Regenerating Society wishes to avoid giving any encouragement to " *turn-outs*," I assure you, sir, and to avoid encouraging any mode of procedure that can by possibility injure the labouring poor, who are the objects of the society's especial care. It is for them that the society has been established, and has recommended applications being made to the masters, accompanied by a request that they will adopt the new regulation, and by a short statement of the reasons, why it is believed the adoption of it would be beneficial to both masters and work-people.* The society disclaims any intention of creating divisions between the employers and the employed ; its motto is " The rights of industry, and peace and good-will," and with it the weapons the society may use shall correspond, and if in its efforts to secure to all in return for moderate labour, a full and ample share of the necessaries and comforts of life, and proper time for education, recreation, and sleep, to which all who labour are justly entitled; if, in its efforts to secure these things for the labourers, and adequate profits to those who employ them, the society has to attack the interests, and contend against the prejudice and opposition of many who do not labour, but get more in return for the fixed income they possess than they are justly entitled to; against these the society has no feeling of resentment or hostility, but it is fully persuaded that their real and true interests

* See Appendix, No. 6.

B 2

would be advanced by the adoption of the measure recommended.

The first of March has been suggested by the society as a desirable period for the new regulation to commence, this being about the time when the new Factory Bill requires that children, under eleven years of age, should not work longer than eight hours a day; and unless this limitation of the time of labour be extended to all, many children will be thrown out of employment altogether; numbers more will have their wages reduced one-third; and much suffering and an increase of dissatisfaction amongst the poor would follow, but may be avoided if the suggestion of the society be acted on. To cause this to be done, the society has recommended the work-people to unite, and respectfully, but earnestly, request their respective employers, to adopt the proposed regulation of "eight hours' work for the present full day's wages."

If the answers of a considerable number of the masters be favourable, and they agree to adopt the regulation, provided it be general, a meeting of the masters may be convened, the question discussed, and resolutions agreed upon and circulated, calculated to bring over the dissentient masters. Other measures, if found necessary, may be agreed on at the meeting, which cannot fail to be efficient in securing the success of this righteous cause. Should the masters, generally, resolutely oppose the adoption of the plan suggested by the society, and the entreaties of their work-people to do them this act of justice, then it will remain for the Regenerating Society, and the work-people, to devise such a legal and peaceable mode of proceeding as they may consider proper to obtain the adoption of the regulation.

It is hoped, however, that the masters will not be so blind to their own interests, and to the interests and comforts of their work-people, by whom they are surrounded, and whose well-being is so manifestly identified with their own, as to refuse their cordial consent to the measure proposed, and for which so strong a necessity exists to allay the discontent among the work-people, and

ensure satisfaction and security to themselves.

For, what becomes of our boast of new acquisitions in mechanical skill, great improvements in machinery, and unprecedented increase in production, all excellent things when rightly directed, if the result which has hitherto followed be to continue, namely, the withdrawal of work altogether from some, and their degradation into paupers; the reduction of wages visited on those who are left to compete with the improved mode of production, consequent upon the adoption of the new machines; from which lessened wages, starvation, misery, and crime, ensue; and the increase of labour, without any increase of remuneration of those comparatively few in number who are fortunate enough to get work on the new machines. If such consequences cannot be avoided, then of one thing I am certain, that all our boasted improvements in machinery are not a blessing, but a curse to the productive classes, whose work is being constantly increased in intensity, and deteriorated in value, by the changes arising from these improvements. But a right direction may, and ought to be given, to those invaluable improvements; and the masters and workmen, by cultivating a good understanding with each other, and by an union of effort, ought to do it for themselves, without seeking for legislative interference on the subject.

To effect this object, the time of labour must be shortened, all must have employment, and the same, or more wages must be paid to each individual, for the reduced time of labour that he had before the hours of labour were abridged. Then the blessings of these improvements will become manifest to every one; the disputes between masters and servants relative to wages, and the introduction of the most improved machines, will cease, because all will participate in the benefits which they confer. Peace, concord, and mutual goodwill, will prevail; and an improvement in the physical, mental, and moral condition of the people, will follow, corresponding with the increase and improvement of the machines put in operation, to aid them in producing what they want.

I have now, sir, at considerable length, endeavoured to answer your letter, and stated my reasons for supporting the Regenerating Society. I have described what has been the state of the cotton trade, during the last eighteen years; what is its present state; and what in my opinion would be its state, if the plan the Regenerating Society recommends should be adopted; and I beg again to repeat, that, although my reasoning has been chiefly confined to the cotton trade, it will apply to other branches of manufacture throughout the country. There is sufficient evidence of this in the inquiry made by the committee of manufacturers, commerce, and shipping, in the last session of Parliament, and especially so in the committee on the state of the silk trade, in 1832.*

The subject is one of which it is difficult to convey clear views to those unacquainted with the nature of it; and in my attempts to do this, I have repeated again and again, some striking and most important

facts, which go to show the lamentable and rapidly declining condition, both of masters and workmen, engaged in the manufactures of this country; facts, which cannot be too strongly impressed on the minds of all who have any anxiety for the comfort and happiness of the labouring people, and for the peace and security of their employers; and, as I am one of the latter myself, and being thoroughly satisfied that the course we have pursued for several years back, cannot be proceeded in much farther, I naturally wish we may in *time* change that course, and avoid the evil consequences, which, I am fully convinced, will otherwise befall us.

If I have succeeded in removing your objections to the plan proposed by the Regenerating Society, for introducing the change, I shall feel amply repaid for the pains I have taken; and if I have not, I am sure we shall agree to differ, without thinking worse of each other on that account.

I am, my dear sir,

Your obedient humble servant,

JOHN FIELDEN.

Waterside, 7, *December*, 1833.

* See Appendix, No. 7.

No. I.

The Average Prices obtained for the second quality of 74 Calico, with the Price paid for the Warp and Weft, and the Sum left for Labour, Expenses, and Profit.

Years..	1820	1821	1822	1823	1824	1825
	s. d.	s. d.	s. d.	s. d.	s. d.	s. d.
Prices obtained for the calico..	12 2	11 3½	10 4½	10 1	9 5¼	10 2
The warp and weft cost	8 0¼	6 10	6 6¾	6 6½	6 3¾	7 3
Sum left for labour, expenses, and profit........	4 1¾	4 5½	3 9¾	3 6½	3 1½	2 11
Decline per cent. from 1820 ..	—	—	8	14	24	30

No. II.

The Average Prices obtained for the second quality of 74 Calico, with the cost of Cotton, and of weaving the same, and the sum left for Labour, Expenses, and Profit per Piece.

Years..	1826	1827	1828	1829	1830	1831	1832	To May 1833
	s. d.	s. d.	s. d.	s. d.	s. d.	s. d.	s. d.	s. d.
Price obtained for the calico	6 10½	6 11	6 9½	6 1¾	6 8	6 7	6 2½	6 4½
Cost of cotton and weaving..	4 6¾	4 9	4 8½	3 11⅜	4 6¾	4 6½	4 4½	4 7½
Sum left for labour of spinning, expenses, & profit	2 3¾	2 2	2 1	2 2	2 1¼	2 0½	1 10¼	1 9
Decline per cent. since 1826		6	10	6	9	11	20	24

No. III.

The Average Prices per Pound, of a common quality of 30 Hanks Water Twist in each year, from 1818 to May, 1833, with the cost of Cotton for the same, and the Sum left for Labour, Expenses, and Profit.

Years..........	1818	1819	1820	1821	1822	1823	1824	1825	1826	1827	1828	1829	1830	1831	1832	To end of May 1833
	d.	d.	d.	d.	d.	d.	d.	d.	d.	d.	d.	d.	d.	d.	d.	d.
Price of 1 lb. of common quality of 30 water twist	33	25	22½	18½	17½	18¾	19¼	19¼	13	12½	12⅛	12½	12¼	10½	11¾	11½
Cost of 18 ounces of cotton for ditto	22½	15¼	13¼	10¾	9	9¼	9½	13¾	7½	7	7	6½	7½	6½	7¼	8
Sum left for labour, expenses, and profit	10½	9½	9¾	7¾	8½	9½	9¾	5½	5½	5½	5⅛	4	4¾	4	4½	3½
Decline per cent. from 1818	0	7	12	26	19	9	7	47	47	47	51	43	55	62	57	66

No. IV.

The Prices obtained for one pound of 40 Hanks Copt Weft, in each year from 1815 to May, 1833, with the cost of Cotton for the same, and the Sum left for Labour, Expenses, and Profit.

Years........	1815	1816	1817	1818	1819	1820	1821	1822	1823	1824	1825	1826	1827	1828	1829	1830	1831	1832	To May 1833
	s. d.	s. d.	s. d.	s. d.	s. d.	s. d.	s. d.	s. d.	s. d.	s. d.	s. d.	s. d.	s. d.	s. d.	s. d.	s. d.	s. d.	s. d.	s. d.
The price obtained for 1 lb. of 40 hanks cop weft	3 0½	2 7½	2 6	2 6	1 10½	1 7¼	1 5¼	1 4¾	1 4¾	1 3½	1 5½	1 1	1 0½	0 11¾	0 11¾	1 0¼	0 11¼	0 11¼	1 0
Cost of 18 ounces of cotton for ditto ..	1 10	1 8¾	1 10½	1 10½	1 3¼	1 1¼	0 10¾	0 9¼	0 9¼	0 9½	1 1¾	0 7½	0 7	0 7¼	0 6½	0 7½	0 6½	0 7¼	0 8
Sum left for labour, expenses, & profit	1 2½	0 10¾	0 7½	0 7½	0 7¼	0 6	0 6½	0 7¾	0 7½	0 6	0 3¾	0 5½	0 5½	0 4½	0 5¼	0 4¾	0 4¾	0 4	0 4
Decline per cent. from 1815	—	26	48	48	50	60	55	46	48	60	74	62	62	69	63	65	65	72	72

No. V.

The Prices obtained for a four-cut Warp in each year, from 1815 to May, 1833, with the cost of Cotton for the same, and the Sum left for Labour, Expenses, and Profit.

Years	1815	1816	1817	1818	1819	1820	1821	1822	1823	1824	1825	1826	1827	1828	1829	1830	1831	1832	To May 1833
	s. d.	s. d.	s. d.	s. d.	s. d.	s. d.	s. d.	s. d.	s. d.	s. d.	s. d.	s. d.	s. d.	s. d.	s. d.	s. d.	s. d.	s. d.	s. d.
Prices obtained for a four-cut warp	28 11¼	26 1½	25 0¾	25 9¾	20 9	18 0½	15 10½	15 2	15 2½	14 10¼	16 3	11 2½	10 3¼	10 0½	9 9¼	10 1½	9 1½	9 8	10 2¼
Cost of 9¼ lbs. of cotton for ditto	15 0¼	14 3	15 5	15 5	10 5	9 3	7 3¾	6 3	6 4½	6 6½	9 5¼	5 2½	4 9¾	4 8½	4 4	5 1	4 4	4 9	5 4¾
Sum left for labour, expenses, and profit	13 11	11 10½	9 7¾	10 4¾	10 4	8 9½	8 6¾	9 2	8 10	8 3¾	6 9¾	6 0	5 5½	5 4	5 5¼	5 0½	4 9½	4 11¾	4 9½
Decline per cent. from 1815	—	15	31	24	24	37	39	34	36	40	51	57	60	61	60	64	65	64	65

No. VI.

The Average Price for Spinning One Pound of Cotton into 36 Hanks Weft on Commission, receiving the same weight of Weft delivered of Cotton, and the decline per Cent. from 1822 to 1833.

Years..	1822	1823	1824	1825	1826	1827	1828	1829	1830	1831	1832	1833
	d.	d.	d.	d.	d.	d.	d.	d.	d.	d.	d.	d.
Prices paid for Spinning	7½	7½	7½	7	6	5⅝	5	5¼	5¼	5⅛	5	5
Decline per cent from 1822				6	20	25	33	30	30	31½	33½	33½

No. VII.

Statement of the prices of Upland Cotton, nine-eight Shirtings, twenty Hanks Water Twist, and three-quarter Velveteens, within the last seven years; showing the average Price per pound or per piece, in each year for Manufacturing each Article.

	COTTON.							20 HANKS WATER TWIST.						
	1827	1828	1829	1830	1831	1832	1833	1827	1828	1829	1830	1831	1832	1833
	d.	d.	d.	d.	d.	d.	d.	d.	d.	d.	d.	d.	d.	d.
January	7¼	6	6¼	6⅜	6½	5¾	7¼	13	11	11¼	11	11½	10⅜	10¾
February	6⅞	6	6⅛	6½	6⅛	5⅞	7¼	12¾	11	11¼	11	11⅜	10⅞	11¼
March.........	6¾	5¾	5⅞	6⅝	6½	6½	7¼	12¾	11	11¼	11⅜	11⅜	11⅛	11¼
April	6½	6	5⅞	7	6⅛	6⅝	7¼	12¼	11¼	11¼	11½	11⅛	11	11¼
May...........	6½	6⅜	5¾	6⅞	6	6½	7¾	12	11¼	11¼	11½	11	11	11⅛
June	6½	6⅝	5¾	6¾	5¾	6½	7⅜	12	11¼	11¼	11½	10¾	10¾	11⅛
July..........	6⅜	6½	5⅞	6⅞	5⅝	6¾	9⅜	11¾	11¼	11	11½	10½	10¾	13
August	6½	6½	5¾	7⅜	5¾	6¾	..	11¾	11¼	11	11¾	10	10¾	..
September	6⅛	6½	5½	7¼	5¾	7	..	11½	11	11	11⅝	10⅛	10¾	..
October	6¼	6½	5¾	7¼	5⅝	7⅜	..	11½	11	11⅛	11⅝	10	11	..
November	6	6⅞	5⅞	6¾	5¾	7⅛	..	11	11¼	11¼	11½	10	11⅛	..
December	6	6⅝	6¼	7	5½	7⅛	..	11	11¼	11¼	11½	9⅞	10¾	..
	77⅞	76¼	70⅝	82⅝	71	79⅞	53½	143¼	133¾	134⅛	137⅜	127⅝	130¼	79¾
Average	6½	6⅜	5⅞	6⅞	5⅞	6⅝	7⅝	12	11⅛	11⅛	11½	10⅝	10⅞	11⅜
Less price of cotton	..	..	..	..	..	..	..	6½	6⅜	5⅞	6⅞	5⅞	6⅝	7⅝
Difference	..	..	..	..	..	..	..	5½	4¾	5¼	4⅝	4¾	4¼	3¾
Less per cent. for spinning in 1833 than in each of the preceding years	..	..	..	..	..	..	..	32	21	28½	19	21	11¾	..

Table VII.—(*Continued*).

	THREE-QUARTER VELVETEENS.							NINE-EIGHT SHIRTINGS.						
	1827	1828	1829	1830	1831	1832	1833	1827	1828	1829	1830	1831	1832	1833
	d.	d.	d.	d.	d.	d.	d.				s. d.	s. d.	s. d.	s. d.
January	..	..	19¾	17½	19¼	18¼	16¾	..	..	..	..	13 3	13 0	13 0
February	..	..	19¾	17½	19½	18¼	17	..	..	..	14 0	13 3	13 0	13 0
March	..	..	19¾	18	20	18	16¾	..	..	..	13 3	13 0	13 0	13 0
April	..	24	19¾	18¼	20¼	18	16¾	..	..	..	13 3	13 0	13 0	13 0
May	..	24	19¾	19½	20	18	17	..	..	..	13 3	13 0	13 0	13 0
June	..	22	19¼	19	19	17¾	17½	..	..	..	13 3	13 0	13 0	13 0
July	..	22	18	19	19	17½	18	..	..	..	13 3	13 0	13 0	13 6
August	..	21½	18	18¾	19	17½	..	..	..	..	13 3	13 0	13 0	..
September	..	21½	18	19½	19¼	17¼	..	..	..	..	13 3	13 0	13 0	..
October	..	21	17¾	19¾	19¼	17	..	..	..	..	13 3	13 0	13 0	..
November	..	20½	17½	19½	18¾	16¾	..	..	..	..	13 3	13 0	13 0	..
December	..	20¼	17½	19½	18	16¾	..	..	..	..	13 3	13 0	13 0	..
	..	196¾	224¾	225¾	231¼	211	119¾	..	..	..	134 0	156 6	156 0	91 6
Average	..	21⅞	18⅛	18⅞	19¼	17⅝	17⅛	..	..	..	13 5	13 0	13 0	13 1
Less price of cotton	..	6⅜	5⅞	6⅞	5⅞	6⅝	7⅝	..	..	..	6 0½	5 1½	5 9½	6 9
Difference	..	15½	12⅝	12	13⅜	11	9½	..	..	..	7 4½	7 10½	7 .2½	6 4
Less per cent. for spinning and weaving in 1813 than in each of the preceding years	..	39	25	20	28½	13½	..	..	..	..	14 0	20 0	12 0	..

The foregoing Tables show that we have had—

32 per cent less for spinning 20 hanks twist in 1833 than in 1827
21 ditto ditto 1828
28½ ditto ditto 1829
19 ditto ditto 1830
21 ditto ditto 1831
11¾ ditto ditto 1832

6)118

19¾ per cent. less in 1833 than the average of the last six years.

32½ per cent. less for manufacturing fustians in 1833 than in 1828
25 ditto ditto 1829
20 ditto ditto 1830
28½ ditto ditto 1831
13½ ditto ditto 1832

5)125½

25½ per cent. less in 1833 than the average of the last five years, and 15½ per cent less for manufacturing nine-eight shirtings in 1833 than the average of the last three years.

No. VIII.

Statement showing the prices paid for Weaving one Piece of second seventy-four Calico, the first seven years; and third seventy-four Calico, for the remaining period, from 1814 to July, 1833, inclusive.

No.	1814	1815	1816	1817	1818	1819	1820	1821	1822	1823
1	7 6 4 0	5 0 3 6	4 6 2 9	3 3 2 9	4 3 3 3	4 0 2 9	3 6 2 9	3 6 2 10	2 9 2 3	2 6 2 0
2	6 6	4 3	3 4	3 0	3 7	3 1	2 11	3 2	2 6	2 4
3	26 0	17 1	13 5	12 1	14 5	12 6	11 8	12 7	10 2	9 4
4	52 0	34 2	26 10	24 2	28 10	25 0	23 4	28 3¾	22 10½	21 0
5	5 3	5 3	5 3	5 3	5 3	5 3	5 3	5 3	5 3	5 3
6	46 9	28 11	21 7	18 11	23 7	19 9	18 1	23 0¾	17 7½	15 9

No.	1824	1825	1826	1827	1828	1829	1830	1831	1832	1833
1	2 3 2 0	2 3 2 0	2 0 1 0	2 0 1 3	2 0 1 3	1 3 1 1½	1 9 1 1½	1 9 1 6	1 6 1 3	1 4 1 4
2	2 1	2 1	1 4	1 7½	1 7½	1 2	1 6	1 7½	1 4	1 4
3	8 6	8 6	5 3	6 6	6 6	4 8	6 0	6 7	5 4	5 4
4	19 1½	19 1½	11 10	14 7½	14 7½	10 6	13 6	14 10	12 0	12 0
5	5 3	5 3	4 3	4 3	4 3	4 3	4 3	4 3	4 3	4 3
6	13 10½	13 10½	7 7	10 4½	10 4½	6 3	9 3	10 7	7 9	7 9

No. 1. The highest and lowest price in each year, per piece.
2. The average price of each year, per piece.
3. The average sum per week a good weaver would earn in each year.
4. The sum a family of six persons, parents, and children, three of the family being weavers, could earn a week in each year.

No. 5. The indispensable weekly expenses of the family of six persons for repair of looms, rent, fuel, light, &c.
6. Sum the family of six persons had left for food and clothing per week.

No. IX

Statement of the Weekly Quantity of Food, of the plainest kind, requisite for a Family of Six Persons; the cost of the same in every year; the surplus weekly sum the Family could earn more than the cost of Food; and the sum per head per day, the earnings of the Family would give, applicable for Food and Clothing, in every year, from 1814 to 1833.

	1814	1833.
35 quarts of blue milk	2s. 2d.	2s. 2d.
2lbs. of bacon	1 5	1 3
20lbs of potatoes	0 6½	0 6½
Coffee, tea, sugar, and treacle..	1 0	1 0
	5 1½	4 11½
25½lbs. of oatmeal at 39s. per 240 lbs.	4 1¾	2 9½
	9 3¼	7 9

No. 1. Milk, bacon, potatoes, coffee, tea, and sugar.
2. Oatmeal, 25½ lbs. or 17 lbs., and the remainder in flour.
3. Weekly amount for food for six persons.
4. The surplus weekly sum the family could earn above cost of food.
5. The full amount of income from wages, applicable for food and clothing for one person per day.

No.	1814		1815		1816		1817		1818		1819		1820		1821		1822		1823	
	s.	d.	s.	d.	s.	d	s.	d.	s.	d.	s.	d.	s.	d.	s.	d.	s.	d.	s.	d.
1	5	1½	5	0½	5	0½	5	1½	5	1½	5	0½	5	1½	4	11½	4	11½	4	11½
2	4	1¾	3	11	3	10	7	6	5	4½	4	1½	4	4½	3	7	3	1½	4	4½
3	9	3¼	8	11½	8	10½	12	7½	10	6	9	2	9	6	8	6½	8	1	9	4
4	37	3¾	19	11½	12	8½	6	3½	13	1	10	7	8	7	14	6¼	9	6	7	5
5	0	13¼	0	8¼	0	6	0	5½	0	6¾	0	5	0	6½	0	6½	0	5	0	4½

No.	1824		1825		1826		1827		1828		1829		1830		1831		1832		1833	
	s.	d.	s.	d	s.	d.	s.	d.	s.	d.	s.	d.	s.	d.	s.	d.	s.	d.	s.	d.
1	4	11½	4	11½	3	8½	4	11½	4	11½	2	5½	4	1½	4	11½	4	5	4	11½
2	4	6	3	10½	3	7½	4	3	3	3½	3	9	4	1½	4	0	3	0	2	9½
3	9	5½	8	10	7	4	9	2½	8	3	6	2½	9	1	8	11½	7	5	7	9
4	4	5	5	0½	0	2¾	0	0½	2	1½	0	0½	0	2	1	7¼	0	1¾	..	
5	0	4	0	3¾	0	2¼	0	3	0	3½	0	1¾	0	2¾	0	3	0	2¼	0	2¼

No. X.

Statement of the Yearly Earnings of six persons, three of whom are Weavers; Yearly Rent, Fuel, Light, &c.; Yearly Food; and surplus remaining per year for Clothing, from 1814 to 1833 inclusive.

Years.	Family of six Persons, three of whom are weavers, their yearly income £. s. d.	Yearly expenditure of a Family of six Persons, rent, fuel, light, soap, repair of looms &c. £. s. d.	Yearly amount for Food for a Family of six Persons. £. s. d.	The Sum remaining for clothing or better food, when rent, fuel, &c. are deducted. £. s. d.
1814	135 4 0	13 13 0	24 2 1	97 8 11
1815	88 16 8	—	23 5 10	51 17 10
1816	69 15 4	—	23 1 6	33 0 10
1817	62 16 8	—	32 16 0	15 7 2
1818	74 19 0	—	27 6 0	30 0 4
1819	65 0 0	—	23 16 8	27 10 4
1820	60 13 4	—	24 14 0	22 6 4
1821	73 12 3	—	22 4 0	37 15 1
1822	59 9 6	—	21 0 4	24 16 2
1823	54 12 6	—	24 5 4	16 13 8
1824	49 14 6	—	24 11 10	11 9 8
1825	49 14 6	—	22 19 4	13 2 2
1826	30 14 3	11 1 0	19 1 4	0 11 11
1827	38 0 6	—	23 18 10	4 0 8
1828	38 0 6	—	21 9 0	5 10 6
1829	27 6 0	—	16 2 10	0 2 2
1830	35 2 0	—	23 12 4	0 8 8
1831	38 10 3	—	23 5 10	4 3 5
1832	30 14 3	—	19 8 0	0 7 7
1833	31 4 0	—	20 3 0	—

No. XI.

Statement of the Average Annual Earnings of a Family of Six Persons in each successive five years, from 1814 to 1833, inclusive; the Reduction per Cent. in their Earnings in each succeeding five years; and the Reduction per Cent. in the three last periods of five years each, as compared with the first five years; and also the Annual Average Cost of provisions, and other outgoings necessary for the Family, and the Reduction per Cent. in the Cost of the same, for the same four periods of five years each.

Years.	The Amount of Earnings of a Family of six Persons, three Weavers, in five years. £. s. d.	The Yearly Average of each five years, from 1814 to 1833, inclusive. £. s. d.	Reduction per Cent. in their Earnings in each successive five years.	Less per Cent. than the first five years in each succeeding five years.	Cost of five years' Provisions, rent, fuel, light, soap, repairs of looms, as to standard quantity fixed. £. s. d.	The yearly Average Cost of each five years, from 1814 to 1833, inclusive. £. s. d.	Reduction per Cent. in the cost of provisions, fuel, &c., in each successive five years.	Reduction per Cent. in Expenditure in the last three periods of five years each, as compared with the first five years.
1814 1818 inclusive	431 12 0	86 6 4¾	—	—	198 16 11	39 15 4½	—	—
1819 1823	313 7 1	62 13 5	27 5-16	27 5-16	184 5 6	36 17 1	8 ¾	8 ⅞
1824 1828	206 4 3	41 4 10	34 ⅞	52 3-16	172 9 4	34 9 10¾	6 5-16	13 10-16
1829 1833	162 16 6	32 11 3¼	21 1-16	62 5-16	157 14 8	31 10 11	8 ¾	21 3-16

No. XII.

Statement of the Comparative Situation of the Hand-Loom Weavers in the Township of Crompton, from 1814 to 1833.

Years..	1814	1815	1816	1817	1818	1819	1820	1821	1822	1823	1824	1825	1826	1827	1828	1829	1830	1831	1832	1833
Price per lb. for weaving, Jan. each year	27 ½d.	23 ½d.	18d.	13d.	17½d.	20d.	18d.	17d.	18d.	19d.	19d.	17½d.	13d.	13d.	14d.	12d.	10d.	10d.	9½d.	9½d.
Sum a fair weaver can earn per week, working ten hours and a half each day.	13 9	11 9	9 0	6 6	8 9	10 0	9 9	8 6	9 0	9 6	9 6	8 9	6 6	6 6	7 0	6 0	5 0	5 0	4 6	4 6
Rents, fuel, light, repairs of looms, winding, &c. &c. per week..............	3 7½	3 3¼	2 9½	2 4¼	2 8½	2 11	2 8¾	2 7½	2 8¼	2 9	2 8¾	2 7	2 1½	2 2¼	2 3	2 0¾	1 10½	1 10½	1 9¼	1 9
Net sum per week for food and clothing	10 1½	8 5¾	6 2½	4 1¾	6 0¼	7 1	6 3¼	5 10½	6 3¾	6 9	6 9¼	6 2	4 4½	4 3¾	4 9	3 11¼	3 1½	3 0½	2 8¾	2 9
Price of flour per peck of 12lbs.	2 8	2 7½	2 10½	2 10¼	3 2½	2 7½	2 6½	2 4	2 1¾	2 1½	2 5¼	2 7½	2 5½	2 6	2 3¾	2 6	2 6¼	2 6¾	2 3¼	2 0½
Ditto oatmeal...............	2 1¼	1 11½	2 0½	2 1	2 5	2 0¾	2 0	1 7½	1 7½	1 8¼	1 11¾	1 11¾	1 11¾	2 1	1 8¾	1 10½	1 11¾	1 11¾	1 7½	1 4½
	d.	d.	d.	d.	d.	d.	d.	d.	d.	d.	d.	d.	d.	d.	d.	d.	d.	d.	d.	d.
Average price of beef and mutton per lb.	9½	7¾	7	7	7⅝	8	8	6⅜	5¼	6½	6¼	7⅜	6⅝	7½	7	6⅝	5¾	6¾	6½	6½
Quantity of flour his wages would procure per week in lbs.	45 9 16	38¾	26	17 5 11	22 3-5	32⅜	29 6-10	30¼	35 3-10	38½	33 1-3	28 3-16	21 1-3	20 7-10	24 7-11	18 9-10	14 5-6	14 2 3	14¼	16 1-6
Ditto of oatmeal, ditto in lbs	57¾	52	36½	24	30	41 1-5	37 2-3	43⅜	46⅝	46⅞	41	37⅜	26½	24⅞	33	15 1-5	19	19	20 1-6	24
Ditto beef or mutton, ditto in lbs.	13 1-7	13⅛	10 2-3	7 1-9	9½	10⅝	9⅜	11	14⅜	12½	13	10	8	6 9-10	8 1-7	7 1-8	6¾	5 5-9	4 8-9	5
General average of flour, meal, and shamble meat..	116	104	73	49	62	84	77	85	96	98	87	76	56	52	66	51	41	39	39	45

The deduction from weavers' wages for rent, fuel, winding, &c. is taken as follows:—

In 1814, rent for a family consisting of, say six or seven individuals, of whom four were workers, £7 7s. 4d. per annum, or per week for each worker, 8½d ; candle-light, 2½ ; fuel, 3d. ; and wear and tear of looms, gearing, shuttles, &c. 2d. ; making together 1s. 4d. per week, which has been gradually reduced to the following in 1833 ; say rent per annum, £5 4s. or per week each weaver, 6d. ; wear and tear of looms, gearing, shuttles, &c., 1½d. ; candle-light, 2d. ; fuel, 2½d. ; together, 1s. per week. The regular price for winding during the whole time has been 2d. per 1s. on the weaver's earnings.

No. XIII.

Statement of Wages paid in the years following, in the month of March of each year, by a very respectable Manufacturer (William Cannon).

Year.	48 Reed. s. d.	56 Reed. s. d.	70 Reed. s. d.
March 1811	10 0	13 0	20 0
1812	11 1	13 6	21 0
1813	13 0	16 0	22 0
1814	20 0	27 0	32 0
1815	11 6	15 0	21 0
1816	9 0	11 0	17 0
1817	6 6	8 6	11 0
1818	8 0	10 0	12 6
1819	7 0	9 0	11 6
1820	6 6	8 0	10 6
1821	8 6	10 6	12 6
1822	6 0	8 6	10 6
1823	6 6	8 6	10 0
1824	6 6	8 6	10 0
1825	6 6	8 0	10 0
1826	5 0	6 6	8 6
1827	4 6	5 6	8 0
1828	4 6	5 6	8 0
1829	4 0	5 6	8 0
1830	3 6	5 0	7 0
1831	3 6	5 0	7 0
1832	3 6	5 0	7 0
1833	3 6	5 0	7 0

The average earnings of men, women, and children, 3s. 6d. per week; allowing 3d. in 1s. for expenses, leaves them clear 2s. 8½d., on an average, for working this kind of cloth.

No. XIV.

Prices of Weaving 6-4ths. 60-Reed Cambric, 120 Picks in one inch for the last 38 Years, taken in the month of June in each Year.

		s. d.			s. d.
June, 1795	....6-4 60 Cam. 20 yds.	33 3	June, 1815	....6-4 60 Cam. 24 yds.	14 0
1796	.... ditto	33 3	1816	.... ditto	12 0
1797	.... ditto .. 24 yds.	29 0	1817	.... ditto	9 0
1798	.... ditto	30 0	1818	.... ditto	9 0
1799	.... ditto	25 0	1819	.... ditto	9 6
1800	.... ditto	25 0	1820	.... ditto	9 0
1801	.... ditto	25 0	1821	.... ditto	8 6
1802	.... ditto	29 0	1822	.... ditto	8 6
1803	.... ditto	24 0	1823	.... ditto	8 6
1804	.... ditto	20 0	1824	.... ditto	8 6
1805	.... 63	25 0	1825	.... ditto	8 6
1806	.... ditto	22 0	1826	.... ditto	7 6
1807	.... ditto	18 0	1827	.... ditto	6 0
1808	.... ditto	14 0	1828	.... ditto	6 0
1809	.... ditto	16 0	1829	.... ditto	5 6
1810	.... ditto	19 6	1830	.... ditto	5 6
1811	.... ditto	14 0	1831	.... ditto	5 6
1812	.... ditto	14 0	1832	.... ditto	5 6
1813	.... ditto	15 0	1833	.... ditto	5 6
1814	.... ditto	24 0			

A weaver working one of these pieces in one week is in full employment, and his earnings will be clear (after all deductions and expenses he has to pay) 4s. 1¾d. per week, for an able-bodied man to live on for a week, to provide him with food, and clothing, and lodging.

From a survey of the condition of the poor in thirty-three townships of the manufacturing district in Lancashire and two in Yorkshire, mostly employed in the manufacture of cotton, of woollen, and of silk, it appears that in these thirty-five townships the population is 203,349 ; the families visited are 8,362 ; the persons in these families 49,294 ; being nearly one-fourth of the whole. The number out of work in the families visited is 2,287 ; the number unfit for work in the same is 23,060 ; the number of workers is 23,947. The total weekly wages which the families visited earn are 4,447*l.* 18*s.* This sum will give for each of those who work a weekly average of 3*s.* 8⅝*d.*, and for each of the whole number of persons visited a weekly average of 1*s.* 9⅝*d.* The rent paid by the families visited is, per annum, 32,693*l.* 17*s.* 5*d.* This sum gives an average of 3*d.* a week for each individual in the families visited. Fuel, light, and wear of implements, will be an average for each individual of at least 3½*d.* a week ; and this, with the average rent of 3*d.* being deducted from 1*s.* 9⅝*d.*, the average income of each individual, leaves for food and clothing, for a week, 1*s.* 3*d.* 1-3.

The whole parish relief given weekly to the families visited is 139*l.* 7*s.*, or for each ⅝ of a penny, and the average income of each for a day, for food and clothing, from both wages and relief, is 2¼*d.*

APPENDIX, No. I.

MR. HOLT'S LETTER TO MR. FIELDEN.

MY GOOD FRIEND,

I think I know enough of thy character, from the efforts thou hast employed with a view to improve the condition of the working classes, particularly those employed in factories, to satisfy me, that I may address thee without giving offence, although I may in some points hold different opinions. Having been in one way or other engaged in the spinning trade more than forty years, and the whole of that time as a mill proprietor, I must have witnessed many changes. It however has always been a maxim with me, that whilst I was pursuing my own interest, not to forget that the people about me, by whose labour that interest must be sustained as well as promoted, were at all times entitled to my esteem and regard, and that in the faithful discharge of their duty, they had claims upon me beyond the fulfilment of the simple contract, as far as wages were concerned, which required that I should be the guardian of their interests and comforts, as well as my own. It never entered my mind that I was at liberty to exact from them either in extent of time or labour, a service that should deprive them of the ordinary comforts of life ; and my pen has been employed many and many a time, in their defence, when I have seen attempts making to diminish the fair earnings of the labouring man in a degree that would impose upon him bodily exertion and long confinement, as well as diminish those comforts and conveniences to which every honest and industrious man has an indisputable claim. I have often addressed the masters, imploring them to consider, both as men and Christians, how far they were, by such conduct, deviating from that sound maxim of " doing to others as they would be done unto"; and how certainly such conduct would recoil, in the long run, upon themselves. I endeavoured to show them, that low wages and inordinate exertion would break down the spirits of the people, and destroy that bond of union which ought ever to subsist between master and servant, and eventually entail poverty and distress upon the whole labouring population.

We are unfortunately arrived at that period, and our rapacity has not only deprived us of the affectionate regard of our servants, but has created a feeling of hatred toward us, as being the authors of all the miseries and privations to which they are exposed ; and who shall say that they are not warranted in this conclusion ? I have asserted many and many a time, that our policy ought to have been to sustain the price of labour at a point that would enable every man with a family, to feed and to clothe them, and that a moderate degree of labour should be sufficient to effect this. If this object had been duly regarded by the mill proprietors and master manufacturers, would not the general consumption have sustained our home trade, and secured those advantages here, which we are so anxiously seeking abroad? But suppose that, for the moment, the profits had been less, they would not have dwindled, as they have done, into comparatively nothing. Another and serious evil has resulted from this wretched policy, which has almost imperceptibly broken down the middle ranks in society, who, in our better days, stood as a wall of defence between the rich and the poor, and we are all become the prey of the speculators and great money dealers, who absorb the wealth of the country; and then, to consummate our ruin and degradation, send their over-grown wealth to other states and people, creating for them a capital by which they become our formidable rivals, instead of making it subservient to the promotion of enterprise and industry at home. This unnatural state of things has been gradually assuming a complexion, which, when viewed dispassionately, becomes appalling. The *many* look upon the *few* as their oppressors, and as they find their appeals disregarded, can we wonder that there should be unions, combinations, and contests between masters and men, which threaten to break up society altogether, and to produce anarchy in a degree that it may be difficult to suppress?

Now, my good friend, is not the association proposed to be formed, at the head of which I see thy name, and those of some other influential men, one, which if carried into effect as intended, must create a sensation of no ordinary character, and may produce a general convulsion in the country, and involve thousands of innocent persons in ruin, and consequent wretchedness? Would it not then be wise to pause even on the threshold of such a measure, and see if some other means quite as effectual, and better calculated to ensure success,

cannot be devised? I am inclined to think that a great number of the mill proprietors and master manufacturers are well disposed, and would most willingly embrace any plan or regulation by which the condition of the working classes through the whole empire might be so improved as to do away with the existing complaints; for we all know, that one rapacious, unprincipled man, who may be extensively engaged in business, can, and not unfrequently has, by his unjust and wicked exactions, brought poverty and distress upon a whole district, by not only robbing the people himself, but compelling his neighbours, who may be engaged in the same business, in their own defence to adopt the same rate of wages. Now, if the plan that I have many a time recommended through our public papers, had been adopted, such attempts could never have succeeded, and the condition of the labouring classes would have been very different to what it is. The plan to which I allude, and which to me appears unexceptionable, is, that in all the spinning and manufacturing districts, the well-disposed masters should unite, and form themselves into committees, for the express purpose of sustaining the labour of the country, and protecting the workmen from those abitrary and unjust attempts, which are, from time to time, made to reduce wages below the level, by which, with moderate exertion, a comfortable subsistence may be gained, as well as to prevent their imposing hours of labour and confinement beyond what are generally considered to be reasonable and proper upon the people under their control.

This is carried to an extreme in many places, and people are compelled to work fourteen, fifteen, or sixteen hours for even less than others are paying for twelve. This is an act of palpable injustice, which, if such committees were formed and organized, would not be practised; and a moment's reflection must convince any reasonable man, that these shifts and contrivances, being founded in dishonesty and sustained by fraud, cannot for any length of time be profitable, and are most dishonourable to those who practise them. I would have all these committees open to every representation that the working classes may feel disposed to make to them, and in all cases grievances should be removed, or they should be convinced that none existed.

Would it not then be wise *first* to try what advantages the operatives could obtain in this way, and thus make the masters themselves the medium through which the improved condition of the people should come? This would prevent that collision which the plan you propose to pursue must, I fear, inevitably produce.

I am decidedly of opinion, that ten hours' labour, whether in or out of a factory, is quite as much as ought to be imposed upon any man, woman, or child, and that no children under ten years of age ought to be employed in any factory. And if any plan can be devised by which the public burdens imposed by the enormous taxation of the country can be so far lessened, as to make the shorter periods of labour, equally or more productive to the operatives, the masters as well as the country itself, would soon partake in the benefit, and we should become a united and happy people, and peace and plenty would again visit our land.

Thou wilt, I trust, pardon the liberty I take in thus placing my opinions before thee, and if thou see any value in them, thou art at liberty to make any use of this letter thou pleasest. We are both interested in, and anxious to promote, the well-being of our fellowmen.

If it would be any gratification to thee to look at these concerns, and thou wouldest do me the favour to partake of a family dinner with me, it would afford pleasure to

Thy very respectful friend,
DAVID HOLT.

Chorlton New Mills, Manchester,
12 *mo.* 16, 1833.

J. Fielden, Esq., M.P.,
Todmorden.

APPENDIX, No. II.

An Extract from William Longston's evidence taken before the Committee on the Factories Bill. (See Minutes of Evidence, 1832, pp. 430, 431, and 432.)

9397. Is the intensity of application and of labour altered, either against or in favour of the operative and of the children employed in mills and factories?—I was a great number of years out of any factory, but those who were my acquaintances during my boyhood have often conversed with me, and they very frequently say that it cannot be less than double in intensity and exertion of physical application.

9398. State why you believe that the labour of those employed has doubled since the first introduction and use of cotton machinery, or at least since you first knew it?—The reason why I believe so is from some calculations which I have been obliged to make, and by my own observation during the time I was manager of a mill in 1830 and 1831, when I had some of the same operations under my own observation.

9399. Have you any objection to put in those calculations?—Certainly not.

[The following document was then put in and read.]

Cotton Manufacture, at Stockport.

	lbs. of slubbing.
1800, 1 billey,* attended by a man and two boys, made....	360
1832, 1 ditto ditto	750

	lbs. of roving.	Wages per score. s. d.
1810, 1 stretcher,† worked by A. Docker, spun	400	1 3¼
1811, 1 —, the same man, ..	600	0 10
1813, 1 —, the same man, ..	850	0 9
1823, 1 —, the same man, ..	1000	0 7½

* Billeys prepare the materials for jennies. The jennies are placed in cellars and other damp places, as the work requires dampness. When the children, who have been thus employed, are removed to the opposite condition in mills, injury must be done to their health.

† In 1810, if at the above rate Abraham Docker's week's work did not amount to 26s. that sum was always made up to him.

C

The same man on another stretcher, the boving a little finer:

1823,	900	0	7½
1825,	1000	0	7
1827,	1200	0	6
1832,	1200	0	6

[*Observation.* To each stretcher, three young women are employed in the previous preparation of the article. Their wages have never been high, and have not been reduced in the above proportion, yet their labour has increased in the same proportion, otherwise the quantities above stated could not have been produced. A little girl is also employed, whose labour is also increased in like proportion, and who, whenever that law can be evaded, is kept at meal-time to clean the stretchers.]

Mule Yarn-spinning.

At Mr. Jesse Howard's:

	Spindles.	Hanks, about 40 to the lb.	Wages per 1000. s. d.
1806	480	6668	9 2
1823	480	8000	6 3
1832	480	10,000	3 10

9400. It appears by this document that the work done is very greatly increased between the years 1810 and 1832; has the machinery been so altered as to produce that amazing difference, or does it result from accelerating the speed of the machinery?—It is from accelerating the speed generally; and another cause is, that more work and more exertion is required from the individual working at the machine; these are two causes.

9401. Those causes, then, prove what you have been asserting, namely, that double the labour and attendance is now requisite that was formerly required?—I think so.

9402. In spite of the improvements of machinery?—Yes; I believe those that are now working in the same employment as I did when I was a boy, do double the work.

9403. So that there may be a great improvement in machinery, and at the same time a great increase in actual labour to each operative?—Yes.

9404. Has that been, as far as your experience has extended, the consonant result of improvements of machinery in those mills, namely, that the labour of the hands has increased with every improvement in the machinery, rather than diminished?—Yes; the improvements in the machinery have been great, and the same physical exertion, and the same attention as was formerly applied, would certainly produce, in proportion to the altered state of the machinery, a *much greater quantity and better articles; but, added to that, the increased exertions make the quantities to be such as just now surprised you.

9405. Are we to understand then that the labour of those employed has been much increased in its intensity?—Yes.

9406. How long were you employed in your boyhood in that way?—About six years.

9407. So that you were quite long enough to form an accurate observation as to the facts to which you have been alluding?—The statement which I have just now given with regard to the increased speed and the increase of physical exertion, I think is sufficient, even, if no weight were laid upon my own experience, to account for the increased quantity. The whole increase of quantity is not produced by increase of labour; that must be considered as combined with the improvement of machinery.

9408. Is not the increase of labour greater now than at the period to which you first adverted?—Yes; it is not only my opinion, but it is the opinion of all those with whom I converse, that it is generally doubled where it could be doubled; and I believe it is generally so. I have to observe from the quantities produced here (referring to the last document put in), that it may be evident, from other witnesses, that the increased speed alone would not produce the quantities here given; that, therefore, there must be an increase of physical exertion; and hence I infer the greater necessity of some law to make the duration of that labour shorter daily.

APPENDIX, No. III.

Instructions to Factory Commissioners, as shown in an extract, from page 3, of a correspondence between Mr. Wilson, Secretary to the Central Board of Factory Commissioners, and Mr. Stuart, one of the Commissioners.

" It is considered highly desirable by " the Central Board, that particular " attention should be paid to obtaining " information in reply to the following " queries, as such information may be " conducive to important results :—
" What would be the objection (if " any), to restricting the employment of " children between the ages of nine and " thirteen, to six or eight hours in the " day, and thus to work in two sets, " according as the whole day's work " might extend to twelve or sixteen " hours ?
" It is suggested that such change of " sets might be made at the hour of " dinner, when the machinery is already " stopped ?
" Would a change of hands so made, " entail any waste or the inferiority of " the work ? If so, describe the nature, " of such waste or inferiority."

APPENDIX, No. IV.

NATIONAL REGENERATION SOCIETY.
The objects intended to be obtained by this Society, are,—
1st. An abridgment of the hours of daily labour, whereby sufficient time may be afforded for education, recreation, and sleep.
2nd. The maintenance of, at least, the present amount of wages, and an advance as soon as practicable.
3rd. A system of daily education, to be carried on by the working people themselves, with the gratuitous assistance of the well-disposed of all parties, who may have time and inclination to attend to it.
N.B. It is suggested that, where other accommodation for schools does not exist, a sufficient substitute may be found in the buildings in which the people work.

This system of instruction to consist in teaching men how to produce the best of every article in the shortest time, at those branches of industry, they are, or may wish to be, engaged in.
In teaching women to wash, bake, brew, and mend clothes and stockings ; and in all other domestic duties appertaining to cottage economy, in which knowledge a large majority of females, in the manufacturing districts, are now so lamentably deficient as to disgrace the age in which we live ; owing to which deficiency of really useful knowledge, the most sad degeneracy has arisen, and will be followed by national evils, unparalleled in our history, unless time be given, and great pains taken to avert them.
And, in addition to this knowledge, it is designed to teach both men and women any other branch of useful knowledge they may be willng to learn, and will labour to acquire; to enjoin on both to abstain from running into debt ; to be economical and industrious, and avoid all manner of intemperance ; we may hope, thus, to train them to be good fathers and mothers, good husbands and wives, and virtuous members of society.
Children to be taught reading, writing, accounts, and other branches of useful knowledge. The female part of them to be taught, in addition, sewing, knitting, and every other branch of learning necessary to fit them for a proper discharge of the duties belonging to their sex.

APPENDIX, No. V.

Mr. Jacob's evidence, from the Select Committee's Report on Agriculture, page 5.
38. Do you conceive, taking the dealers from the great dealers in seaport towns, to the small dealers in market towns, there is a lessening in the stocks such persons hold ? — Certainly, of English wheat.
39. Could you state in what proportion to the time the stocks were considered high ? — I did suppose at one time, when we had a harvest in

1816, which was so very deficient, we had then six months' consumption in the country; I do not think that there has been a month's consumption in the country, at the time of the harvest, since 1829.

64. Can you form any opinion of what was the cause of the reduced stock in the hands of the farmers? — I suppose, in some measure, the reduction of capital; they have been paying a great deal of rent out of their capital.

51. You say that in 1816, preceding the bad harvest of that year, you think there were six months' consumption in store, and recently not more than one month; supposing the harvest of 1816 was to come over again, from whence do you contemplate the supply? — It could not be supplied from all the world. My opinion is, that if we were to diminish the growth of English wheat by one-tenth part of that now produced, we should not be in a safe state in case of a deficient harvest, for all the world could not make up the deficiency. We are now about four weeks in the year deficient in our growth on the average; last year the harvest was one month earlier than the year previous, so that we were enabled to get to the end of the year. The harvest of 1832 ought to supply 13 months, and I dare say it will do so; but if we have a deficient harvest, and the next harvest gives us but 11 months' supply, and owing to bad weather it be deficient one-tenth more, there would then be such a deficiency as all the world could not easily supply at any price, for wheat is not the food of man in any other country to the same extent as in England.

In France, even where wheat is much more used than in the north and east of Europe, Chaptel states that there are only about 17,000,000 of quarters a year grown, of which near 3,000,000 are wanted for seed, and that for a population of 30,000,000 persons, while we require nearly as much for half that number of persons.

————

APPENDIX, No. VI.
RIGHTS OF INDUSTRY.

Sir,—We have been appointed as a deputation, by our fellow workmen, in your employ, to wait on you, and earnestly to request, that on the 1. day of March next you will have the goodness to fix eight hours per day as the time for us to work, such eight hours to be between the hours of six o'clock in the morning and six o'clock in the evening, and that you will also agree to pay us the wages we now earn per day, for the said eight hours' work.

We believe your interest, as well as our own, would be promoted by such a regulation, for it has been established by evidence that cannot be confuted, given before the committee on manufactures, shipping, and commerce, in the last session of Parliament, that, in the cotton trade (and we believe a similar investigation would prove it to be the same in other trades), the master manufacturers and their work-people received 72 per cent. less for labour, expenses, and profit for manufacturing articles from cotton, in 1832, than they did in 1815, and that for manufacturing six leading articles of cotton manufacture, which are a fair criterion of the state of the trade, the manufacturers now get an average of 30 per cent. less for labour, expenses, and profit, for producing these six leading articles, than they got in 1826, when the consumption of cotton was about 12,000 bags a week—the consumption which it would be again reduced to by the proposed alteration. And it can be demonstrated, that in 1815, for working up 6,500 bags of cotton a week, of 300 lbs. each, into four leading articles of cotton manufacture, the masters and their men received after the rate of 13,000,000l. per annum for the whole quantity, for labour, expenses, and profit; whereas in 1832, for working up 17,300 bags a week, of 300lbs. each, into the same four still leading articles, they only got after the rate of 10,250,000l. per annum, for the whole quantity, for labour, expenses, and profit; and that, too, notwithstanding the amazing increase of the number of persons engaged in this manufacture, and dependent upon it for subsistence in 1832, as compared with 1815. Besides, the time we now labour is too long to be endured, and deprives us of the opportunity of getting education, and of having that relaxation from a cessation of toil which rational beings ought to have. We respectfully wish to be informed whether you are disposed to adopt this new regulation, provided others in the trade agree to do the same.

APPENDIX, No. VII.

Extracts from J. Brocklehurst, jun. Esq.'s evidence, taken before the Select Committee on the Silk Trade.

11,350. You were led to expect there would be a very large increase by the alteration of the law?—The Minister told us we should go on and make the silk equal to the cotton trade; he only considered the silk trade to be the younger sister, and that he should place the silk trade on a par with her sister;—that was one expression of Mr. Huskinson's.

11,404. Can you state how many failures occurred between 1814 and 1826, of silk throwsters and manufacturers?—They were of so rare occurrence, I can only recollect one or two; and though a banker the last nine years of the time, I should think 9l. would cover our losses.

11,405. Since 1826, how many failed?—Somewhere about 40, as nearly as my recollection serves me, besides a great many in minor trades.

11,406. How large a proportion is that of the whole?—Two-thirds at that time.

11,407. How many establishments may there be at the present time?—There are now about as many left as have failed; I have a list of the parties who failed, but I think it is not desirable to go into those particulars.

11,408. To what do you attribute so many failures?—Some few might probably have been from unsuccessful competition, but I am confident the bulk of those have been ruined by the reduction of duties on foreign thrown silks, and the general bad effects of the measures that came into operation in the year 1826.

11,409. They were in it, and could not get out of it?—Men cannot get out of a trade they are embarked in so rapidly as some political economists imagine.

11,410. If you had 20,000l. invested in a silk mill, do you know any mode of realizing your property when the throwing of silk is unprofitable?—At the time when individuals wish to get out of trade, they find that the moment of all others no one wishes to get into it.

11,411. Does not that observation peculiarly apply to manufacturing establishments, where there are large buildings, a plant and machinery, peculiarly adapted to that trade?—Yes; but political economists conceive that we can turn from the manufacture of cotton or silk, or any thing else, with the rapidity they proceed to conclusions.

11,412. Can the machinery be applied to any purpose?—To no purpose but firewood; I have seen property sold (if in fact it may be so called) that cost 60s. for 3s.

11,413. Do you know of any instance of mill property being offered for sale?—I know an instance of a mill originally costing 6,000l. or 7,000l. that was purchased in 1827 for 1,700l., and I stated the fact to the Board of Trade in 1828 or 1829; a few weeks ago I met the late proprietor in London, and asked him what that mill actually cost; he said 7,000l. independently of machinery, and that the machinery cost him above 4,000l. more; altogether that property which cost 11,000l., was knocked down for 1,700l., and about 200l. for the machinery.

11,414. When was that mill erected?—In 1822, I believe.

11,415. It was not old or worn out?—No; it was, and is still, as good and as perfect a mill as any in the kingdom.

11,416. Was that man ruined?—He was, and has since been reduced to the necessity of trying to maintain himself and his family by keeping a petty shop in London.

11,417. Supposing that mill to be erected in 1827, as it was in 1822, what would it have cost to have built that mill, and stored it with machinery?—Perhaps 10 per cent. less.

11,418. It would have cost about 10,000l. in the year 1827?—Yes; and it would now.

11,419. What may be the prices of throwing silk at Macclesfield?—There are no fixed prices; throwsters, who engage work, are too often obliged to take the prices offered without reference in any way to cost, and then find themselves compelled to turn round on their wages and expenses, to see whether they can make contract pay.

11,420. Can wages be reduced any lower?—Most assuredly not; for at this time they do not afford subsistence or common household necessaries, much less clothing, putting aside rent.

11,451. What has been the condition of the weavers since 1826?—Since 1826 their condition has undergone such a transition from comfort and regular employment to so great a degree of distress, as hardly to be known to be the same trade as it was before interfered with.

11,452. Have you any statement of wages that will show the alteration you describe?—I have a table of some of the principal articles made at Macclesfield, and the prices from 1821 to 1831, which I will deliver in; the average earnings of the weavers in 1821 to 1826 amounted to 16s. 6d., but as soon as the change took place their earnings decreased to 7s. 9d., and they are now reduced to 6s. per week.

The statements of wages of weavers include the weaving of the richer kinds of handkerchiefs, not made by all manufacturers, and therefore rather exceed the actual average of earnings of the weavers.

[The same was delivered in and read.]

Statement of leading articles made at Macclesfield.

	Mounture Handkerchiefs.	Figured stage-harness of 100 Shafts.	Black Figured Handkerchiefs.	Grey Bandanna Handkerchiefs.	Single Sarsnets.	Gros de Naples.	Average Earnings, clear of all deductions.
	per dozen	per dozen	per dozen	per piece.	per yard.	per yard.	
	s. d.	s. d.	s. d.	s d.	d.	s. d.	s. d
1821	30 0	14 0	10 0	3 6	9	1 1	16 6
1822	30 0	13 0	10 0	3 6	9	1 1	16 0
1823	24 0	14 0	10 0	3 6	9	1 1	16 0
1824	22 0	12 6	9 0	3 6	9	1 0	15 6
1825	24 0	13 6	9 6	3 6	9	1 0	16 7
1826	16 0	12 0	8 0	2 6	8	0 10	7 9
1827	14 0	12 0	7 6	2 6	6	0 8	7 4
1828	14 0	12 0	7 0	2 6	6	0 8	7 4
1829	12 0	10 0	6 6	2 6	5	0 6	7 0
1830	11 0	9 0	6 6	2 3	5	0 7	6 6
1831	9 0	7 6	6 3	2 3	4	0 6	6 0

11,543. Have you any further information to give to the committee, or any table to wish to put in?—I have a table here of the earnings of weavers in our employ, their comparative earnings in 1824 and 1831, showing also the quantities of silk consumed at each period. In 1824, I find from our books, that 500 weavers, in one week, worked 620 lbs. of silk, and wages amounted to 370l.; the earnings being 15s. a week, from which have to be deducted the usual expenses for a quill winder, loom standing, and other incidental expenses of 2s. 6d., their earnings would then be 12s. 6d.; the quantity of silk used in each loom averaged 1 lb. 4 ounces; the cost of weaving that silk would be 9d. per ounce. In 1831, taking the average work of that year, I find that 500 weavers worked up 875 lbs. of silk per week, and that their wages were 171l.; the average earnings of these weavers would be 7s. a week, from which are to be deducted the same expenses of quill winding, loom standing, and other incidental expenses, leaving the net earnings of 500 weavers to be 4s. 6d. per head.

Extracts from Mr. Thomas Johnson's evidence, taken before the Select Committee on the Silk Trade.

11,564. What wages did you pay in 1823, and what in 1832?—The wages for a man in 1823 were 15s.; for a young man from fifteen to twenty, about 8s.; for a young woman from fitteen to twenty, 7s.; children from ten to fifteen, about 5s.; and children from seven to ten, about 2s. 9d. In 1832, the wages of men were about 10s.; young men, 5s. 6d.; a young woman from fifteen to twenty, 5s.; children about 3s.; and the younger children 1s. 6d.; that is for six days per week; but as they have been at a reduced time, the wages have been reduced in proportion.

11,565. What was the number of hands employed in 1823, and what is the present number?—In 1823, there were 3,961, and in 1832, 2,219.

11,566. How many hands are out of employment?—From the best information I can obtain, about 1,700; pro-bably not quite that number; they have been getting a little more into work since the East India Company's Sale.

11,567. How do these hands subsist?—Some on the poor-rate, others by begging, others by thieving, and many of the females by prostitution.

11,577. What would be the effect of a still further reduction of the import duty?—Destruction of the British throwster; we are all but annihilated as it is; our property is made useless. I have a capital of 15,000l. sunk in a silk mill and machinery; the mill is of no more value to me than this piece of paper; it gives me no return. I have not only sacrificed my own labour, but I have sacrificed funds and property which I derive and draw from other sources; it all seems to sink, and I am keeping this mill in action in hopes of better and improved times.

11,578. When did you erect this mill?—In 1810.

11,579. Is your mill as favourably situated as any other?—It is beautifully situated as a mill, and has water power; nothing can excel the situation.

11,580. Is the labour as cheap with you as in other parts of the kingdom?—Most decidedly.

11,581. Is it as cheap as it is at Manchester?—Cheaper, I should think.

London: Printed by William Cobbett, Johnson's-court, Fleet-street.

British Labour Struggles:
Contemporary Pamphlets 1727-1850

An Arno Press/New York Times Collection

The Factory Act of 1833. 1833-1834.
Richard Oastler: King of Factory Children. 1835-1861.
The Battle for the Ten Hours Day Continues. 1837-1843.
The Factory Education Bill of 1843. 1843.
Prelude to Victory of the Ten Hours Movement. 1844.
Sunday Work. 1794-1856.
Demands for Early Closing Hours. 1843.
Conditions of Work and Living: The Reawakening of the English Conscience. 1838-1844.
Improving the Lot of the Chimney Sweeps. 1785-1840.
The Rising of the Agricultural Labourers. 1830-1831.
The Aftermath of the "Lost Labourers' Revolt". 1830-1831.